The Theology and Pastoral Ministry of Pastor Yong-Gi Cho

The Theology and Pastoral Ministry of Pastor Yong-Gi Cho

As Seen by a Catholic Theologian for the Pastoral Renewal of the Church

| Chung-Myung Son |

DONG YEON

Preface

One might wonder why a Catholic theologian would research the theology and pastoral ministry of Pastor Yong-Gi Cho. Some years ago I read a small book about the Pentecostal movement written by Massimo Introvigne[1], while I was preparing a thesis on the Pentecostal movement. It gave me a big surprise. So many Catholics who were baptized but do not practice the faith, are transferring continuously to the Pentecostal churches or to other religions in Latin America and in Africa.[2] I wanted to know the reason for this movement. According to the Document of Aparecida, 'it is not because they like to follow faith of non-Catholic groups. They agree with the catechism and the theology of Catholic Church, but they are not happy with the way of the pastoral ministry in the Catholic Church.' My heart ached for them, especially because they are truly seeking God rather than simply leaving the Catholic Church.[3]

One of the actual problems of the Catholic Church in Seoul Korea is there are many people who are recently baptized but the number of the faithful who are not attending Sunday Mass is increasing too.

---

[1] Massimo Introvigne was born in Rome Italy in 1955. He is an author and co-author, editor of many books, head of CESNUR (il Centro Studi sulle Nuove Religioni), and co-edited Encyclopedia of Religions in Italy.

[2] Massimo Introvigne, *Pentecostali*, Elledici, Torino, 2004, 86.

[3] Tecle Vetrali, *Verso Una lettura francescna dell'incontro con il Fratello pentecostale*, in Studi Ecumenici, 27 (2009), Venezia, 439-440.

However, they do not move to the Pentecostal churches or to the Protestant churches as in Latin America.

With this situation in mind, I came to have a big desire to know how the Pentecostal churches do pastoral ministry. I also felt it was important to study the Pentecostal movement considering its rapid growth and influence. According to D.B. Barrett, statistician, 24.5% among all the Christian population (more than 1,950,000,000 people) in 1996 are Pentecostal. According to the statistics in 2000, 27.7% of all Christians of the world are Pentecostal. In 2025 the Pentecostal faithful will be 37% (1,140,000,000 people) of the approximately 3,000,000,000 Christian people and it will become a central power of Christianity in the world.[4]

Since the Pentecostal movement is an experience-centered faith movement, not a theological movement, their theology is not well developed systematically. Therefore, for the purpose of this study, I thought I would summarize his theology and ministry, focusing on Yong-Gi Cho (1936~2021), who has had a significant international impact in the Pentecostal world. Even though Yong-Gi Cho was not a theologian, his typical theology and pastoral method are well known. Many theologians have presented thesis on his theology and ministry. It is also true that it is not easy to talk about Yong-Gi Cho, since his theology has been evaluated positively by some people, but others have had a negative evaluation.

---

4 Jea-Cheol Yang, *Hankug Osunzol Kyohoiui Sinangkwa Sinhak (Pentecostal Churches in Korea)*, Hanulmokzang, Seoul, 2005, iv, 374.

The purpose of this book is to help both Catholics and Protestants alike to lead God's entrusted sheep to Him for His glory. The theology of Yong-Gi Cho is limited because he was a pastor, not a theologian. So it is not easy to compare his theology directly with the Catholic theology that has developed since the early Church. Therefore, each topic, if it is possible will be presented according to how Catholic theology understands and interprets the same topic, in order to offer a broader view. And in the field of pastoral ministry, especially in terms of preaching and the Small Christian Community, I hope that we can see the good aspect of the other side by looking at what the Korean Catholic Church is doing in comparison to Yong-Gi Cho's pastoral methods.

In the Ecumenical movement, we can notice easily the difference of the theological interpretation on the same topic according to the Confession. Therefore, I hope that any prejudice or misunderstanding between Protestants and Catholics, will be diminished even a little through this book. I also hope that they respect each other's theology and life practice, and live more faithfully according to their own religious tradition. Even though there are many ways to live the Christian life, the most important aspect is to produce the fruit of the Holy Spirit and the fruit of Love. Therefore, in the conclusion there will be suggestions for the pastoral renewal of the Catholic Church together with the words of Pope Francis and the ideas for spiritual growth and practice.

A note on Methodology, a summary of the original text will be provided and then if it is possible the original text will be presented.

This is out of consideration for those who want to read the original text, because some of the materials are out of print or not easy to find.

Chung-Myung Son (Cecilia)

Table of Contents

Preface   5
Introduction   13

PART I ı Yong-Gi Cho and Yoido Full Gospel Church

1. Yong-Gi Cho, called to be a pastor   21
2. The Pioneering period (1958~1961)   24
3. The Developing period (1961~1973)   26
4. The First period of expansion (1973~1982)
    — Growth of the church and the Holy Spirit movement   28
5. The Second period of expansion (1982~2000)   29

PART II ı Theology and Doctrine of Yong-Gi Cho

1. Theology of the Threefold Redemption and the Threefold
   Blessing   33
    1) Theology of the Threefold Blessing
    2) Scholarly Debates on the Theology of the Threefold Blessing
2. Divine healing   59
    1) Theology of Divine healing
    2) Arguments on Yong-Gi Cho's Divine healing
3. Theology of the Reign of God and Ecclesiology
   of Yong-Gi Cho   93
    1) The Concept of the Reign of God
    2) Different Paradises and How to Get Them
    3) Jang-Hyun Ryoo's Evaluation of Yong-Gi Cho's Reign of God
    4) The Ecclesiology of Yong-Gi Cho

5) Some Protestant Theologians' Interpretation of Yong-Gi Cho's Ecclesiology
   6) The Catholic Church's Understanding of the Reign of God
4. Conclusion   123
   1) Threefold Blessing
   2) Divine healing
   3) The Reign of God

PART III ı Pastoral Challenge

1. Anthropology and the Fourth Dimension Spirituality
   of Yong-Gi Cho   147
   1) The Pneumatological Anthropology of Yong-Gi Cho
   2) Thought
   3) Faith
   4) Dream
   5) Word
2. Preaching   199
   1) Yong-Gi Cho's preaching method
   2) Pope Francis' recommended method for delivering homilies
3. The Cell system as a pastoral strategy   235
   1) The Cell system of Yoido Full Gospel Church
   2) The Small Community of the Catholic Archdiocese of Seoul
   3) The Dure Community of Won Jun
   4) The Saranbang Meeting of Jae-Ul Lee
4. Conclusion   287
   1) Spirituality of the Fourth dimension
   2) Thought
   3) Faith
   4) Dream
   5) Word

6) Preaching
7) Cell group

PART IV ǀ Conclusion
— Proposals for the Pastoral Renewal of the Catholic Church

1. Pastoral activity	326
2. Discernment	337
3. A special place for the poor	349
4. Pastoral care for young people in the age of scientific omnipotence	356

References   367

Introduction

Yoido Full Gospel Church founded by Yong-Gi Cho is a Pentecostal church. There is no Pentecostal church as a denomination, but it is called collectively all the churches influenced by Pentecostal theology. Among Pentecostal theologians, there are several viewpoints about when and where the Pentecostal movement began. Historians often trace the origins of Pentecostalism in the United States to a revival that began on January 1, 1901, at Charles F. Parham's Bethel Bible School in Topeka, USA.[1]

Charles F. Parham (1873~1929) founded Bethel Bible School in October, 1900 to train missionaries. Charles Parham gave an assignment to his students to find the evidence of Baptism in the Holy Spirit. The students discovered that it was the speaking in tongues (Glossolalia) in the Acts of Apostles. Parham and his students prayed so hard day and night. In January 1, 1901 Agnes Ozman spoke in tongues, experiencing Baptism in the Holy Spirit. This was the be-

---

[1] Stanley M. Burgess, ed., *Introduction, in The New International Dictionary of Pentecostal and Charismatic Movements (revised and expanded edition)*, Zondervan, Michigan, 2003, xviii.

ginning of Pentecostalism in the 20th century.

William J. Seymour (1870~1922), a black Holiness preacher from Louisiana in the USA, was a student of Charles F. Parham. He contributed to the spread of Pentecostalism across the nation and around the world as a protagonist of the revival at the Azusa Street Mission (1906~1909) of Los Angeles.

In 1906 William J. Seymour invited by black Holiness in Los Angeles, preached Baptism in the Holy Spirit. But he had a big difficulty to continue preaching because people could not accept the doctrine about glossolalia as evidence of Baptism in the Holy Spirit. Therefore, the assembly was done in a family house instead.

On April 9, 1906 some of the black people gathered in the poor family house, started speaking in tongues (Glossolalia) receiving the Baptism in the Holy Spirit. They prayed day and night for three days with screaming, and a crowd of people arrived from everywhere because the rumor spread out.

The Azusa Street Revival continued for three years day and night and there was glossolalia, interpretation of glossolalia, prophecy, Divine healing, and exorcism. The fire of Pentecostalism was diffused all over the world through the pilgrims who visited Azusa Street[2].

Modern Pentecostalism spread in 1906 to Canada, in 1907 to

---

2 Jea-Cheol Yang, *Hankug Osunzol Kyoboiui Sinangkwa Sinhak (Pentecostal Churches in Korea)*, 118-122.

England, Denmark, Norway, Sweden, Netherlands, Germany, Poland, India, in 1908 to China, and in 1913 to Africa, South America, Mexico, and Japan. Since the 1960s the New Pentecostalism, namely Charismatic movement began, and since the 1980s, the Pentecostalism has become more widespread, with rising up the Third Wave movement.³

Pentecostalism is a faith movement. It has several groups: Classical Pentecostals, Charismatics, Third Waves (Neo-charismatics). Each group has unique aspects. The Classical Pentecostals refer to those participating in Classical Pentecostal denominations, such as the Assemblies of God, the Church of God (Cleveland, TN), the Church of God of Prophecy, and the International Church of the Foursquare Gospel. Charismatics, refer to persons with connections to mainline denominations. Neo-charismatics are participants in independent, interdenominational, nondenominational indigenous groups or organizations, such as the Vineyard Christian Fellowship.⁴ Neo-charismatics include the Third-wave which is spreading in the USA. The Vineyard church and New Apostolic movement belong to the Third-wave. Since the Third-wave movement includes so many independent, indigenous churches and groups, it could be seen, with a broader perspective, as a part of the Neo-charismatic movement.⁵ According to D.B. Barrett the number of Neo-char-

---

3 Jea-Cheol Yang, *Hankug Osunzol Kyohoiui Sinangkwa Sinhak (Pentecostal Churches in Korea)*, 124.
4 Stanley M. Burgess, Introduction, xxi; Jea-Cheol Yang, *Hankug Osunzol Kyohoiui Sinangkwa Sinhak (Pentecostal Churches in Korea)*, 142.
5 Jea-Cheol Yang, *Hankug Osunzol Kyohoiui Sinangkwa Sinhak (Pentecostal Churches in Korea)*, 146.

ismatics in 2000, were about 295,000,000 people worldwide. This number is larger than Classical Pentecostals (about 66,000,000 people) and Charismatics (about 180,000,000 people) combined. Therefore, Neo-charismatics appear to be a powerful influence in the Pentecostal movement.[6]

The basic form of Pentecostal thought and sprit is the Fourfold Gospel, namely, four Christological themes: 1) Christ as Savior, 2) Christ as Baptizer in the Holy Spirit, 3) Christ as Healer, and 4) Christ as Coming King. This Fourfold Gospel is the heart of Pentecostalism.[7]

Yoido Full Gospel Church (YFGC) belongs to the Assemblies of God, the biggest denomination among Classical Pentecostal denominations. In 1958, pastor Yong-Gi Cho (1936~2021) founded the Yoido Full Gospel Church located in Seoul; at the end of 2007, this church became the largest single congregation in the world with 755,000 members.[8]

Yong-Gi Cho studied theology at the seminary of Assemblies of God, where he was ordained. His theology has common aspects with the theology of Assemblies of God even though his theology has unique, distinctive aspects that have greatly influenced many other churches.

---

6 Ae-Cheol Yang, *Hankug Osunzol Kyohoiui Sinangkwa Sinhak (Pentecostal Churches in Korea)*, 152.

7 Donald W. Dayton, *Theological Roots of Pentecostalism*, Hendrickson, 1996, 173-174.

8 Young-Hoon Lee, *The Holy Spirit Movement in Korea: Its Historical and Theological Development*, Regnum Books International, Oxford, 2009, 93.

The first part of this book, will present the basic stages of his vocational journey as a minister, and of YFGC. The second part will present his doctrinal and theological contents. Finally, the third part will discuss some of pastoral challenges between YFGC and the Catholic Archdiocese of Seoul in Korea.

PART I

Young-Gi Cho
and Yoido Full Gospel Church

1. Yong-Gi Cho, called to be a pastor

Knowing how Yong-Gi Cho, born in a Buddhist family, became a Christian and how he overcame the difficulties of opening up a church, can provide an important key to understand his theology. The characteristics of every stage in the early history of Yoido Full Gospel Church, show how he guided the sheep, those who were in poverty and suffering, towards the hopeful life with prayer and pastoral zeal.

Yong-Gi Cho was born in February, 1936 in Buddhist family in Seoul, Korea.[1] His father, Doo-cheon Cho, who ran for the national Parliament in general election in May 30, 1950, was not elected, and found himself without money. In June 25, less than one month after election, the war between South and North Korea began. As a result, his eleven family members suffered from hunger.[2]

In 1953, during his second year of high school, Cho was diagnosed with late stage (Terminal) tuberculosis (TB) and was told that he had less than six months to live.[3] A friend of his older sister came to visit him with a Bible and prayed every day for a week. She invited him persistently to read the Bible so he would know who Jesus is, welcome Jesus as his Savior and be saved and cured. In the beginning, Cho refused strongly, but after a week he started to read the

---

1 International Theological Institute, *Yoidoui Mokhoiza (The Pastor of Yoido)*, Seoul Logos, Seoul, 2010, 63.
2 International Theological Institute, *Yoidoui Mokhoiza (The Pastor of Yoido)*, 127-134.
3 International Theological Institute, *Yoidoui Mokhoiza (The Pastor of Yoido)*, 149-154.

New Testament following her suggestion.

Yong-Gi Cho observed the New Testament was about Jesus curing the sick, bringing the dead back to life, and giving food to the hungry; there was no mention about philosophy or morals. Reading the Bible he realized that Jesus could save him from TB and death. In that moment he remembered how his sister's friend prayed in his room kneeling down. Cho also tried kneeling down, putting his hands together and prayed with tears, asking his greatest need: "Mr. Jesus, if you cure me I will be a person for you. Please save me!" After praying this way for a long time, he felt joy flowing over from deep within his heart, and his body became very hot. Feeling the vital energy coming from deep in his heart, Cho danced and sang with joy "Silaui Dalbam (Korean pop song)" for a long time while his family members were worrying. His mother embraced him strongly, crying and crying. Since that day Cho never stopped reading the Bible.[4] Since he could not go to school, he continued to read books and study English alone at home.[5]

Yong-Gi Cho, meeting by chance Kenneth Tice, a missionary of the Assemblies of God, began to interpret his sermons for him as well as the sermons of Lou Richards, another missionary. Lou Richards taught the Bible to Cho. While Yong-Gi Cho was reading about Divine healing in the Bible, he was touched by it and repented for not having fully believed in it. He kept a fasting prayer for three

---

4 International Theological Institute, *Yoidoui Mokhoiza (The Pastor of Yoido)*, 163–171.
5 International Theological Institute, *Yoidoui Mokhoiza (The Pastor of Yoido)*, 175.

days.[6] He wanted to see for himself if he could really be blessed and healed if he believed in Jesus.[7] On the third day of fasting prayer, he saw a vision of Jesus, in which he was called to be a preacher: "I will cure you and do you want to become my servant in your whole life?" According to Cho, he responded to this call and he was fully healed from tuberculosis.[8]

In 1956 Cho entered the seminary of the Assemblies of God in Seoul, and met Ja-sil Choi,[9] his classmate, who later became associate pastor and also his mother in law.[10] Ja-sil Choi, who was already experiencing glossolalia (Speaking in tongues) at that period, visited her spiritual director, pastor Sung-bong Lee to discuss her future. Pastor Sung-bong Lee proposed she enter the seminary of the Assemblies of God to continue speaking in tongues. Under his direction, she entered into this seminary.[11] Yong-Gi Cho began to speak in tongues in 1957,[12] and married the daughter of Ja-sil Choi on March 1, 1965.[13]

---

6 Young-Hoon Lee, *The Holy Spirit Movement in Korea*, 94.
7 International Theological Institute, *Yoidoui Mokhoiza (The Pastor of Yoido)*, 189.
8 International Theological Institute, *Yoidoui Mokhoiza (The Pastor of Yoido)*, 193-197.
9 The mother of Ja-sil Choi was a Buddhist, but Ja-sil Choi and her mother became Christian when Ja-sil Choi was attending elementary school. Ja-Sil Choi, *Nanun Halleluia Azummayutda (I was Halleluia Woman)*, Seoul Logos, Seoul, 2010, 16-24.
10 Young-Hoon Lee, *The Holy Spirit Movement in Korea*, 94.
11 Ja-Sil Choi, *Nanun Halleluia Azummayutda (I was Halleluia Woman)*, 83; Yung-Gi Hong, Cho Yong-Gi Moksaui Yungsongkwa Leadership (Spirituality & Leadership of Rev. Yong-Gi Cho), Kyohoisongzang-yunkuso, Seoul, 2003, 215.
12 International Theological Institute, *Yoidoui Mokhoiza (The Pastor of Yoido)*, 236-241.
13 Ja-Sil Choi, *Nanun Halleluia Azummayutda (I was Halleluia Woman)*, 316.

According to the study of the International Theological Institute of Yoido Full Gospel Church about the characteristics of Yong-Gi Cho and Ja-sil Choi: Ja-sil Choi was influenced by protestant leaders of Pentecostal movement born in Korea. Therefore, she emphasized some typical Korean styles: the 'Prayer of dawn (Sebyuk Kido)', fasting prayer, and a strong spirit for evangelization. While Ja-sil Choi had the elements for the revival style of inculturation in Korea, Yong-Gi Cho was spreading positive messages underlining the Redemption of Cross, based on the Scriptures. These two spiritual elements contributed greatly to the growth of Yoido Full Gospel Church.[14]

2. The Pioneering period (1958~1961)

In May of 1958 two evangelists, recently graduated from seminary, Yong-Gi Cho and Ja-sil Choi, pitched a tent and planted a church in Daejo-dong, at that time an absolutely poor area in the outskirts of Seoul. Daejo-dong was a place of absolute poverty, home to many poor people from the countryside who flocked to the city to fill their hungry bellies. Yong-Gi Cho gave them news of hope by telling them if they live with faith in Jesus, they might receive not only the spiritual blessing, but also enjoy abundant mate-

---

14 International Theological Institute, *Yoido Sunbokumkyohoiui Songnyungundong Ihe (A Comprehension about the Holy Spirit Movement of the Yoido Full Gospel Church)*, Seoul Logos, Seoul, 2001, 48-49.

rial blessing, and the environmental blessing of God. They believed in this message of hope, and indeed, it is said that a paralysis was healed, a drunkard stopped drinking, a shaman was converted and became a Christian, and blessings fell upon the poor. The news of this hope spread and many began to gather in tent church.[15]

According to the International Theological Institute of Yoido Full Gospel Church, during this period, Yong-Gi Cho considered Divine healing and exorcism as visible signs of the kingdom of God and he placed Divine healing as one of the central elements of his pastoral ministry. Many miraculous cures made Yong-Gi Cho very well known as an evangelist through Divine healing.[16] The International Theological Institute says that emphasizing the presence of the Holy Spirit became the central aspect of all pastoral activities in the Yoido Full Gospel Church, since its foundation. Therefore, they prayed earnestly for the help of the Holy Spirit before the church did anything, and they believe the result was the sovereign work of the Holy Spirit.

---

15 International Theological Institute, *Yoido Sunbokumkyohoiui Songnyungundong Ihe (A Comprehension about the Holy Spirit Movement of Movement of the Holy Spirit of the Yoido Full Gospel Church)*, 49–51.

16 International Theological Institute, *Yoido Sunbokumkyohoiui Songnyungundong Ihe (A Comprehension about the Holy Spirit Movement of the Yoido Full Gospel Church)*, 53.

3. The Developing period (1961~1973)

Three years after planting the tent church, it was necessary to have a second church planting due to lack of space.[17] On October 15, 1961, a groundbreaking service was held for the construction of the second church in Seodaemun, and it was completed on February 18, 1962 under the name of 'the Full Gospel Revival Centre.' In April 26 of the same year Yong-Gi Cho was ordained as pastor, and in May he changed the name of church into the Seodaemun Full Gospel Central Church (Seodaemun Sunbokum Jungang Kyohoi). In 1964, its membership reached 3,000 people.[18]

The International Theological Institute of YFGC has compared the characteristics of the Daejo-dong and the Seodaemun Full Gospel Central Church periods as follows. Whereas the work of the Holy Spirit in the pioneering period in Daejo-dong (the tent church) was an experiential work of personal faith, the work of the Holy Spirit in the developing period in the Seodaemun Full Gospel Central Church was a revival and renewal of the church community. Two characteristics are found in the period of the Seodaemun Full Gospel Central Church. One is that the work of the Holy Spirit continued to be manifested at the individual and church community levels, and the other is that the Guyuk Yebe (Cell group worship)

---

17 International Theological Institute, *Yoido Sunbokumkyohoiui Songnyungundong Ihe (A Comprehension about the Holy Spirit Movement of the Yoido Full Gospel Church)*, 54.

18 Young-Hoon Lee, *The Holy Spirit Movement in Korea*, 96.

organization was put in place to better manage and reproduce the church that grew as a result.[19] In this period, Yong-Gi Cho and all his faithful understood the Holy Spirit as a personal existence, and began to have a deep personal relationship with Him and did pastoral ministry with Him. According to the International Theological Institute, in this way, they moved from believing in the Holy Spirit as an object of experience to believing in the Holy Spirit as a person, and co-operating with the Holy Spirit, the whole church was filled with the Holy Spirit and overflowed with living faith. They claim that thanks to the Guyuk Yebe (Cell group worship) system of the Seodaemun Full Gospel Central Church, their church's growth became concrete, and through this system the church showed its dynamic power.

The International Theological Institute also says three things about the importance and necessity of the Guyuk Yebe (Cell group worship) system: 1) it enables discipleship formation; 2) it creates the faith community through communion among the faithful; 3) it can function as an organization through the organic relationship among the faithful.

According to the study of the International Theological Institute, Yong-Gi Cho began the Guyuk Yebe (Cell group worship) system by realizing the dual ministry of the church: temple ministry and

---

19 International Theological Institute, *Yoido Sunbokumkyoboiui Songnyungundong Ihe (A Comprehension about the Holy Spirit Movement of the Yoido Full Gospel Church)*, 56.

house-to-house ministry. This is related to the early church's life: the disciples had regular meeting in the temple, and the faithful had daily meeting together in their house breaking bread in communion (Act 2:46-47). Therefore, the International Theological Institute evaluates that Yong-Gi Cho made lay leaders participate in the pastoral ministry so that they can give formation to many other lay people, and these lay leaders could also administer the Guyuk Yebe (Cell group worship) for a more organized and effective church growth.[20]

4. The First period of expansion (1973~1982)
― Growth of the church and the Holy Spirit movement

In 1968 the Seodaemun Full Gospel Central Church had 8,000 members, consequently it was necessary to construct a third church, Yoido Full Gospel Church (YFGC), which was opened in 1973 with 10,000 seats and 18,000 members in Seoul. In 1978, the Sunbokum Kyoyuk Yunkuso (Present International Theological Institute) for the faith education of the faithful was founded, and soon after, the Bible school and university were opened.

Regarding the explosive growth of Yoido Full Gospel Church in the 1970s, the International Theological Institute points to several

---

[20] International Theological Institute, *Yoido Sunbokumkyohoiui Songnyungundong Ihe (A Comprehension about the Holy Spirit Movement of the Yoido Full Gospel Church)*, 57-58.

key factors: based on God's work, the messages and leadership of Yong-Gi Cho, the formation of leaders through education and prayer movement in the fullness of the Holy Spirit.[21]

5. The Second period of expansion (1982~2000)

Since 1984 the Yoido Full Gospel Church has offered free assistance to poor children with heart disease. In 1988 the church opened the Elim Welfare Town for the aged without family and also Job Related Training for the youth in need as a social welfare projects. On December 10 of the same year Cho founded Kukmin Daily (Kukmin-ilbo).[22] In 1998 the church started the Sunbokum Internet Bangsongkuk (Young-san Internet Broadcast, www.FGTV.com). On March 28, 2000, YFGC founded DCEM (David Cho Evangelistic Mission) to centralize the Cho's evangelical conference with a net-work of many organizations throughout the world to have a more effective mission.[23] In 1993 YFGC was listed as a biggest congregation of the world in the Guinness Book of Records for having more than 700,000 members.

---

21 International Theological Institute, *Yoido Sunbokumkyohoiui Songnyungundong Ihe (A Comprehension about the Holy Spirit Movement of the Yoido Full Gospel Church)*, 59-62.

22 International Theological Institute, *Yoidoui Mokhoiza (The Pastor of Yoido)*, 535-538.

23 International Theological Institute, *Yoido Sunbokumkyohoiui Songnyungundong Ihe (A Comprehension about the Holy Spirit Movement of the Yoido Full Gospel Church)*, 68-70.

In 1999 an NGO, Good People was founded. Its purpose is to make known the reality of underprivileged neighbors in the global village who face the extreme danger of poverty, sickness, and calamity, and to offer them systematic and professional help, transcending borders and race (Eg. Black and White). Good People is active with various projects for the poor areas in the world: children protection, education, drinking water sanitation, disease prevention and treatment, regional development, and emergency relief.

Activity of YFGC for those who are in the blind spot of social welfare, is going on continuously. The Scholarship Institute was founded to support youth from orphanages who are more than 18 years old until they can be independent with a place to live and a job. The declining birthrate is a serious problem that threatens the very existence of the human race. That is why YFGC is absolutely opposed to abortion and have policies that actively encourage and support childbearing. Since 2012, maternity benefits are offered to families having children.

PART II

Doctrine and Theology of Yong-Gi Cho

The doctrine and the theology of Yong-Gi Cho have common aspects with the Assemblies of God to which he belongs, but there are also Cho's unique and distinctive aspects. Therefore, there coexist positive and negative evaluation about this theology. In this section we will see the Threefold Blessing and the Divine healing, the theology of the reign of God and the ecclesiology according to Yong-Gi Cho's teaching. And we will see also the viewpoints of other theologians about each topic. In particular, the reign of God part will be presented according to how the Catholic Church understands it. In the conclusion, if the topic is shared in common between the Catholic Church and Young-gi Cho, we will also see the Catholic Church's theology.

1. Theology of the Threefold Redemption and the Threefold Blessing

1) Theology of the Threefold Blessing

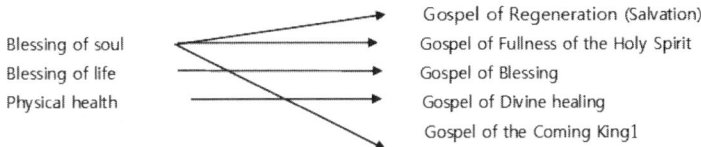

Blessing of soul
Blessing of life
Physical health

Gospel of Regeneration (Salvation)
Gospel of Fullness of the Holy Spirit
Gospel of Blessing
Gospel of Divine healing
Gospel of the Coming King[1]

The doctrine of the YFGC (Yoido Full Gospel Church) is summarized in the Fivefold Gospel and the Threefold Blessing, based on Pentecostal theology and Evangelical theology. This doctrine is a pastoral principle and a canon of faith which Yong-Gi Cho applied in his pastoral ministry for over 40 years as a foundation of the YFGC.[2] The Fivefold Gospel of Yong-Gi Cho indicates five aspects in the Gospel: the Regeneration (Salvation), the Fullness of the Holy Spirit, Divine healing, the Blessing, and the Second Coming of Jesus Christ.[3] The Fivefold Gospel represents a theory and doctrine of faith, while

---

[1] Yong-Gi Cho, *Ozung Bogumkwa Samzung Chukbok (Fivefold Gospel and Threefold Blessing)*, Seoul Logos, Seoul, 2009, 263.

[2] International Theological Institute, *Hananimui Songhoi Kyohoisa (The History of The Assemblies of God)*, Seoul Logos, Seoul, 2008, 250.

[3] International Theological Institute, *Yoido Sunbokumkyohoiui Songnyungundong Ihe (A Comprehension about the Holy Spirit Movement of the Yoido Full Gospel Church)*, 91.

the Threefold Blessing is a practice and application of this theory and doctrine.⁴ The doctrine of the Threefold Blessing could be understood as the holistic salvation of a person. Being a saved and blessed man includes all the aspects related to him: his soul and body, all things related to him and his environment.⁵ Mun-hong Choi explains that the soteriology of Cho is the Threefold redemption through Jesus Christ. Namely, it claims that to be saved is to be redeemed not only from sin but also from sickness and curse/poverty. Mun-hong Choi underlines that the Cross of Christ is the starting point, the root of Cho's theology and the center of his soteriology because Yong-Gi Cho's understanding of salvation is based on the Cross of Christ.⁶

According to Yong-Gi Cho, the Threefold Blessing means a blessing approached as a result of the holistic salvation of person. Namely, when Jesus saves a person he does not save only soul but also their whole life including their body.⁷ He says that the Threefold Blessing indicates first, a blessing of the soul related to Regeneration with

---

4 Yong-Gi Cho, *Ozung Bogumkwa Samzung Chukbok (Fivefold Gospel and Threefold Blessing)*, 250.

5 International Theological Institute, *Yoido Sunbokumkyohoiui Songnyungundong Ihe (A Comprehension about the Holy Spirit Movement of the Yoido Full Gospel Church)*, 101.

6 Mun-Hing Choi, *Young Sanui Kuwon Ihe (Understanding of Young San about Salvation)*, in *Young Sanui Mokhoiwa Sinhak (Ministry & Theology of Young San)*, vol. 1, ed. Young San Theological Institute, Hansei University Logos, Gunpo, 2008, 352.

7 Yong-Gi Cho, *Ozung Bogumkwa Samzung Chukbok (Fivefold Gospel and Threefold Blessing)*, 251.

salvation of soul, and then, a blessing of all circumstances and of physical health. It means that soul will be blessed first, and after which there will follow prosperity in all circumstances and physical health.

Yong-Gi Cho explains how the Threefold Blessing can be practiced concretely, based on the Fivefold Gospel: Christians are those who have been forgiven, given eternal life, justified and sanctified, who received the fullness of the Holy Spirit through Jesus Christ on the Cross and the Risen Lord, and who received the spiritual blessing to communicate with God. Christians should pray, study the Bible, and worship God to unfold this spiritual veil. God gives a big blessing when Christians live the God-centered life with honest, fidelity and diligence. For physical health, Christians should keep away from sin, cast out demons, avoid too much eating and working, and cultivate good personal hygiene. Yong-Gi Cho emphasizes that in case of illness, they should repent of sin and disobedience and practice a fasting vigil prayer to be healed.[8]

Threefold Blessing theology originated from the miserable situation of Yong-Gi Cho himself and from his pastoral ministry field. During his high school period, Yong-Gi Cho crossed life and death with extreme despair and suffered from tuberculosis (TB). His pastoral field where he went after being cured from TB and being called to be a servant of the Lord, was also full of suffering and despair,

---

8 Yong-Gi Cho, *Ozung Bogumkwa Samzung Chukbok (Fivefold Gospel and Threefold Blessing)*, 262-264.

with desperate poverty and sickness. Yong-Gi Cho had to propagate the good news of forgiveness of sins and the curing of the sickness, and the blessing of the Threefold redemption to satisfy their desperate need. As a natural conclusion, he gave the message of hope to those who fall into despair. Therefore, Yong-Gi Cho confessed that his central pastoral motive was to give absolute hope to those who were in absolute despair, and the Threefold redemption theology came out from enlightenment through an urgent Bible study:

> While I was reading from the Gospel of Matthew till the Acts of the Apostles, I discovered a surprising fact that Jesus is different from Jesus learned in the seminary. Jesus filled up the necessary things to those who were in a desperate situation, not only crying out the ideal or fantastic Gospel. ... From that moment, what I began to cry out is the Threefold Blessing. "Beloved, I hope you are prospering in every respect and are in good health, just as your soul is prospering." (3Jn 1, 2).[9]

Mun-Hong Choi sees that the Threefold Blessing theology of Yong-Gi Cho is based on the idea of 'Good God.' Yong-Gi Cho realized that his God is a 'Good God', through receiving the Word, 3Jn 1:2, while he was studying carefully the Bible, and praying with a desperate heart in a despairful and painful reality. And Yong-Gi Cho, understanding that God the Creator created man as a perfect creature without any deficit in spirit, soul, or body, explains: the

---

9 Yong-Gi Cho, *Sonkyowa Mokhoi (Mission and Pastoral Ministry)*, vol. 4, 1988, 26–27.

spirit is an instrument to communicate with God as a container to serve God, and to live following what the bright conscience instructs, and to understand His will; the soul has a personality and is the place of intelligence, sentiments, and the will which can think, feel and decide; the body, through five organic senses (Sight, Hearing, Smell, Taste, Touch), allows the soul to recognize the world. Yong-Gi Cho affirms that when God created man there was an order among spirit, soul, and body: spirit dominates soul according to the will of God; soul dominates body; and body obeys spirit and soul. This beautiful order was collapsed completely with the falling of Adam and Eve against God. Therefore, Yong-Gi Cho says that as a result, three kinds of fatal death began.[10]

Yong-Gi Cho explains the Threefold corruption as the spiritual death, the physical death, and the environmental death of man: When Adam and Eve ate the forbidden fruit, they died spiritually. Spiritual death means being separated from God. The next is physical death. When man sinned, disease came upon man, which is the beginning of death, the return of man's flesh to the dust. Also environmental death came. Through the fall of Adam and Eve the cursed ground began to produce thorns and thistles. As a result of this fall, the world has sprouted thorns and thistles of misery, thorns of hatred, thorns of anxiety and fear, thorns of frustration and despair, and human beings are writhing in pain. Yong-Gi Cho says

---

10 Mun-Hong Choi, *Young Sanui Kuwon Ihe (Understanding of Young San about Salvation)*, 353-356.

that this is a holistic corruption (or the punishment of Threefold corruption). (Gen 3:17-19).[11]

Yong-Gi Cho argues that because humans are triply and completely depraved, a Threefold atonement through Jesus is necessary. Cho first speaks of the spiritual atonement, explaining that Jesus alone bore the Threefold punishment as a result of Adam's fall, and through his death on the Cross and Resurrection, he made the Threefold atonement.[12] Regarding the atonement of the spirit, he often quotes Is 53:5 ("He bore the punishment that makes us whole, by his wounds we were healed"). Traditionally, Christianity has understood the event of Jesus' crucifixion to be limited to the atonement for sin, but Yong-Gi Cho also includes the atonement for physical sickness. For him its biblical foundation is Mt 8, 17 (Is 53:4) and 1Pt 2:24 (Is 53:5). And also 1Pt 2:24b ("By his wounds you have been healed"). Furthermore, Yong-Gi Cho insists that the atonement of Jesus includes the atonement from malediction and poverty. This is the unique aspect of his soteriology. As the basis of this claim he often quotes Gal 3:13-14 and 2Cor 8:9.[13]

Yong-Gi Cho explains that humanity received the atonement

---

[11] International Theological Institute, *Yoido Sunbokumkyohoiui Songnyungundong Ihe (A Comprehension about the Holy Spirit Movement of the Yoido Full Gospel Church)*, 102-104.

[12] Mun-Hong Choi, *Young Sanui Kuwon Ihe (Understanding of Young San about Salvation)*, 357.

[13] Mun-Hong Choi, *Young Sanui Kuwon Ihe (Understanding of Young San about Salvation)*, 358-359.

from the physical, environmental curse and death, could receive spiritual, environmental, physical blessings through the work of the precious blood of Jesus Christ, culminating in the Cross. He says that, with this, humans could resume their lost fellowship with God, mentioning Gal 3:13 related to the atonement of curse: Christ ransomed us from the curse of the law by becoming a curse for us, for it is written, "Cursed be everyone who hangs on a tree." He tells also that the Blessed Son of God shouldered the curse and bleed for us to destroy the curse's power. According to Yong-Gi Cho, if we believe in Jesus, all the thorns (Which are hatred, anxiety, restlessness, fear and desperation, frustration and death, guilt, condemnation), will be removed. And then the river of peace flows in the heart, and we receive the blessing of Christ so that the river of peace will flow in life. Therefore, the physical death that came through the Fall of Adam, is recovered thoroughly through the atonement of Jesus. Yong-Gi Cho says that while we live out the rest of our physical lives, we can claim healing and restoration of health for the diseases that cling to our bodies and destroy us on the basis of the ransom of Jesus Christ.[14]

Yong-Gi Cho uses several biblical bases in the New Testament to support his Threefold redemption theology. Only 3Jn 1:2 is used as a signature passage to express clearly his Threefold redemption

---

14 International Theological Institute, *Yoido Sunbokumkyohoiui Songnyungundong Ihe (A Comprehension about the Holy Spirit Movement of the Yoido Full Gospel Church)*, 105–107.

theology. 3Jn 1:2 changed definitively his eye for reading the Bible. Therefore, Cho interpreted the Bible based on this Word. In other words, the Threefold redemption was Cho's 'key to interpreting the Bible.'[15]

Yong-Gi Cho expresses clearly that the Threefold Blessing is based on the unshakable Cross because it came to us through the redemptive suffering of Jesus. Cho interprets 3Jn 1:2 in this way: the word **'Beloved'** presents the precondition to receive the Threefold Blessing. Namely, to receive blessing, we need to become a person beloved by God through the atonement of Jesus, for this, we need to welcome Jesus Christ personally. The word **'Just as your soul is prospering'** expresses that we need to choose the prospering of our soul first in everything because the soul is eternal. **'Prospering in every respect'** demonstrates that when soul is prospering, everything will be prospering, because the blessing of God is with us. It is because Jesus said "Seek first the kingdom of God and his righteousness and all these will be given you besides" (Mt 6:33). **'You are in good health'** means that you can be healed by praying a prayer of faith and relying on the precious blood of Jesus, the great healer.

> **'Beloved'**: To receive the blessing of God, first, we need to become 'beloved' by God through the atonement of Jesus Christ. We are 'beloved' obtained with the blood price of His only Son of God, and

---

15 Mun-Hong Choi, *Young Sanui Kuwon Ihe (Understanding of Young San about Salvation)*, 359-360.

we are chosen people in Christ. Therefore, the precondition of the Threefold Blessing is to become beloved children of God, who welcome Jesus Christ personally.

'**Just as your soul is prospering**': Why is the soul's problem mentioned first? Because soul is eternal. ... We need to choose first the way for the soul's prospering in everything. There is a proper order in Christian life: serve God first and live a God-centered life as a main occupation, and then worldly life as a side occupation. Today, there are so many Christians whose main occupation is with worldly life, considering the belief in God an accessory.

'**Prospering in every respect**': If our soul is prospering, the blessing of God is with us, therefore, (We) will be prospering in every respect. Jesus said clearly: "Seek first his kingdom (of God) and his righteousness, and all these things will be given you besides" (Mt 6:33). When we go forth praying in faith, these things will be added to our life.

'**You are in good health**': Jesus is a great healer. Because of this, if we pray with faith relying on the precious blood of Jesus, we can be freed from the bond of disease. This Threefold Blessing given to his beloved people was accomplished with the precious blood of Jesus. Therefore, the Threefold Blessing, today, is based on the unshakable Cross because Jesus gave us this blessing through his redemptive suffering.[16]

---

16 Yong-Gi Cho, *Ozung Bogumkwa Samzung Chukbok (Fivefold Gospel and*

To summarize the Threefold Blessing of Yong-Gi Cho, "The blessing taught in the Bible is not only spiritual salvation, but it is also blessings in abundance for all; it promises earthly blessings as well as afterlife blessings. And this blessing is to be enjoyed only by those who had a relationship with God, Jesus and the Holy Spirit. The blessings of visible and temporary circumstances can be true happiness when combined with the blessings of eternity within."17

Yong-Gi Cho mentions that the blessing of God for man began since the creation of the world. God created the material world first, and then created man. The day after man's birth was the Sabbath of Yahweh. Therefore, Yong-Gi Cho interprets that man, in the first day of his life, could only enjoy the material world with God and rest by entering into the Sabbath of Yahweh (Gen 1:28). According to Cho this was the fundamental will of God towards man.

> The blessing of God began since the creation of the world (Gen 1 and 2). God created first the material world of this world before the creation of man. On the last day of the creation of the material world, God created man according to His image and shape. And God blessed them saying this: "Be fertile and multiply; fill the earth and subdue it." Have dominion over the fish of the sea, the birds of the air, and all the living things that crawl on the earth (Gen 1:28). ... The day after man's birth was the Sabbath of Yahweh. Man, in the first day of his life, could only enjoy the abundant

---

Threefold Blessing), 266-270.

17 Yong-Gi Cho, *Ozung Bogumkwa Samzung Chukbok (Fivefold Gospel and Threefold Blessing)*, 179-180.

material world with God and rest by entering into the Sabbath of Yahweh. This was the fundamental will of God towards man.[18]

Yong-Gi Cho, interpreting the Bible that the poverty of Jesus was to give us richness (2Cor 8:9), emphasizes that we need to enjoy the richness accomplished by Jesus already, and we also need to share this blessing with others as Christians. Yong-Gi Cho, speaking about the curse of Jesus and our blessing (Gal 3:13-14), explains that the purpose of Jesus being cursed, is that the blessing of Abraham might be extended to the Gentiles in Jesus. According to Cho, believers in Christ are redeemed already from the curse, and are the people who will receive the blessing of Abraham. And especially he specifies that the core of the Christian blessing is to share it with the poor and the marginalized, not to stockpile it.

> For you know the gracious act of our Lord Jesus Christ. For your sake he became poor although he was rich. By his poverty you might become rich (2Cor 8:9).
> We are already ransomed people through Christ, not only from eternal sin, but also from poverty. Therefore, if we don't enjoy the blessing according to this Word, we make the poverty of Jesus in vain. So, we need to enjoy the richness accomplished by Jesus already, and to become believers who share the received blessing with others. This is

---

18 Yong-Gi Cho, *Ozung Bogumkwa Samzung Chukbok (Fivefold Gospel and Threefold Blessing)*, 183.

the biblical will of God, it is the way to glorify Christ.

Christ ransomed us from the curse of the law by becoming a curse for us, for it is written, "Cursed be everyone who hangs on a tree." The blessing of Abraham might be extended to the Gentiles through Christ Jesus, so that we might receive the promise of the Holy Spirit through faith (Gal 3:13-14).

Jesus not only ransomed our poverty but also redeemed our curse. ... Roman soldiers made the crown of thorns and crowned Jesus. These thorns symbolize curse. And also the Cross of Jesus symbolizes curse. It shows that all the curse, which came to man with the Corruption of Adam, were moved onto the body of Jesus. The Bible says that the purpose for which Jesus was cursed in this way was that the blessing of Abraham might come to the Gentiles in Jesus (Gal 3:14).

The believers in Jesus are already redeemed from the curse, and are the people who will receive the blessing of Abraham. For the believers there is no reason at all to be cursed again. Therefore, we become not only redeemed heirs because our spiritual body is freed from the curse, but also we need to enjoy the blessing to glorify Christ, being redeemed from the environmental curse. ...

The core idea of the Christian blessing is to receive the abundant blessing of God, and to share it with others, not to stockpile it.[19]

According to Cho, after having the Threefold redemption theory

---

19 Yong-Gi Cho, *Ozung Bogumkwa Samzung Chukbok (Fivefold Gospel and Threefold Blessing)*, 187-189.

as a central philosophy of his pastoral ministry, he had enlightenment about the precious blood's power. Yong-Gi Cho said that Jesus poured his blood four times and the meaning of the blood can be interpreted differently according to the place. The first was the precious blood shed in the Garden of Gethsemani, to obey his Father, and to ransom our disobedience. The second was the precious blood that was shed in Pilate's courtyard, for the healing of our sick body. The third was the precious blood of the crown of thorns, shed to ransom our curse and to give us blessing. The fourth was shed on the Cross, to ransom our souls. In this way Cho interpreted the precious blood of Christ relating directly with the Threefold Blessing.

> The first precious blood shed was in the Garden of Gethsemane (Lk 22:44). The precious blood shed in the Garden of Gethsemane was the blood to obey to God against his own will. Namely, it was the blood to ransom our disobedience. The great strength to live in God's will is in this precious blood.
> Secondly, the precious blood shed in Pilate's courtyard. The precious blood that was shed here is the blood that was shed for the ransom of our flesh. The Bible says that "He bore the punishment that makes us whole, by his wounds we were healed" (Is 53:5). Therefore, the precious blood was meant to heal the body that was diseased by lust or disease. Jesus took upon himself our infirmities and bore our diseases (Mt 8:17).
> Thirdly, the precious blood that was shed while crowned with thorns.

By placing the crown of thorns on Jesus' head, God atoned for the curse that had come to the earth through wrong thinking. The precious blood that Jesus shed while crowned with thorns not only atones for our curse, but also brings us blessing (Gal. 3:13-14).

Fourthly, the precious blood shed on the Cross. The precious blood that Jesus shed on the Cross was the blood that saves from the place of abandonment. He ransomed our souls, which were destined to be destroyed forever and cast into the fires of hell. On the Cross, Jesus said, "It is finished" (John 19:30), which means "It is paid in full", meaning that He has paid for all of our original sins and personal sin. Jesus didn't just redeem our souls, He also redeemed our sicknesses, curses, and disobedience. Therefore, when we preach the Gospel of Jesus, we shouldn't just preach the redemption of the soul. We must preach all that Jesus has ransomed. In doing so, we must give hope and change the hearts of those who are suffering, despairing, sick, and lacking joy in their lives.[20]

We can ask a question here: "Does the Threefold Blessing emphasize only material prosperity and healing, while excluding believers' suffering or their life carrying the cross?" Yong-Gi Cho answered clearly. "There are two kinds of hardship in the faith life of believers: hardship to fight and win, and hardships to bear." Namely, he said, because Jesus ransomed sin, sickness and the curse through his Cross, believers should not suffer for these without any especial

---

[20] Yong-Gi Cho, Nanun Iroke Solkyohanda (I preach like this), Seoul Logos, Seoul, 2010, 404-405.

reason. On the other side, there is a cross which the believers should carry to live according to the will of the Lord, rejecting their own will. Yong-Gi Cho explains that this is a hardship to shoulder voluntarily to follow the Lord; and when we carry this cross, there is an abundant paschal life and the reward of paradise.[21]

There is some criticism that Korean Protestantism is influenced by Shamanism and pursues the "Faith for blessings (Gibok Sinang)." Yong-Gi Cho sees that Shamanism is a typical appearance of the "Faith for blessings." Therefore, he compares the "Blessing faith of Christianity" and the "Faith for blessings" of Shamanism, and discusses their similarities and differences.

Praying for material prosperity is a similarity between the "Blessing faith of Christianity" and the "Faith for blessings" of Shamanism. But there are also differences:

With or without Salvation.

The most important point in the differences among the "Blessing faith of Christianity" and the "Faith for blessings" is whether there is salvation or not. The "Faith for blessings" does not presuppose salvation because it has no concept of salvation. But the "Blessing faith of Christianity" presupposes the salvation of Christ, and blessing is a fruit of that salvation which appears concretely in reality.

---

21 Mun-Hong Choi, *Young Sanui Kuwon Ihe (Understanding of Young San about Salvation)*, 363-364.

Egocentric blessing and ethical blessing.

Since the "Faith for blessings" has no concept of salvation, there is no afterlife aspect or ethical aspect. We can say that the "Faith for blessings" is temporal, and is an egocentric blessing for a living person. The "Blessing faith of Christianity" pursues to be as light and salt, by living an ethical life with the blessing from God in this world, rather what the traditional "Faith for blessings" is pursuing: wealth and honor, prosperity, being healthy and longevity. And the "Blessing faith of Christianity" hopes, considering that the resurrection of the afterlife and the eternal happiness are more precious.

Fluke blessing, and Blessings based on covenant and promise.

The "Faith for blessings" of Shamanism follows a fluke aspect because it has no ethical aspect. According to Shamanism, since receiving or not receiving blessings depends on the will of the spirits, people can only hope that the spirits will release their wrath and bestow many blessings. There is no solid basis for receiving blessings. It becomes a fatalistic faith that blames everything that happens in life on one's own Chinese horoscope (Sazu Palza). The "Blessing faith of Christianity" is based on God's covenants and promises. God blesses because there is a promised Word to those who come into his covenant of salvation, namely, the covenant of blessing (Galatians 3:13-14).

Superstitious Blessing and Blessing of faith.

The shaman has a mediator role between the human world and

spirit world, calling the spirits through incantations and encouraging them to bestow their blessings upon the worshipper. In this way, the "Faith for blessings" asks for blessings through certain superstitious spells or incantation. A Christian blessing is a religious blessing. We can only be blessed by living a beautiful and good life according to God's promised Word of blessing. The Bible teaches that we are truly blessed not only when we receive blessings from God, but when we share them with our neighbors and use them for God's glory.[22]

2) Scholarly Debates on the Theology of Threefold Blessing

Myung-Soo Park says that the Holy Spirit transmits the Threefold salvation for us, interpreting the Threefold salvation of Yong-Gi Cho as the work of God in Trinity. But Mun-Hong Choi raises an objection to this interpretation. Namely, according to Mun-Hong Choi, Myung-Soo Park emphasizes that "the person in the fullness of the Holy Spirit will be saved from spiritual weakness, from mental weakness and from corporal weakness, through the power of the Holy Spirit." In other words, it seems that Myung-Soo Park attributes not only spiritual blessings but also good health (Perhaps including prosperity) to the role of the Holy Spirit. Therefore, Mun-Hong Choi

---

22 Yong-Gi Cho, *Ozung Bogumkwa Samzung Chukbok (Fivefold Gospel and Threefold Blessing)*, 195-198.

asks regarding the opinion of Myung-Soo Park: "Is the role of the Holy Spirit for the good of soul a soteriological Spirit in the Threefold redemption (Blessing) theology of Cho? Or is it the Spirit who comes upon the saved person in the fullness of the Holy Spirit?" Furthermore, Mun-hong Choi presents how he understands Yong-Gi Cho in this way: Even though it is true that, when Yong-Gi Cho explains the Threefold redemption (Blessing), he mostly speaks of the Cross, it does not mean that he excludes the role of the Holy Spirit. According to Mun-Hong Choi, Cho understands the role of Holy Spirit in two ways: 1) as having a role in salvation, and 2) having a Pentecostal role that empowers the saved person with baptism in the Holy Spirit / Fullness of the Holy Spirit.

> When Young-San (Yong-Gi Cho) explains the Threefold redemption (Blessing), he mostly speaks of Cross of Jesus Christ, and not so much about the role of Holy Spirit. But it is a big mistake to think that Young-San excludes the role of the Holy Spirit in the Threefold redemption (Blessing) theology. Because according to the Young- San's understanding of the Holy Spirit, salvation is possible only through the grace of the Holy Spirit. But if we speak only of this, we can create misunderstanding about the Pneumatology of Young-San. Namely, the Pneumatology of Young-San remains in the dimension of the Holy Spirit for salvation regarding the conversion of unbeliever. When he says that the salvation is only possible through supernatural work, Young-San keeps in mind the understanding of Paul and John about the Holy Spirit. Going further, based on the text of Luke and the Acts of the Apostles,

Young-San understands that the Holy Spirit of Pentecost is the one who gives power to the saved person, namely, with baptism in the Holy Spirit / Fullness of the Holy Spirit. When we speak of the Pneumatology of Young- San, we need to distinguish these two roles of the Holy Spirit.[23]

Applying Yong-Gi Cho's understanding of the Holy Spirit to his theology of the Threefold redemption (Blessing), Mun-Hong Choi explains that: First, Mun-Hong Choi emphasizes that the role of the Holy Spirit is presupposed for the theology of the Threefold Blessing of Cho. And he distinguishes two kinds of role: the role of the Holy Spirit in the salvation from sin to make the person born again; and the role of making the person full of the Holy Spirit in order to enjoy the Threefold Blessing. Going further, according to the Pneumatology of Yong-Gi Cho, to have the abundant enjoyment of the Threefold Blessing, it is necessary to have a personal communion with the Holy Spirit.

When Young-San (Yong-Gi Cho) speaks of salvation through Jesus, not only from sickness or curse / poverty, but also from sin, the role of the Holy Spirit is surely to make man born again. But when he talks about the enjoyment of the Threefold Blessing of the saved person, the role of the Holy Spirit is to make man full of the Holy Spirit. But to go further, when we see in the light of the personal Pneumatology

---

23 Mun-Hong Choi, *Young Sanui Kuwon Ibe (Understanding of Young San about Salvation0*, 365.

of Young-San, we might say that the enjoyment of the Threefold Blessing can be abundantly realized through the communion of the Holy Spirit who is a personal Spirit. In short, we can say that in the theology of the Threefold Blessing of Young-San, the role of the Holy Spirit is presupposed.[24]

Mun-Hong Choi talks about the salvation of society and the salvation of nature as related to the Threefold Blessing of Yong-Gi Cho in this way. Mun-Hong Choi says that Yong-Gi Cho declared that in the Year of Social Salvation, the devil is ultimately behind social and natural evils, but that the salvation of Christ's Cross is effective in eliminating social and natural evils, so we should actively carry out the work of social and natural salvation.

According to Mun-Hong Choi, this declaration demonstrates a big change of direction from Cho's previous attitude. Namely, while Yong-Gi Cho mostly has been emphasized that, to realize the social salvation, those who received the Threefold Blessing will practice love for neighbor personally in the society, Mun-Hong Choi sees that according to Yong-Gi Cho, from 'the Year of Society Salvation', the social salvation will be more outspreading actively in the church dimension. Therefore, Mun-Hong Choi expects that the social salvation ministry related to the theology of the Threefold redemption (Blessing) will not fail, unlike Minjung theology or Liberation theol-

---

24 Mun-Hong Choi, *Young Sanui Kuwon Ihe (Understanding of Young San about Salvation)*, 366.

ogy which in the past have claimed social salvation. Because Yong-Gi Cho declared that spiritual war with the devil who is behind social evil and natural evil, and also the social salvation ministry will be developed with prayer movement.[25] In reality, Yoido Full Gospel Church is trying to make a world where everybody is happy without suffering, through supporting the people who need to be saved from poverty, disaster, sickness, and to become self-reliant through a 'Good People', NGO.

Won-Suk Ma evaluates that the Yong-Gi Cho's theology of blessing is soteriologically motivated by the Christological process, namely through the atoning work of Christ. Consequently, Won-Suk Ma points out that it needs to be supplemented more by pneumatological study. Considering that the theological framework of Cho's theology of blessing has been developed in the Fivefold Gospel, Won-suk Ma presents a chart to compare Yong-Gi Cho's Fivefold Gospel with the Pentecostal Fourfold Gospel. The 'Fivefold' terminology is accepted almost as a professional theological language by Pentecostals. It is very important to check the content of the 'five', because if one fails to check the content of the 'five', Yong-Gi Cho's Fivefold theology can be easily misunderstood as the Fivefold of the Holiness Pentecostal system.

---

25 Mun-Hong Choi, *Young Sanui Kuwon Ibe (Understanding of Young San about Salvation)*, 369.

Pentecostal Five	Pentecostal Four	Yong-Gi Cho's Five
Jesus as Savior		
Healer		
Sanctifier		Blesser
Baptizer		
Coming King		

In presenting Jesus as Saviour in diagram, Won-Suk Ma makes it clear that Yong-Gi Cho's theology is decidedly Christo-centric, like that of traditional Pentecostals. According to Won-Suk Ma, it is noteworthy to say that Cho's theology is Christo-centric because Cho has been criticized often by non-Pentecostal Christians in Korea. They said that Cho's theology emphasizes the Holy Spirit, while minimizing Christ's work of salvation. Won-Suk Ma explains that Cho's Fivefold theology goes along with the Pentecostal Fourfold theology, which is the theology of the Assemblies of God to which he belongs, and that 'the Blesser' element has been added to the Pentecostal Fourfold theology. Won-Suk Ma considers that the addition of the fifth element, 'the Blesser', has been contextually motivated as Cho applied the traditional Pentecostal theology to the unique socio-cultural context of Korea. Likewise, some groups consider that Cho's blessing theology has creatively brought the Pentecostal tradition into the Korean context. But there are also disagreements about his theology of blessing, and some popular writers readily label Yong-Gi Cho as "shamanistic." Won-Suk Ma asks a question, at this point, toward the theological intent of Yong-gi Cho's theology of blessing: Is it self-serving? Or is it kingdom-serving?[26]

Won-Suk Ma points out that Yong-Gi Cho's theology of blessing, which was often treated as the Prosperity Gospel, has no clear theological goal or intent. Namely, a clear theological direction is not sufficiently clear in answer to the question, "What is the blessing for?" Won-Suk Ma asks, "Is the Christian concept of blessing any different from, let's say, the shamanistic or secular idea?"[27] Yong-Gi Cho insists that our salvation includes the removal of the curses of sin. According to Cho, once the curse is removed, blessings will come to every area of our lives; the cursed land will turn into a good land flowing with milk and honey and God's blessings; every area of our lives will be recovered to live in newness of life. Yong-Gi Cho makes clear that there is a decisive role of the Holy Spirit in this process. But Won-Suk Ma sees that in Yong-Gi Cho's theology of blessing, the direct role of the Holy Spirit in making our lives whole needs to be studied, because restoration and blessings has not been developed as a pneumatological theme.[28]

Won-Suk Ma strongly opposes the highly individualized notion

---

26 Won-Suk Ma, *Yong-Gi Cho's Theology of Blessing: New Theological Basis and Directions, in Young San International Theological Symposium (2003)*, ed. Full Gospel Theological Institute of Hansei University, Hansei University, Gunpo 2003, 188-191.

27 Won-Suk Ma, *Yong-Gi Cho's Theology of Blessing: New Theological Basis and Directions*, 195.

28 Won-Suk MA, *Yong-Gi Cho's Theology of Blessing: New Theological Basis and Directions*, 194.

of the modern theology of blessing. And he insists that the coming of the Holy Spirit is "upon us", thus, it cannot be ignored in its social and communal context. Since justice, righteousness, peace, security, and trust are the result of the Holy Spirit's presence, and are related to the community, if my blessings are not understood in the context of the community, they have little significance. For this reason, Won-Suk Ma thinks that it is encouraging to see an increasing discussion of the Pentecostal notion of social service.[29]

Some Korean scholars criticize Yong-Gi Cho. Yong-Sub Chung emphasizes that the theory of the Threefold Blessing is a lie, namely, according to Yong-Gi Cho, if one believes in Jesus well, this person will receive the Threefold Blessing; the Word of 3Jn 1:2 is only conventional phrase that was often used in the correspondence of that time without any especial meaning.[30] Yong-Sub Chung objects to the Threefold Blessing, saying that even though its appearance seems like a blessing, in reality, it has a high probability of acting as a malediction. And he presents an example, saying that because faith and theology are fundamentally based on common sense, this problem can have an answer: when the people who cannot escape from poverty, participate in public worship, if the pastor's sermon associates faith and material blessings together, saying that a man of faith receives material blessing, it is clear that the poor will be

---

[29] Won-Suk MA, *Yong-Gi Cho's Theology of Blessing: New Theological Basis and Directions*, 196.

[30] Yong-Sub Chung, *Sokbinsolkyo Kwagchansolkyo (Hollow preaching and Full Preaching)*, The Christian Literature Society of Korea, Seoul, 2006, 298.

hurt deeply.31

According to Yong-Sub Chung, the sermon of Yong-Gi Cho makes people become attached to riches, health, and success rather than to their salvation. Therefore, Yong-Sub Chung says that Yong-Gi Cho is destroying fundamentally the depths of Christian spirituality and the historical character of God's kingdom. Yong-Sub Chung gives an example of Yong-Gi Cho encouraging people to be a race winner in their life.32

> The life will be forgotten quickly, if a person gets out from the rank of life or is abandoned. Therefore, we should not be a failure always. In the race of life, we must be a winner, stand in the front group and run with it.33

Yong-Sub Chung affirms that, according to Yong-Gi Cho, Christians must cling to God in order to be victorious in this world, so they must pray for good business, good health, and for the demons to go away. Yong-Sub Chung says that, eventually, the Christian faith could become a kind of magical channel for personal productivity and competitiveness in this world. Chung continues in saying that according to Yong-Gi Cho, since winning or losing

---

31 Yong-Sub Chung, *Sokbinsolkyo Kwagchansolkyo (Hollow preaching and Full Preaching)*, 299.

32 Yong-Sub Chung, *Sokbinsolkyo Kwagchansolkyo (Hollow preaching and Full Preaching)*, 303.

33 Yong-Gi Cho, *Silpezanun Solgosiopda (Failure has no place to stand[Sept. 11, 2005])*, Sunday Sermon, (Sept. 2012), http://yfgc.fgtv.com.

this competition depends on church life, believers have no choice but to cling to church life in order to get ahead in the world. Therefore, Yong-Sub Chung points out that this fixation on logic ends up disempowering people' lives, asking the question: "Can we say that Yong-Gi Cho's sermon is a fundamentally Christian Gospel?" It is clear that Yong-Sub Chung is against the theory of the Threefold Blessing of Cho.[34]

Won-Kun Park argues that notable pastors of the theology of Prosperity have some negative aspects in common: a church hereditary to their family, sexual scandals and denominational division. Won-Kun Park gives the example of Robert H. Schuller, founder of the Crystal Cathedral Church in the USA, who followed the theology of Positive Thinking of Norman Vincent Peale. After the retirement of Robert H. Shuller this Crystal Cathedral Church went bankrupt in 2010. With this in mind Won-Kun Park poses the question: "For whom is the church's growth?" According to Won-Kun Park, the Korean Protestant church grew a lot with the supremacy of church's growth; but it became a leafy fig tree without fruit; it goes along the corruption way, losing the essence of the church. Won-Kun Park says that if church's growth is the supreme aim, then the pastor and the faithful and even God will become mere tools for growth. Therefore, Won-Kun Park asks: "What are they doing after making a megachurch even using secular way?"[35]

---

[34] Yong-Sub Chung, *Sokbinsolkyo Kwagchansolkyo (Hollow preaching and Full Preaching)*, 304.

[35] Won-Kun Park, *Yebe-esoui Kibok Sinang Muosi Munjeinga? (What's wrong with*

Even though Yong-Gi Cho was so famous for founding the largest church community in the world, but he also had a shadowy side. His decision to allow his family to run the church's institutions and schools led to major conflicts with the church elders and social controversy. As a result, he was also judged by the courts over his financial affairs. Ki-Suk Yun criticizes that the cupidity problem, such as the astronomical wealth of Yong-Gi Cho and his family members, expresses the shame and the corruption of the Korean Protestant Church. He affirms that a pastor who has lost his morality and ethics is not a pastor anymore, and insists that pastor and church elders should have high standards of morality and ethics.36

2. Divine healing

Saying that, since pastoral ministry of Yong-Gi Cho is oriented towards healing, they cannot think the worship without healing in the Yoido Full Gospel Church. This church has an image as a place where to go for healing.37 Yong-Gi Cho thinks of church community basically as a healing community. For Yong-Gi Cho, the word, "When

---

believing in good luck in worship?), in Hoibo, June (2011), The Presbyterian Church in the Republic of Korea, Seoul, 70-71.

36 Ki-Suk Yun, *Hankug Kyohoiui Kehyuk (1) (The Renewal of Korean Church [1])*, in Hoibo, May (2012), The Presbyterian Church in the Republic of Korea, Seoul, 14.

37 Hong-Keun Kim, *Young Sankwa Ciyumokhoi (Young San and Divine Healing), in Dr. Yonggi Cho's Theology: A theological Paradigm of the 21st Century*, ed. Full Gospel Theological Institute of Hansei University, Hansei University, Gunpo, 2003, 71.

a believer lays hands on the other believer, this believer is cured", needs to be interpreted, that the church should pray for each other's Divine healing. Therefore, the YFGC is so active for the pastoral ministry of healing through the participation of whole church.[38]

1) Theology of Divine healing

Yong-Gi Cho defines Divine healing as being healed by divine ability, namely, by the power of God. Therefore, Divine healing means a supernatural healing involved by the power and the providence of God, not through the ordinary medical practice. According to Yong-Gi Cho, the medical healing is also grace of God, but it cannot be defined as Divine healing. Because Divine healing means a healing of omnipotent God who is curing directly our body through his supernatural power.[39]

For Yong-Gi Cho, Divine healing is a gift of God, which should be certainly testified, being included in the atonement of Jesus Christ. It is not a gift which is good to have or not to have.[40] Cho observes, further, that the two third of ministry of Jesus on earth was constituted by healing, and Jesus has ordered disciples to ex-

---

[38] Hong-Keun Kim, *Young Sankwa Ciyumokhoi (Young San and Divine Healing)*, 87.
[39] Yong-Gi Cho, *Sinyuron (Divine Healing)*, Seoul Logos, Seoul, 2009, 9.
[40] Sang-Bok Lee, *Kungzong Simribak Kwanzomesobon Osunzol Ciyusinhak: Young San Cho Yong-Gi Moksaui Ciyusinhakul Zungsimuro (Pentecostal Healing Theology from the Positive Psychology Perspective: on the Dr. Yonggi Cho's Healing Theology)*, in *Korean Journal of Pentecostal Studies*, vol. 5, ed. Society for Pentecostal Studies in Korea, Hansei University Logos, Gunpo, 2007, 246.

ercise such ministry: 1) when he sent the 12 disciples (Mt 10:8), 2) the 70 disciples (Lk 10:9), 3) before the Ascension (Mk 16:18). Yong-Gi Cho declares that the healing is the core of Christianity. And he confirms, if Christianity ignores a healing, that is not Christianity.[41]

> Christianity, which ignores healing, is not Christianity. Christianity, which believes in Jesus Christ, is a religion of healing. Therefore, if we testify the moral and ethical Christianity only, ignoring healing, this is an action against the grace prepared by Christ on the Cross.[42]

Following the Word, "Jesus Christ is the same yesterday, today and forever" (Hebrews 13:8), Yong-Gi Cho insists that if today's church forbids or not practices the Divine healing ministry, it is like not to follow the command of God. Cho believes that Divine healing is never limited to the apostolic age, but has been a phenomenon throughout the church history and is a gracious act of God that is even more powerful and active in today's age of widespread disease.[43]

According to Hong-Keun Kim, Cho's sermons generated the most enthusiastic response from his congregation because he was con-

---

[41] Dawk-Mahn Bae, *Ciryo-hasinun Yesunim: Ciryoza Yesu Cristorul Tonghebon Yong Sanui Gidoknon Yunku (Healing Jesus: A Study on Young San's Christology Focusing on Jesus Christ as a Healer)*, in Young Sanui Mokhoiwa Sinhak (Ministry& Theology of Young-San), vol. 1, ed. Young San Theological Institute, Hansei University Logos, Gunpo 2008, 226.

[42] Yong-Gi Cho, *Chiryoui Kang (Healing River)*, complete works of Dickens, vol. 8, 154-155.

[43] Yong-Gi Cho, *Sinyuron (Divine Healing)*, 12-13.

vinced of the healing of diseases. Yong-Gi Cho, understanding that Satan, sin and malediction as three powers which brought us sickness, explains the sin of Adam and Eve, the death of the soul, the death of the body, the sickness in this way:

> Because of the sin of Adam and Eve, the death sentence was suddenly imposed on man, who had never known sickness or death. In the crime and corruption of man, the soul was killed before the body (Separation of relationship with God). Therefore, the death of the soul is the beginning of death. The death of the body comes from the death of the soul, which is the firstborn of death, and the beginning of this death is disease.[44]

Yong-Gi Cho also understands that sin and Satan are two in one, always together, and says that where there is Satan, there is sin, and where there is sin, there is certainly Satan. Cho affirms that Satan is behind sickness, so Jesus healed by casting out Satan. By seeing the sickness as a curse from God, Cho explains sin and Satan, sickness and curse, and Jesus' healing in this way:

> Where there is Satan, there is sin, and where there is sin, there is certainly Satan. At the behind of this disease there is Satan to supply the vitality and destructive power of the disease. Therefore, if this Satan is cast out, as a dead body without a soul, the disease without Satan's spirit becomes a dead disease. Behind all the sicknesses healed by Jesus, Stan was sup-

---

44 Hong-Keun Kim, *Young Sankwa Ciyumokhoi (Young San and Divine Healing)*, 83.

plying life. When Jesus threw out this Satan's spirit, the power of sickness was broken, and the life of health was given to the wounded body, and it was healed cleanly. In general, sickness comes from the curse of the law due to sin, and is a snare of Satan who is a prison officer of sin, curse and death. This sickness is approaching as a curse from God.[45]

Pointing to the Bible, which says, "By his wounds you have been healed" (1Pt 2:24), Cho shows that the healing of sickness lies in the atonement of Jesus. "If Divine healing is in the fact of atonement of Jesus on the Cross, all the believers in Christ should be healed. But why some faithful are healed, while others are not?" Responding at this question, Yong-Gi Cho explains that the healing is a gift given by God for us without cost, but not all the persons get this, because there are many factors involved: plan of God, man's sin, and faith. Yong-Gi Cho advices, that to receive Divine healing, first thing to do is to examine oneself, and then go forward to God with humility and faith.

The healing of sickness is a gift given by God for us without cost. Therefore, our healing is also given not because of our righteousness, but Jesus bought with payment on the Cross.[46] Divine healing is also a grace certainly which God permits for us, but not everybody will be

---

[45] Hong-Keun Kim, *Young Sankwa Ciyumokhoi (Young San and Divine Healing)*, 84.
[46] Yong-Gi Cho, *Sinyuron (Divine Healing)*, 13.

healed. Because there are many factors involved: plan of God, man's sin, and faith. Sometimes, for God's time, he withholds for a while or leaves it for his good will (2Cor 12:9). Therefore, to receive Divine healing, first thing to do is to examine oneself, and then go forward to God with humility and faith.[47]

Dawk-Mahn Bae, saying that Cho's understanding of Christ unfolds in various forms and directions around the event of the Cross, summarizes this way. First, Yong-Gi Cho declares that the suffering of Christ on the Cross was to cancel out the sins of humanity. Second, he argues that Jesus Christ was the only one who was born without sin and lived without sin, so he was able to take on the sins of humanity and go to the Cross. Third, Yong-Gi Cho believes that only the precious blood of Christ enabled to solve the sin of humanity. Therefore, Cho underlines that all the human efforts to obtain the salvation are only extremely foolish actions, and error based on ignorance and unbelief. Only the precious blood of Christ is the perfect righteousness of human being. Finally, Yong-Gi Cho is convinced that Jesus Christ, who solved man's most fundamental problem of sin on the Cross, also healed the problem of sickness. Therefore, Cho says that when we go up to the Cross and look at wounded Jesus, it is said that we can see Jesus healing there. Therefore, Dawk-Mahn Bae observes that the forgiveness of sin and healing

---

47 Yong-Gi Cho, Sipzaga Wiesobon Yesu (Jesus seen on the Cross), complete works of Dickens, vol. 4, 315. , *Sinyuron (Divine Healing)*, 14.

of diseases, in the Christology of Yong-Gi Cho, are not separated, but go hand in hand, like two sides of the same coin. This can be found in his words.[48]

When we go up to the Cross and look at wounded Jesus, we can see Jesus healing there.[49]

Yong-Gi Cho highlights more the real meaning and value of Resurrection, affirming the presence of Risen Jesus Christ. And he interprets the Resurrection as a current ongoing event, not only a one-time event in the past. Therefore, Dawk-Mahn Bae says that for Yong-Gi Cho, it is accepted as an unshakable truth, namely, that the healing event of Christ before 2,000 years, can be repeated now.[50]

The Resurrection of Christ is not the historical event or Bible story in the past. The Resurrection event of Christ is what is realistic. Jesus is Resurrection, life, and he is present among us. When you welcome this Christ, the dynamic history of Resurrection appears in your life. All the power of death in your life will be abolished and paradise history of

---

48 Dawk-Mahn Bae, *Ciryo-hasinun Yesunim: Ciryoza Yesu Cristorul Tonghebon Yong Sanui Gidoknon Yunku (Healing Jesus: A Study on Young San's Christology Focusing on Jesus Christ as a Healer)*, 227-229.
49 Yong-Gi Cho, *Sipzaga Wiesobon Yesu (Jesus seen on the Cross)*, complete works of Dickens, vol. 4, 315.
50 Dawk-Mahn Bae, *Ciryo-hasinun Yesunim: Ciryoza Yesu Cristorul Tonghebon Yong Sanui Gidoknon Yunku (Healing Jesus: A Study on Young San's Christology Focusing on Jesus Christ as a Healer)*, 230-231.

God's glory will begin.[51]

Yong-Gi Cho explains that Jesus Christ is the Lord of reconciliation. Dawk-mahn Bae summarizes it in this way: Jesus Christ was an excellent mediator of peace, breaking down the wall between God and man, making dramatic reconciliation between these two. As two foundations of this reconciliation, Yong-Gi Cho presents the event of Christ's Cross and the Resurrection of Christ. First, Cho picks up the sacrifice as a necessary condition for reconciliation, and believes that Christ satisfied it bleeding on the Cross. Second, Cho explains that the dissension between God and man was overcome through Resurrection of Christ. Namely, after Adam's sin there was only complete disconnection and dissension between God and man, and this dissension means death for man. Yong- gi Cho underlines that because Christ conquered death through Resurrection, the dissension between God and man was healed automatically. Therefore, he said that those who rely on Jesus Christ can be reconciled with God and can receive love of God. Yong-Gi Cho declares that the first fruit of this reconciliation was rightly healing. It is based on the fact that Jesus Christ was suffered for humanity. In other words, when Christ took up the sins of humanity and suffered on the Cross, humanity was freed from the snare of sin, and as a result, the problem of humanity's sin was solved.[52]

---

51 Yong-Gi Cho, *Yesunimui Buhwal, Nomuna Kippun Sosik (Resurrection of Jesus, So Good News)*, complete works of Dickens, vol. 19, 83.

52 Dawk-Mahn Bae, *Ciryo-hasinun Yesunim: Ciryoza Yesu Cristorul Tonghebon Yong*

The first fruit of reconciliation is healing. All the people of today are sick. Man is sick in spirit and in mind, in body and in life. ... We can experience the healing grace in spirit and in mind, in body and in life through the suffering of Jesus. When we rely on Jesus, God's healing power will overflow in us. Because we have a reason to be reconciled to God through Jesus.[53]

For Yong-Gi Cho, Jesus Christ is not only the historical person in the First century, but also who is carrying out the same ministry here and now as before. Therefore, who is not only the object of worship, but who is also a close companion of our life. Dawk-Mahn Bae makes up in three aspects, how Yong-Gi Cho understood the existing way of Christ and content of his ministry:

First, Yong-Gi Cho insists that Jesus Christ is present here today through the Holy Spirit.

Today, Jesus is present not only in the bodies of those who believe and love the Lord through the Holy Spirit, but also wherever two or three are gathered in the name of the Lord. Jesus who has come among us is the same yesterday, today, and forever. The same Jesus who came to earth 2,000 years ago in the flesh of a man of Nazareth has come to you today as the Holy Spirit, to be with you wherever you get up and sit down, in your home and workplace.[54]

Sanui Gidoknon Yunku ("Healing Jesus: A Study on Young San's Christology Focusing on Jesus Christ as a Healer"), 232-233.
53 Yong-Gi Cho, *Hwahe (Reconciliation)*, complete works of Dickens, vol. 11, 283.

Secondly, Yong-Gi Cho is convinced that Jesus is the same person in eternity. Therefore, if he is present among us through the Holy Spirit, he is doing the same work now. On this basis, Yong-Gi Cho proclaimed the gospel of healing and continued the ministry of Divine healing, against the attack of the Reformed orthodox who oppose the Pentecostal movement and Charismatic movement by insisting on the Cessation Theory of the gifts.

Finally, Yong-Gi Cho is sure of the real possibility of miraculous healing, based on the continuous presence of Jesus Christ through the Holy Spirit. And he urges the faithful to participate in this experience, affirming that Jesus Christ is that "the source of healing who gives us eternal life."55

> Even today, when we are sick, if we look to Jesus, river of healing flow from Jesus. So we should look to Jesus to be cured from our spiritual sickness, mental sickness, moral sickness, family sickness, life sickness, and all other sickness. Jesus is the source of the healing that gives us eternal life.56

Dawk-Mahn Bae evaluates that Yong-Gi Cho enriches his Christology, depicting messianic work of Jesus Christ with a variety

---

54 Yong-Gi Cho, *Nohui-ane Kyesin Christ (Christ present in you)*, complete works of Dickens, vol. 7, 296.

55 Dawk-Mahn Bae, *Ciryo-hasinun Yesunim: Ciryoza Yesu Cristorul Tonghebon Yong Sanui Gidoknon Yunku (Healing Jesus: A Study on Young San's Christology Focusing on Jesus Christ as a Healer)*, 237-238.

56 Yong-Gi Cho, *Zu Yesurul Baraboza (Let us look at Lord Jesus)*, complete works of Dickens, vol. 7, 332.

of tropes. And Dawk-Mahn Bae mentions three typical things related to Divine healing: Cross, Precious blood, yoke. First, Yong-Gi Cho uses the **Cross** of Jesus Christ as a symbol of healing. He presents the healing power of Christ through the Cross, symbolically identifying the Cross carried by Christ and Jesus Christ. Second, Yong-Gi Cho chooses the **precious blood** of Jesus Christ as another symbol of Christ healer. He insists that the suffering of Christ is the original basis for healing of humanity's sickness, relating the Book of Isaiah 53 with the figure of suffering Christ. And he chooses the precious blood of Jesus Christ as a symbol of this suffering. Finally, he compares the healing through Jesus Christ with yoke. **Yoke** is not only instrument for suppression and control, but it has positive function to prevent a bigger wound and to have higher work efficiency. Especially, Yong-Gi Cho accentuates that the yoke of Jesus Christ has positive meaning to offer us healing and rest through lightening the load of sickness. In this way Yong-Gi Cho explains Christ's ministry as a healer with rhetorically, using the visual tools like Cross, precious blood, and yoke.[57] But Yong-Gi Cho claims that if Christ shed the blood of ransom for healing, there will never exist the real meaning of Divine healing for non-Christian. Because the presupposition of Divine healing is to accept Christ, who is a healer.[58]

---

[57] Dawk-Mahn Bae, *Ciryo-hasinun Yesunim: Ciryoza Yesu Cristorul Tonghebon Yong Sanui Gidoknon Yunku (Healing Jesus: A Study on Young San's Christology Focusing on Jesus Christ as a Healer)*, 239-240

[58] Lok-Young Hong, *Young San Cho Yong-Gi Moksaga Mannan Ciyuhasinun Yesu Cristo (Understanding of Young San's Divine Healing)*, in *Young Sanui Mokhoiwa Sinhak (Ministry & Theology of Young San)*, vol.1, ed. Young San Theological

2) Arguments on Yong-Gi Cho's Divine healing

Yong-Gi Cho declares that the Resurrection of Jesus Christ is a clear historical fact. He is sure that as a result of this, death has been overcome, and all the tears that have been penetrated in the world because of malediction of death have also been overcome, and remained only the glory. According to Dawk-Mahn Bae, pentecostal scholar, this conviction on the Resurrection is the theoretical basis which permits to call the theology of Yong-Gi Cho as a 'theology of hope'. And Dawk-Mahn Bae evaluates that theological base, namely which Fivefold Gospel can be embodied in Threefold Blessing, is deeply connected with his firm belief in the Resurrection.[59]

Dawk-Mahn Bae sees that while Christology of Yong-Gi Cho can be approached from many different perspectives and in many different ways, the specificity of Chos' ministry context naturally led him to place the image of Jesus the healer in relation to healing. Dawk-Mahn Bae, cannot deny that the image of healer Jesus is the main point to understand Yong-Gi Cho's Christology. But Dawk-Mahn Bae evaluates that Cho's Christology is very limited in depth and width. For example, in the sermon of Yong-Gi Cho (May 9, 1982), based on Lk 4:16-21, denying the political and economical interpretation about the Gospel proclaimed to the poor,

---

Institute, Hansei University Logos, Gunpo, 2008, 255.

59 Dawk-Mahn Bae, *Ciryo-hasinun Yesunim: Ciryoza Yesu Cristorul Tongbebon Yong Sanui Gidoknon Yunku (Healing Jesus: A Study on Young San's Christology Focusing on Jesus Christ as a Healer)*, 230.

PART II _ Theology and Doctrine of Yong-Gi Cho **71**

the captive, the oppressed, the blind, he was only consistent for the personal interpretation. And Dawk-Mahn Bae, points out also that even though there is environmental redemption in the Threefold Blessing of Yong-Gi Cho, the environmental and ecological issues are not touched enough in his Christology or Divine healing theology or soteriology. But Dawk-Mahn Bae thinks that because already in the theology of Yong-Gi Cho, the understanding of social dimension and ecological dimension are conceived, if one pays more attention in this aspect, a very deep and influential theology can be developed in this field.[60]

Vinson Synan sees that one of the cross Yong-Gi Cho have to bear is the charge that he is practitioner of Shamanism in the Korean context. Some who have made this charge are Walter Hollenweger and Harvey Cox. For many conservative Christians, these are considered "liberal critics." On the other hand, are such "conservative" anti-pentecostal critics see Yong-Gi Cho as a deceiver as well as a shaman. But Vinson Synan agrees with Myung-Soo Park and Donald Dayton, saying that Yong-Gi Cho was not influenced by Korean Shamanism, but that the main source of his healing message came from Pentecostalism presented within the historical context of Korea.[61]

---

60 Dawk-Mahn Bae, *Ciryo-hasinun Yesunim: Ciryoza Yesu Cristorul Tonghebon Yong Sanui Gidoknon Yunku (Healing Jesus: A Study on Young San's Christology Focusing on Jesus Christ as a Healer)*, 241-242.
61 Vinson Synan, *Young San Cho Yong-Gi Moksaui Ciyu Sinhakui Puri (Roots of*

Another scholar, Dong-Soo Kim, expresses his opinion about *Han* in this way, relating the Minjung theology and Shamanism, and also Korean Pentecostal worship and overnight prayer of Yoido Full Gospel Church: According to Dong-Soo Kim, *Han*[62] is typical Korean feelings. It does not mean that this kind of feeling only exists in Korean, but it is inherent to the majority of Koreans. *Han* is a kind of 'broken heart.' It means that a heart becomes broken by mistreatment and violence. When the mind is wounded, there is pain, and when the pain continues, there is suffering, and when this continues, *Han* will take place in the heart. Dong-Soo Kim insists that the Pentecostal theology is not influenced by Shamanism, but it has more common aspects with Shamanism than Minjung theology in the way to eliminate *Han*. Therefore, Dong-Soo Kim says that the Korean Pentecostal faith includes the '*Han* releasing theology', which most appropriately solves the Korean's *Han* problem. Dong-Soo Kim affirms that shaman has a role of '*Han* healer' or

---

Yong-Gi Cho's Theology of Healing), in *Young San International Theological Symposium (2006)*, ed. Young San Theological Institute of Hansei University, Hansei University, Gunpo, 2006, 19.

62 The *Han* often appears traditionally in the women who are weak in the society. There is endless story of the women's *Han* in Zoson, the reign founded in XVI century. For common example, if a woman does not give birth a son after some period of getting married, she has all the responsibility of it. In this time, her only way is divorce or should look for concubine or a woman who will give birth to a son to continue that family. In this situation, suffering and sadness inherent in her heart, she is hurt deeply. This is the Han.; Dong-Soo Kim, *Hebanui Sinhakurosoui Young San Sinhak (The Pentecostal Theology as a Theology to make free from Han)*, in *Dr. Yong-Gi Cho's Theology: A Theological Paradigm for the 21st Century*, ed. Full Gospel Theological Institute of Hansei University, Hansei University, Gunpo, 2003, 58–59.

'priestess of *Han*', seeing that the Korean's *Han* is dissolved usually, not with revenge, but with being sublimated through the religion or the arts. And he affirms that shaman celebrates various types of rite ('Gud') to dissolve Han, respecting the cause of *Han*: for the healing from sickness, for the dead, for the drowned dead, for asking the rain, etc. For example, in performing a 'Gud' for a drowned dead, the shaman invokes the spirit of this drowned dead to complain of his injustice, and afterwards declares that the spirit has been freed from the resentment and is at rest. And the grief and sorrow of the surviving family are also consoled by the 'Gud.'[63]

Dong-Soo Kim sustains that the starting point of Minjung theology was the problem of *Han*, and it is the contribution of Munjung theology to make *Han*, which is the psychological and cultural problem of Koreans, the theological subject. According to Young-hak Hyun, the Minjung theology is even a theology of *Han*. This can be seen in the words of Nam-dong Suh, Minjung theologian:

> We must put *Han* as our theological subject. Actually, *Han* is a language of Minjung (People), and their real experience. If we do not listen to the moan of Minung's *Han*, we cannot listen to the Christ's knocking on our door.[64]

---

63 Dong-Soo Kim, *Hehanui Sinhakurosoui Young San Sinhak (The Pentecostal Theology as a Theology to make free from Han)*, 59-62.

64 N.D. Suh, *Toward a Theology of Han, in Minjung Theology: People as the Subjects of History (The Christian Conference of Asia)*, ed. Young-Bock Kim, Singapore, 1981, 65; Dong-Soo Kim, *Hehanui Sinhakurosoui Young San Sinhak (The Pentecostal Theology as a Theology to make free from Han)*, 62.

According to Dong-Soo Kim, Minjung theologians interpret the *Han* as "the willpower for the life of repressed people" being influenced by Liberation theology, not understanding with traditional concept of Korean.[65] Dong-Soo Kim sees that for the Minjung theologians, *Han* is the driving force for the social revolution. Namely, they understand that the main cause of *Han* is with unfair social structure, therefore, to heal *Han*, they insist the revolution of social structure through fighting against unequal social structure.

Dong-Soo Kim evaluates that the Minjung theology is a theology which did not get a favorable response from minjung (People), and he explains the reason why he evaluates this way: First, Dong-Soo Kim says that Minjung theology could not get close to minjung (People) because of distance between Minjung theology's understanding of *Han* and minjung's traditional understanding of *Han*. Second, according to Dong-Soo Kim, Korean 3.1 Movement and 4.19 Movement, which were considered by Minjung theologians as the minjung movement against unjust social structure in Korea, were not the minjung movement, but it was a movement of the intellectual elite.[66] As a result, Dong-Soo Kim recognizes that the Minjung theology could not heal *Han*, even though *Han* was the starting point of their theology.

On the other side, Dong-Soo Kim sees that the Pentecostal theol-

---

65 N.D. Suh, *Toward a Theology of Han*, 55; Dong-Soo Kim, *Hehanui Sinhakurosoui Young San Sinhak (The Pentecostal Theology as a Theology to make free from Han)*, 63.

66 Dong-Soo Kim, *Hehanui Sinhakurosoui Young San Sinhak (The Pentecostal Theology as a Theology to make free from Han)*, 63.

ogy has a role to release properly the problem of *Han*, which is the traditional Korean people's problem, even without using the word *Han*. Dong-Soo Kim affirms that the Threefold Blessing theology of Yong-Gi Cho, especially in the late 1950s, was a theology that uprooted *Han* and solved the salvation of the soul, even the problem of poverty and disease. And Dong-Soo Kim sees that the main concern of Minjung theology to heal *Han*, was the revolution of social and political structure which made *Han* arouse, while Shamanism and Pentecostal theology in Korea, try to heal *Han* through casting out demons and proclaiming the material blessing. Dong-Soo Kim mentions that non-Pentecostals doubted this way to remove *Han*, saying that "Korean Pentecostal theology is influenced by Shamanism."[67]

Dong-Soo Kim confirms that Korean Pentecostal theology has evangelically enculturated the releasing *Han* of Shamanism; Pentecostal theology took over the role of releasing *Han*, which was traditionally a role of Shamanism. Furthermore, Dong-Soo Kim says that Korean Pentecostal church has the elements to make people experience in releasing *Han* naturally, and he summarizes it in two aspects.

First, Dong-soo Kim affirms that most Pentecostal pastors in Korea have experienced *Han*, but they overcome it with faith, and also they have clear sense of vocation as a 'priest of *Han*.' According

---

67 Dong-Soo Kim, *Hebanui Sinhakurosoui Young San Sinhak (The Pentecostal Theology as a Theology to make free from Han)*, 64-65

to Dong-Soo Kim, usually the suffering people with *Han*, are looking for a person with *Han* experience, but it is not enough to be a 'priest of *Han*' even though there is a pastor with *Han* experience. Because a 'priest of *Han*' must have clear sense of vocation. Dong-Soo Kim affirms that Pentecostal theology puts forward the experience of Holy Spirit and sense of vocation as a qualification to be a pastor; therefore, this point is very well-connected with the qualification to be a 'priest of *Han*.'[68]

Secondly, Dong-Soo Kim sees that the Pentecostal worship in Korea and glossolalia (Speaking in tongues) have a role of releasing *Han*. Especially because Pentecostal worship creates an atmosphere in which the faithful can approach easily to God with their own problem, seeking to be free in the Holy Spirit, rather than dominated by the form of worship. Furthermore, Dong-Soo Kim underlines that the prayer with speaking in tongues of Pentecostal movement has a capacity to make the sickness of the heart free from the chain of *Han* through prayer. Cyrill G. Williams affirms that speaking in tongues has a healing function to relieve stress and internal conflicts by releasing energy.[69] Also, Dong-Soo Kim says that overnight prayer, which began in the Yoido Full Gospel Church, has the function of releasing *Han*. Because when a person is in difficulty to express

---

68 Dong-Soo Kim, *Hehanui Sinhakurosoui Young San Sinhak (The Pentecostal Theology as a Theology to make free from Han)*, 67.
69 Cyril G. Williams, *Tongues of the Spirit: A Study of Pentecostal Glossolalia and Related Phenomenon*, University of Wales Press, Cardiff, 1981, 166; Dong-Soo Kim, *Hehanui Sinhakurosoui Young San Sinhak (The Pentecostal Theology as a Theology to make free from Han)*, 68.

his or her own feelings in front of people, overnight prayer provides a place to pray to God for one's problems without being aware of others during a special time, and to release *Han* psychologically. Dong-Soo Kim concludes that the theology of Yong-Gi Cho, without using the word *Han*, appropriately presents the evangelical healing method of *Han* familiar to the public. And Kim evaluates that the theology of Yong-Gi Cho is the '*Han* releasing theology, saying that his theology contains the element of releasing *Han*. Dong-Soo Kim hopes an ecumenical theological dialogue with the subject, 'to solve the problem of *Han*', to have a wider mutual understanding between Pentecostal and no-Pentecostal theologians, and between believers.[70]

According to Harvey Cox (1929~), wherever there is a Pentecostal movement, healing is part of the basic message of the Pentecostal movement; therefore, the Pentecostals are not uncomfortable with the fact that YFGC (Yoido Full Gospel Church) has grown through the spiritual healing. But Harvey Cox sees that what worries Western Pentecostals is that the church has grown explosively by absorbing Korean Shamanism and demonic possession into its worship services. According to Harvey Cox, what they take issue is: the degree of importation is so extensive, therefore some wonder comes out, what has absorbed what. Namely, what Korean Pentecostal church absorbed from Shamanism is so wide range. As a result,

---

70 Dong-Soo Kim, *Hehanui Sinhakurosoui Young San Sinhak (The Pentecostal Theology as a Theology to make free from Han)*, 68-70.

Harvey Cox asks: "Is the growth of Pentecostal movement in Korea an example of the success of indigenization of Christianity in an Asian culture? Or is it merely the continuation of the most salient forms of previous Korean folk religion wearing a Christian mask?" As debate goes on, Harvey Cox affirms that the Yoido Full Gospel Church is a particularly vivid case in point.[71]

Harvey Cox notes that the elements of Shamanism are present in the worship of YFGC and of some Pentecostal churches in Korea: ecstatic trances, demon possession, exorcism. And Harvey Cox stresses that in Yoido Full Gospel Church there is a massive importation of shamanic practice into a Christian ritual. But Harvey Cox affirms that the majority of Korean Pentecostals deny this point, saying that despite superficial similarities to Shamanism, something very different is going on. For this, Harvey Cox gives an example from a dialogue between Cox and a Korea pastor:

> One Korean pastor pointed out to me that in Paul's description of his experience of hearing words so secret "no human lips could repeat them", the apostle says that he did not know whether he was "in the body or apart from it." He asked me "What did they need Shamanism for if it was all in the New Testament?"

Harvey Cox evaluates positively this pastor, saying that he got

---

[71] Harvey Cox, *Fire from Heaven*, Addison-Wesley Publishing Company, New York, 1995, 222.

to the heart of the matter using the experience of St. Paul. Namely, according to this pastor, the criticism that Pentecostal church in Korea has received too many shamanic elements, is not correct. Harvey Cox says, "In fact, recent biblical scholarship has suggested that St. Paul may have been much more of a mystic, more steeped in the Jewish 'hekhalot' literature with its descriptions of celestial journeys, than more conservative interpreters of the apostle are willing to admit."[72]

Anyway, when "Fire from Heaven" ("Youngsung, Eumak, Yousung") was translated in Korean, Harvey Cox mentioned something very important in the 'Writing to the readers.' Namely, when he wrote this book, he never visited Korea. Therefore, Harvey Cox confessed that he had a great difficulty in understanding the Korean church because, not knowing the language, he had to rely mainly on the tape and the secondhand source, and also a few translated theological materials.[73] Therefore, it can be seen that Harvey Cox recognized the limitation of his writings on the Korean Pentecostal church.

Assemblies of God, where Yong-Gi Cho belongs to, selected their creed on the Divine healing like this:

Divine healing[74]

---

[72] Harvey Cox, *Fire from Heaven*, 225-226.
[73] Harvey Cox, *Yungsong, Umak, Yusong (Fire from Heaven)*, translated in Korean by Yu Ji-Hwang, Dong Yeon, Seoul, 1998, 5-6.
[74] William Menzies, *Anointed to Serve: The Story of the Assemblies of God* (Springfield,

Divine healing is an integral part of the Gospel. Deliverance from sickness is provided for in the atonement, and is the privilege of all believers (Is 53, 4-5; Mt 8, 16-17; James 5, 14-16)

According to Vinson Synan, despite this creed, there is a criticism, "Yong-Gi Cho is so contextualized by Korean culture that he owes little to his Pentecostal roots." But some scholars reject this criticism, saying that Yong-Gi Cho is the one who is most close to the Pentecostal doctrine of healing. For example, Allen Anderson, Donald W. Dayton (1942~2020), and Myung-Soo Park see that Yong-Gi Cho's doctrine of healing came mainly from Classical Pentecostal movement. Vinson Synan evaluates that Yong-Gi Cho is true to the teaching of his denomination, saying that in all his writings on healing, Yong-Gi Cho freely accepts the teaching that Divine healing is in the atonement. But Vinson Synan points out that yet, in most of his writings, Yong-Gi Cho prefers to say that healing is part of 'redemption' and rarely uses the term 'atonement.'[75] Donald W. Dayton affirms that Yong-Gi Cho's theology is away from the categories of 'syncretism' and furthermore he evaluates that Yong-Gi Cho's theology has rootedness in larger themes of both Pentecostalism and the larger Christian movement.[76]

MO: Gospel Publishing House, 1971). The statement on healing is on page 389.

75 Vinson Synan, *Young San Cho Yong-Gi Moksaui Ciyu Sinhakui Puri (Roots of Yong-Gi Cho's Theology of Healing)*, 27-28.

76 Donald W. Dayton, *The "Good God" and The "Theology of Blessing" in the Thought of David Yong-Gi Cho*, in *Young San International Theological Symposium (2005)*, ed. Young San Theological Institute of Hansei University, Hansei University,

Vinson Synan recognizes that Yong-Gi Cho is well known as a pastor who is in charge of the largest congregation, YFGC, and he is a Pentecostal pastor in communion with the Assemblies of God, the largest Pentecostal denomination in the world. But Vinson Synan evaluates that less well known the theological contributions that Cho has made to the contemporary church, especially in the area of Divine healing. Vinson Synan also notes that in developing Cho's theology of healing he was helped by many teachers who had come before him and says, "but his most original contribution was his emphasis on the Threefold Blessings of salvation, healing, and prosperity as part of his Fivefold Gospel, most of which was standard Classical Pentecostal teaching that he had inherited from the Assemblies of God."[77]

Vinson Synan explains the original aspect of Yong-Gi Cho in his theology as follows. The Assemblies of God has Fourfold Gospel (1. Salvation 2, Baptism in the Holy Spirit, 3. Divine healing, 4. Second coming). But when Yong-Gi Cho became a minister and founded his congregation in 1958, Cho added a new article in the statement of faith of YFGC, called 'blessings' which became now another Fivefold Gospel (1. Salvation, 2. Baptism in the Holy Spirit, 3. Divine healing, 4. Second coming, 5. Blessing). According to Vinson Synan, this marked Yong-Gi Cho as an original theologian who added a new element to Korea Pentecostalism, and it seems

---

Gunpo, 2005, 37.
[77] Vinson Synan, *Young San Cho Yong-gi Moksaui Ciyu Sinhakui Puri (Roots of Yong-Gi Cho's Theology of Healing)*, 16.

that this is a singularly Korean contribution to the world of Pentecostal theology because it appears only in Korean Pentecostal church. Saying that healing is the most important aspect of Yong-Gi Cho's theology, Vinson Synan thinks that Yong-Gi Cho's distinctive teaching on healing is influenced by Christian tradition, by Korean Buddhist and Confucian traditions, by the indigenous Korean healers who preceded Yong-Gi Cho, and the development of healing teachings from Europe and America that influenced his thinking.[78]

Yong-Gi Cho acknowledges that miraculous healings did sometimes occur among Buddhists. He also received these questions from Christians: "How can we call the Jehovah God, the unique creator in heavenly places? We see miracles in Buddhism, miracles in Yoga and in 'Chang-ga Hakhoi.' We see many miracles in the Oriental religions." Yong-Gi Cho solved this dilemma through the insights of his Fourth dimension. And Cho says that pagan miracles could come only through human intervention, not divine intervention.[79]

Vinson Synan sees that Yong-Gi Cho added to the standard Pentecostal views on healing that Yong-Gi Cho received from the Assemblies of God, he was greatly influenced by the ministry and teachings of the American healing evangelist Oral Roberts (1918~2009). According to Oral Roberts, in 1947, his eyes fell on a verse of Scripture that revolutionized his ministry: "Beloved, I wish above all things that

---

78 Vinson Synan, *Young San Cho Yong-Gi Moksaui Ciyu Sinhakui Puri (Roots of Yong-gi Cho's Theology of Healing)*, 17.

79 Vinson Synan, *Young San Cho Yong-Gi Moksaui Ciyu Sinhakui Puri (Roots of Yong-gi Cho's Theology of Healing)*, 19.

you may prosper and be in health even as your soul prospers." (3Jn 1:2). It became a central point in Roberts' 1948 book, *If You Need Healing, Do These Things*. Through the American friends, Yong-Gi Cho got a copy of this book and became a devoted follower and friend of Oral Roberts. In 1958, when Yong-Gi Cho started his church in a poor area of Seoul, added the statement called 'Blessings' to his official statement of faith. Through this his church has grown into a global church, Yong-Gi Cho confesses it this way.[80]

> Since that time this truth has been the foundation of all my sermons and I have laid the foundation of my ministry on this Scripture. When I interpreted all Scripture in light of the truth of this particular portion, God began to manifest Himself not only as the God of the past and the future, but as the God of the present —who lives in the present time. Furthermore, because of the power of this message, our church has grown into an international church and will continue to grow in the future.[81]

Vinson Synan sees that Yong-Gi Cho in later years adapted the teachings of the Faith movement to his understanding of healing. Following Kenneth Hagin (1917~2003), Yong-Gi Cho accepted the Rhema-Logos teachings of the Faith movement as his own. Vinson

---

80 Vinson Synan, *Young San Cho Yong-Gi Moksaui Ciyu Sinhakui Puri (Roots of Yong-Gi Cho's Theology of Healing)*, 28-29.
81 David Yong-Gi Cho, *Salvation, Healing & Prosperity, Creation House*, Westmonte Drive, 1987, 12.

Synan thinks in this sense, Yong-Gi Cho could also be called a word faith teacher. According to Vinson Synan, Yong-Gi Cho is influenced by Kathryn Kuhlman (1907~1976) on the prayer methods for the sick. Because while Oral Roberts and other early faith healers placed their hands directly on the patients' body and lay hands on them, Yong-Gi Cho followed Kuhlman by using the 'word of knowledge.' Namely, calling out sicknesses from the platform. This enabled him to minister healing to thousands of people from the pulpit without exhausting effort of laying hands on each one. But leaving the platform after each service, Yong-Gi Cho would continue to lay hands on the sick. One observer mentioned that 7 out of 10 members of the Yoido Full Gospel Church, has experienced healing after prayers ministered by Yong-Gi Cho. Therefore, Vinson Synan concludes that Divine healing has probably been the most important reason for the enormous growth of his congregation, even more than speaking in tongues.[82]

Yong-Gi Cho has some difficulties to accept the evaluation of Vinson Synan: namely, Yong-Gi Cho is much influenced by the ministry and teaching of Oral Roberts, regarding the declaration called 'Blessings'; Yong-Gi Cho has accepted the theory of Rhema-Logos following Kenneth Hagin in healing; he follows the method of Kathryn Kuhlman in the way of healing prayer. Replying to my personal letter as an interview, Yong-Gi Cho expressed about this argu-

---

82 Vinson Synan, *Young San Cho Yong-Gi Moksaui Ciyu Sinhakui Puri (Roots of Yong-gi Cho's Theology of Healing)*, 32-33.

ment through the official letter form, he clearly refused for being influenced by Oral Roberts, Kenneth Hagin and Kathryn Kuhlman. Yong-Gi Cho wrote me this way:

> I am not influenced by the *Word of Faith Movement*, Oral Roberts, Kenneth Hagin, Kathryn Kuhlman. Several Classic Pentecostals, belongs to Assemblies of God, have influenced to my Pentecostal theology and Pentecostal ministry. Of course, I respect the pastoral ministry of Oral Roberts, who was my good friend. Nevertheless, the direction of my theology and pastoral ministry is set up according to the traditional position and orthodox stand of Assemblies of God to which I belong, not other effects. If there are common points between me and Oral Roberts, Kenneth Hagin, Kathryn Kuhlman, because they could be influenced by Classic Pentecostal Movement like me. The *Word of Faith Movement* also not irrelevant with effect of Classic Pentecostal Movement.[83]

Likewise, Yong-Gi Cho confirms clearly that he is not influenced by Oral Roberts and Kenneth Hagin, Kathryn Kuhulman, but his theological and pastoral direction is influenced by the Classic Pentecostals of Assemblies of God. Yong-Gi Cho explains that if there are common aspects between Yong-Gi Cho and these three individuals, because they could be influenced by Classic Pentecostal Movement like him. Yong-Gi Cho affirms, moreover, that the *Word*

---

[83] Yong-Gi Cho, *The response of pastor Yong-Gi Cho to the personal letter of Sr. Chung-Myung Son*, 4 December of 2012.

of Faith Movement is not irrelevant also from the influence of Classic Pentecostal Movement. Therefore, reflecting on the theology of Yong-Gi Cho, is necessary to know something also regarding the *Word of Faith Movement*.

The forerunner of the *Word of Faith Movement (Faith Movement, Positive Confession Movement)* is Essek William Kenyon (1867~1948). E.W. Kenyon was an evangelist, pastor, educator and author, pioneer in radio evangelism with broadcasts. Although E.W. Kenyon was not a Pentecostal, his writings became seminal for the ministry of Kenneth Hagin in the *Word of Faith Movement (Positive Confession)*.[84]

E.W. Kenyon got his vision attending the *Emerson College of Oratory* in Boston, a spawning ground for *New Thought philosophical ideas*. The major tenets of the New Thought movement are health, healing, wealth, prosperity, and happiness. *New Thought Philosophy* can be traced back to Phineas P. Quimby (1802~1866). Quimby studied spiritism, occultism, hypnosis, and parapsychology, among other things. A view of God emerged from Quimby, William Branham, E.W. Kenyon and John G. Lake that was supported by Kenneth Hagin, Copeland, Capps. John G. Lake asserted, "Man is not a separate creation detached from God, he is part of God Himself ... God intends us to be gods. The inner man is the real ruler. The true man that Jesus said was a little god."[85]

---

[84] R.M. Riss, *Kenyon, Essek William*, in *The New International Dictionary of Pentecostal and Charismatic Movements (revised and expanded edition)*, ed. Stanley M. Burgess–Eduard M. Van Der Maas, Zondervan, Michigan, 2003, 819-820.

Some of E.W. Kenyon's direct disciples and those who were influenced by his teaching began the *Word of Faith Movement*. The base of this movement is the theology of *Positive Confession*. Namely, "What I confess, I possess." Therefore, by proclaiming with enough faith what is necessary to get the health and prosperity, Christian has the assurance to get them. This movement quotes Rm10: 8-10.

> The word is near you, (that is, the word of faith that we preach), for, if you confess with your mouth that Jesus is Lord and believe in your heart that God raised him from the dead, you will be saved. For one believes with the heart and so is justified, and one confesses with the mouth and so is saved (Rm10:8-10).

According to the interpretation of the *Word of Faith Movement*, in this paragraph, 'be saved' includes not only eternal salvation, but also physical health and welfare. Sometimes the *Word of Faith Movement* is called '*Hagin current*', named after Kenneth Hagin (1917~2003) who is one of the early promoters of this movement. Kenneth Hagin founded, in 1974, *Rhema Bible Training College*.[86]

The idea of omnipotence of the '*Positive Confession*' brought the preachers of the *Word of Faith Movement* to insist on fact that the Christians can obtain literally all, pronouncing (with sincerity) the words of faith, and moreover, can become 'little gods' which has

---

[85] L. Lovett, *Positive Confession Theology*, in *The New International Dictionary of Pentecostal and Charismatic Movements (revised and expanded edition)*, ed. Stanley M. Burgess – Eduard M. Van Der Maas, Zondervan, Michigan, 2003, 992.

[86] Massimo Introvigne, *Pentecostali*, 154.

provoked more polemic. The *Word of Faith Movement* has also a unique demonology, giving a particular importance to the descent to the hell of Jesus Christ after being crucified. Therefore, they insist that all the sickness and material hardships have a demoniac origin.[87]

The *Rhema* doctrine is the primary key of *Positive Confession* theology. Rm10:8 is its primary passage. The word *Rhema*, in its classical Greek usage, has to do with stating something specifically. E.W. Kenyon recognized two types of knowledge: 1) revelation or faith knowledge; 2) sense knowledge. Revelation knowledge is 'the knowledge that deals with things that the senses cannot discover or know without assistance from revelation knowledge.' For E.W. Kenyon and *Positive Confession* supporters, revelation knowledge, is the realm above sense knowledge. To give the credibility for the *Rhema* doctrine, *Positive Confession* supporters use these as the basic Scriptures: Prov. 6:2; Rom 10:8; 4:17; 3Jn 1:2. Especially 3Jn 1:2 is one of the biblical foundations of Threefold Blessing of Yong-Gi Cho. For *Positive Confession* theology, 3Jn 1:2 is essential, and also Oral Roberts mentions 3Jn 1:2. Therefore, it can be seen that there is a common aspect.

Critics of *Positive Confession* point out that these Scriptures are used improperly: Prov. 6:2; Rom 10:8; 4:17; 3 Jn 1:2. To be "ensnared by the words of your mouth" in Prov. 6:2 is related with a financial transaction that involves a security deposit within a contractual

---

[87] Massimo Introvigne, *Pentecostali*, 156.

relationship. According to them, Rom 4:17 is a description of Abraham's faith, specifically, not ours: "I have made you father of many nations. He is our father in the sight of God, in whom he believed, who gives life to the dead and calls into being what does not exist."

They affirm that Rom 10:8 ("The word is near you, that is, the word of faith that we preach"), must be read related to 9-11v ("for, if you confess with your mouth that Jesus is Lord and believe in your heart that God raised him from the dead, you will be saved, For one believes with the heart and so is justified, and one confesses with the mouth and so is saved. For the Scripture says, 'No one who believes in him will be put to shame.'"). If not, the true meaning will be lost, because, the passages cited refer primarily to the truth that comprises the message of salvation as proclaimed in the apostolic tradition.

Those who disagree with *Positive Confession* theology affirm that 3Jn 1:2 is a formal greeting and not a promise; neither can it be evoked as God's will for all believers to be "healthy and prosperous." They point out that within the Christian faith the biblical meaning of the noun and the associated verb "to believe" denotes the criterion of right relationship with God: 1) In the NT it appears that love is given primacy over faith, especially in the Pauline literature. Positive confessionists reverse this emphasis. Faith is never presented as a tool to manipulate God for our selfish ends, and nowhere in the teachings of Jesus is it given primacy; 2) St. Paul, in the hymn of love in 1 Corinthians 13, gives primacy to love as the greatest of faith, hope, and love; 3) At the heart of our being is the need to be loved by the one who created us for his glory and who alone as perfect love can fully satisfy our deepest needs.[88]

Vinson Synan affirms a connection between Yong-Gi Cho and Kathryn Kuhlman regarding the healing method. Therefore, we will see Kathryn Kuhlman mentioned by R.A.N. Kydd, to compare with Yong-Gi Cho. Kuhlman went into evangelism in the U.S. in 1928. After traumatic events in her personal life, she found herself with a healing ministry near Pittsburgh in 1947. Kuhlman quickly became so famous, established another base in California, went on radio and television, and became the leading proponent of healing evangelism in the 1960s, a position she maintained until her death. The most outstanding feature of Kuhlman's ministry was her insistence on absolute dependence on the Holy Spirit.

R.A.N. Kydd says that no one before Kuhlman had highlighted the importance of the role the Holy Spirit played in healing to the degree to which she did. She insisted that she did not do anything for the apparent healings. God performed the miracles according to His purposes and plans, of which she absolutely did not know anything. Her role was simply to serve as a 'handmaiden', announcing what the Holy Spirit had shown her. She would not begin what she called a 'miracle service' until she was sure she felt the 'anointing' of the Spirit. The most fundamental point in her healing theology:

---

88 L. Lovett, *Positive Confession* Theology, 993-994.

"Healing is the sovereign of God"; the responsibility for healing rests entirely with God; Humans are only his servants, helping people accept what he does. Kuhlman preached, emphasizing the love and faithfulness of God and encouraging people to believe in him. Then, under a sense of the anointing, she would begin to announce what the Holy Spirit showed her: "Someone in the balcony just had a deaf ear opened." She would then invite whoever had received that healing to come to the platform to share this experience with the congregation.[89]

Lok-Young Hong explains the relation of Yong-Gi Cho with Jesus Christ healer in this way: Lok-Young Hong makes it clear that God did not give the healing techniques or method to Yong-Gi Cho. Therefore, Yong-Gi Cho is present as an appealer who appeals and persuades God to heal, remaining between Jesus the healer and a patient or a group of patient. The uniqueness of Yong-Gi Cho as an appealer for healing is that he could only recognize the person suffering from sickness. Another characteristic is that Yong-Gi Cho prays courageously and powerfully, presenting the Gospel of Christ's healing against Satan who has brought sickness. But he emphasizes that the prayer appeal to God must be done logically, like an adult child touching the heart of a parent, but not to throw a tantrum.

---

89 R.A.N. KYDD, *Healing in the Christian Church*, in *The New International Dictionary of Pentecostal and Charismatic Movements (revised and expanded edition)*, ed. Stanley M. Burgess – Eduard M. Van Der Maas, Zondervan, Michigan, 2003, 709-710.

Yong-Gi Cho insists that the appealer for healing must have firm faith and proclamation; namely, faith is absolutely necessary as an important element of healing. The faith, underlined here, is to believe in Christ who has the power of healing, but not suffering person's faith. Finally, Yong-Gi Cho says that the kingdom of God begins the moment it is proclaimed that Jesus, as the Son of God, came to earth to free humanity from disease, and through this the healing work of Jesus is revealed. Therefore, according to Yong-Gi Cho, the Gospel should be proclaimed and the one who wants to be healed should believe the fact: if a person only accepts the Gospel, he could be healed. And it is important for Yong-Gi Cho that the appealer for healing should teach this reality to the person suffering with sickness.[90]

The role of Kuhlman as a servant with passive attitude in front of God, is different from the active prayer method of Yong-Gi Cho as an appealer to God, as if touching the heart of parents logically. But these ways were really so helpful for healing. There is a common aspect between these two: as it was seen before, Kathryn Kuhlman was announcing from the platform who is cured using the 'word of knowledge', Yong-Gi Cho, could heal thousands of people from the platform with same method. In short, according to Vinson Synan, Yong-Gi Cho is influenced by Oral Roberts, Kenneth Hagin and Kathryn Kuhlman, but Yong-Gi Cho refuses clearly such evaluation.

---

90 Lok-Young Hong, *Young San Cho Yong-Gi Moksaga Mannan Ciyubasinun Yesu Cristo (Understanding of Young San's Divine Healing)*, 261-263.

Anyway his opinion needs to be respected. But it is true that exist the common aspects between Yong-Gi Cho and Kathryn Kuhlman, and also between Yong-Gi Cho and Oral Roberts, Kenneth Hagin and the Faith Movement.

3. Theology of the Reign of God and Ecclesiology of Yong-Gi Cho

1) The Concept of the Reign of God

According to Jang-Hyun Ryoo, the reign of God, as understood by Yong-Gi Cho, is 'the place where God's sovereignty is exercised', or 'the fullness of the dominion and mighty rule of the living God. It is an entirely new state in which God claims, dominates, and rules individuals and history, not any nation, system, or organization. Yong-Gi Cho explains three characteristics of the reign of God:

First, the reign of God is a 'heaven after death.' It means the transcendental world where the soul goes and lives after one's death. Second, the reign of God is 'the New heaven and New earth. Namely, a new changed world which will come at the end of the world. It is the 'forever new world' where there is no suffering, sadness, death and sickness. Third, the reign of God is in the 'heart of human being.' God is present in the human heart through Holy Spirit, when we welcome Jesus Christ as a Savior and be forgiven, be saved (Jn 14:16-20).[91] According to Cho, the reign of God is therefore both the transcendental world and the present world.[92] Yong-Gi Cho thoroughly affirms the present state of the reign of God and says that if a believer thinks that the reign of God does not exist in the scene of our life, but only in another world, he is an unhappy believer. Because the reign of God will be realized eschatologically with Jesus Christ, but the transcendental and future blessing of the reign of God should be experienced beforehand now in this world. Here, Yong-Gi Cho affirms not only God of the past and the future, but also God of the present in the human heart through the Holy Spirit.[93]

Jang-Hyun Ryoo sees the reign of God that Yong-Gi Cho speaks of is a realistic world that must be fulfilled in this world. According to him, the beautiful world created by God became the fallen world for the sin of Adam and Eve. Therefore, God decided to establish a reign in which his sovereignty would be exercised, and he came into the world with human body to fulfill his Will. Therefore, Yong-Gi Cho explains that the reign of God and his Will began to be realized in this world through Jesus Christ.[94] Yong-Gi Cho con-

---

91 Jang-Hyun Ryoo, *Young Sanui Zongmalone Kwanhan Bipanzok Gochal (A Critical Study of Dr. Yong-Gi Cho's Eschatology)*, in *Journal of Young San Theology, Vol. 13*, Young San Theological Institute of Hansei University, Gunpo, 2008, 168-169.

92 Jang-Hyun Ryoo, *Young Sanui Zongmalone Kwanhan Bipanzok Gochal (A Critical Study of Dr. Yong-Gi Cho's Eschatology)*, 170.

93 Jang-Hyun Ryoo, *Young Sanui Zongmalone Kwanhan Bipanzok Gochal (A Critical Study of Dr. Yong-Gi Cho's Eschatology)*, 175.

94 Jang-Hyun Ryoo, *Young Sanui Zongmalone Kwanhan Bipanzok Gochal (A Critical Study of Dr. Yong-Gi Cho's Eschatology)*, 171.

nects the reign of God with the concept of the Trinity and government.

> The reign of God means that the government of God is present among us. Namely, the Father, the Son and the Holy Spirit, the Triune God is among us.[95]

Yong-Gi Cho says that the concept of divine rule through connection with the Triune God is as follows. The reign of God became the reign of God's beloved Son, Jesus, who became the sovereign King of heaven and now reigns as King on earth after the event of the Cross. Jesus is our 'spiritual king' and 'our king', 'king of our heart' who is present in our heart. God's power is the Holy Spirit, who is the power of Jesus. The Holy Spirit is the 'Spirit of paradise', or the 'Spirit of the 'kingdom of heaven' and extends paradise on earth, and man can experience the immanent paradise in the Holy Spirit. According to Hee-Seong Kim, therefore, Yong-Gi Cho understands the reign of God which has two aspects: the reign of God as both transcendent and immanent to the world.[96] Yong-Gi Cho interprets the work of the Holy Spirit as a driving force to bring people to faith in Jesus Christ, and to witness to the reign of God.[97]

---

95 Yong-Gi Cho'S SERMON, *"Narai Imhaopsimyo" ("Thy Kingdom Come")*, (1986, 8, 31).

96 Hee-Seong Kim, *Cho Yong-Gi Moksaui Hananimui Nara (Rev. Yong-Gi Cho's Kingdom of God)*, in *16th Young San International Theological Sym-posium*, ed. Young San Theological Institute of Hansei University, Hansei University Logos, Gunpo, 2008, 89.

And he emphasizes that we cannot spread the reign of God with knowledge about Jesus alone, but the power of the Holy Spirit is necessary.

> We cannot spread the reign of God in the world with knowledge about Jesus alone. It is necessary the power of Holy Spirit. Because of this, the disciples were staying in that place without leaving Jerusalem until the Pentecost. All of them received the fullness of the Holy Spirit at Pentecost. ... They experienced the power of God. Therefore, they could become powerful witnesses.[98]

Jang-Hyun Ryoo presents, the five attributes of the reign of God preached by Jesus, according to Yong-Gi Cho: First, the reign of God is a reign without sin. For the reign of God to come, one must first receive the forgiveness of sins through a repentance movement and be justified before God (Mt 4:17; Lk 15:7). Second, the reign of God is a reign that heals the sick. Jesus Christ preached the Gospel and healed various patients as evidence (Mt 4: 23-25; 11: 4-5). Third, the reign of God drives out the demons that oppress humans. When Jesus Christ preached the Gospel, the demon screamed and left (Lk 11:20). Fourth, the reign of God is a rich reign. When Jesus Christ

---

[97] Pan-Ho Kim, *Ozungbokumkwa Samzung Chukbok Sasang-e Natanan Hananim Nara (The Kingdom of God Appeared in the Doctrines of Fivefold Gospel and Threefold Blessing)*, in *16th Young San International Theological Symposium*, ed. Young San Theological Institute of Hansei University, Hansei University Logos, Gunpo, 2008, 221-223.

[98] Yong-Gi Cho, *Song-nyung Gang-nimkwa Hananim Nara*, in *Sermon Collections*, vol. 16, 199-200.

proclaimed the reign of God, poverty was removed (2Cor 8:9). Fifth, the reign of God is a reign of eternal life. By preaching the reign of God, Jesus Christ opened the way to eternal life, which can be obtained by faith (Jn 6:40).[99]

2) Different Paradises and How to Get Them

According to Hee-Seong Kim, Yong-Gi Cho's understanding of paradise is diverse. Yong-Gi Cho first explains the reign of God in two ways: the eternal paradise and the immanent paradise on earth. He expresses the eternal paradise as a central office (Headquarters) and the immanent paradise as a branch office. According to Yong-Gi Cho, the eternal paradise is the paradise that will appear at the end of the world and is the eternal heaven where we will live in after death. The immanent paradise is the place where the grace of Jesus Christ is extended to the earth, and it includes the spiritual paradise and the church paradise. The spiritual paradise is the paradise that exists in the heart of a person when he welcomes Jesus Christ as his Savior. The church paradise is a "spiritual paradise on earth", and it is a paradise that exists in the church, where the believers welcome Jesus Christ as their Savior together.[100] According to Yong-Gi Cho, the kingdom of heaven is the place where Jesus, the

---

99 Jang-Hyun Ryoo, *Young Sanui Zongmalone Kwanhan Bipanzok Gochal (A Critical Study of Dr. Yong-Gi Cho's Eschatology)*, 172.
100 Hee-Seong Kim, *Cho Yong-Gi Moksaui Hananimui Nara (Reverend Yong-Gi Cho's Kingdom of God)*, 91.

king of heaven, is welcomed as the Savior.[101] Cho also says that when we believe in Jesus our souls are saved and we become God's people, our heart becomes a temple. Because the Father, Son, and Holy Spirit are in our hearts, the kingdom of heaven is in our hearts.[102]

Yong-Gi Cho emphasizes the Millennial kingdom. The Millennial kingdom is the kingdom of Jesus' return and reign between the immanent paradise and the eternal paradise. Hee-Seong Kim sees that Yong-Gi Cho especially emphasizes the immanent paradise in the world among these different paradises. Hee-Seong Kim gives an example in his sermon calling for attention to be interested in the immanent paradise (1986, 8, 31):[103]

> Ordinary people think that the 'reign of God' is in heaven, and we can go up to heaven when we leave this world and take off the "veil of the body." Such a thought is not wrong at all. But Jesus teaches us a more realistic paradise. The paradise that Jesus tells us about is the reign of heaven that came right next to us.[104]

Yong-Gi Cho affirms that although the reign of God is eschatologically accomplished with Jesus Christ, the blessings of this reign of God must be experienced in advance in this world now. In other

---

101 Yong-Gi Cho, *Maum Hanul (Heaven in Heart)*, Church Growth Institute, Seoul, 2009, 18.

102 Yong-Gi Cho, *Maum Hanul (Heaven in Heart)*, 16.

103 Hee-Seong Kim, *Cho Yong-Gi Moksaui Hananimui Nara (Reverend Yong-Gi Cho's Kingdom of God)*, 93.

104 Yong-Gi Cho'S SERMON, *Narai Imhaopsimyo (Thy Kingdom Come)*, (1986. 8. 6.).

words, the reign of God must be 'realized in the lives, families, and environment' of God's people. To emphasize the reality like this is because God is not only God of the past and the future, but also God of present who is now in the heart of man through the Holy Spirit. Jang-Hyun Ryoo understands that this blessing of the reign of God means the blessing of Threefold redemption of Yong-Gi Cho.[105] But the blessings of the reign of God that we experience in advance in the present are a prelude to the end, not the completion. Namely, the blessing of Threefold redemption lies in the tension between "already" and "not yet."[106] Therefore, it is interpreted that the Threefold Blessing of Yong-Gi Cho could be partially enjoyed today and will be completed with the Second Coming of Jesus Christ.[107]

According to Yong-Gi Cho, Jesus came into the earth to establish the reign of God, so he began to destroy the work of Satan, and since that time, the fierce fight between the reign of God and the earthly reign has begun. Therefore, Cho emphasizes that Jesus droved out the demons, healed the sick, and nourished the hungry, invaded the reign of Satan. He invites the faithful to invade and to deprive the paradise which Jesus got on the Cross.[108] Namely, even

---

[105] Jang-Hyun Ryoo, *Young Sanui Zongmalone Kwanhan Bipanzok Gochal (A Critical Study of Dr. Yong-Gi Cho's Eschatology)*, 175-176.

[106] Jang-Hyun Ryoo, *Young Sanui Zongmalone Kwanhan Bipanzok Gochal (A Critical Study of Dr. Yong-Gi Cho's Eschatology)*, 178.

[107] Pan-Ho Kim, *Ozungbokumkwa Samzung Chukbok Sasang-e Natanan Hananim Nara (The Kingdom of God Appeared in the Doctrines of Fivefold Gospel and Threefold Blessing)*, 213.

though Jesus prepared the paradise on the Cross, it cannot be possessed automatically, therefore, the faithful must deprive the paradise from the hands of Satan. And Yong-Gi Cho affirms that the believers are in the situation of an ongoing war on this world with Satan and devils, and he underlines that only a strong person can win (Mt 12:29). Mentioning some methods to invade the paradise, first, he presents that we need to know the truth (Jn 8:32). Namely, he affirms that faithful should know clearly these truths: those who believe in Jesus are the forgiven righteous persons; they are the sealed persons with the Holy Spirit; they are the healed persons from the sickness; they received the blessing of Abraham being freed from the curse; they have a citizenship of paradise being moved from death to life. Next, they should testify the precious blood of Jesus Christ and the Gospel, and should fight through the power of the Holy Spirit. Here, emphasizing the word 'deprive', Yong-Gi Cho affirms that the 'strong and determined fighting spirit and determination' are necessary to deprive them. Yong-Gi Cho says that believers should fight against Satan and the spirits by relying endlessly on the Holy Spirit, emphasizing that Jesus won the war with Satan on the Cross, it is already a 'finished war.' Therefore, he points out that what remains is not the war, but the 'problem of faith and obedience.' And he says that we must get the paradise already pre-

---

108 Mun-Hong Choi, *Young-San Cho Yong-Gi Moksawa Hananimui Nara (Young-San Rev. Yong-Gi Cho and the Kingdom of God)*, in Journal of Young San Theology, Vol. 14, Young San Theological Institute of Hansei University, Gunpo, 2008, 193.

pared by Jesus, and get the booty of the Fivefold Gospel and the Threefold Blessing.[109] Therefore, according to Yong-Gi Cho it is very important to know that the faithful are in the middle of spiritual war with Satan.

Mun-Hong Choi sees that in the Yong-Gi Cho's understanding of the reign of God, the ultimate goal is the expansion of that reign.[110] Yong-Gi Cho emphasizes that the people who entered into the paradise, must show not only the fruits of paradise to the people but also share it with the neighbor.[111] According to him, the fruit of the reign of God which the faithful will enjoy are the Fivefold Gospel and the Threefold Blessing, and the faithful can enjoy this fruit through the spirituality of the Fourth dimension. It is obvious that Yong-Gi Cho's concept is very much related to the Fivefold Gospel and the Threefold Blessing, to the spirituality of the Fourth dimension.[112]

Yong-Gi Cho, who maintains that the present era is at the end of the church age and the end of the world is near, presents several proofs of the end of the world: the historical evidence is the independence of Israel and the birth of Europe Economic Community;

---

[109] Mun-Hong Choi, *Youn-San Cho Yong-Gi Moksawa Hananimui Nara (Young-San Rev. Yong-Gi Cho and the Kingdom of God)*, 194-196.

[110] Mun-Hong Choi, *Youn-San Cho Yong-Gi Moksawa Hananimui Nara (Young-San Rev. Yong-Gi Cho and the Kingdom of God)*, 176.

[111] Mun-Hong Choi, *Youn-San Cho Yong-Gi Moksawa Hananimui Nara (Young-San Rev. Yong-Gi Cho and the Kingdom of God)*, 197.

[112] Mun-Hong Choi, *Youn-San Cho Yong-Gi Moksawa Hananimui Nara (Young-San Rev. Yong-Gi Cho and the Kingdom of God)*, 175.

the ecclesiastic evidence is the Pentecostal movement began in 1900; the evidence of the times are the appearance of false prophet, the ecclesial division, wars, famine, persecution, earthquake. Interpreting literally Daniel 9:24-27, Yong-Gi Cho affirms that at the end of the world, there will be the seven-year tribulation after the end of the time of the church, and at that time the church (or the believers) will be raptured.[113]

Yong-Gi Cho explains the Second Coming of Christ in relation to the paradise of the Millennial kingdom in two ways: the Second Coming in the air and the Second Coming on earth. The Second Coming in the air is to get the faithful who prepared the oil in waiting and really wanting for the Coming of Jesus Christ.[114] The Second Coming in the air will take place before the Tribulation. At that time the church (or faithful) and the dead faithful, those who died and participated in the first resurrection, will be raptured and participate in the wedding feast. While they are participating in the seven-year wedding feast, there will be the seven-year tribulation on earth. The Second Coming in the air is not to judge, but it is to pick up the bride who has prepared oil by being filled with the Holy Spirit.[115]

Yong-Gi Cho, who sees the seven-year tribulation as the last op-

---

[113] Jang-Hyun Ryoo, *Young Sanui Zongmalone Kwanhan Bipanzok Gochal (A Critical Study of Dr. Yong-Gi Cho's Eschatology)*, 183.

[114] Mun-Hong Choi, *Youn-San Cho Yong-Gi Moksawa Hananimui Nara (Young-san Rev. Yong-gi Cho and the Kingdom of God)*, 189.

[115] Jang-Hyun Ryoo, *Young Sanui Zongmalone Kwanhan Bipanzok Gochal (A Critical Study of Dr. Yong-Gi Cho's Eschatology)*, 187.

portunity for the conversion given by God to the disobedient people, explains the seven-year tribulation, the Second Coming on earth, the Armageddon war, the Millennial kingdom in this way:

According to Yong-Gi Cho, during the seven-year tribulation some faithful will be martyred for the faith or will trust in God nevertheless extreme suffering. He emphasizes that this salvation of the last gleaning is the expression of God's tenacious love.[116] After seven-year tribulation Jesus will return to earth with the raptured people in the air clouds (Mt 24:30) with celestial angels (Mt 25:31), to realize the promised word (Jn 14:3), to judge the world (Mt 16:27; 25:31-33), to make the faithful transformed in glory (Philippians 3:20-21). Yong-Gi Cho says that although we do not know the exact time (Mt 25:36) the symptom can be known because it will be foretold by many signs. Yong-Gi Cho affirms, when Jesus returns to earth, the Armageddon war will break out (Rev 19:19). According to Yong-Gi Cho, the Armageddon war is the last war on earth (Daniel 11:40-45, Rev 19:17-21).[117] When Jesus returns to earth, he will catch the antichrist and the false prophet and cast them into the lake of fire and brimstone, and Stan will be tied up in the abyss for a thousand years (Rev 20:2-3). And then, Jesus will be King of this earth, the faithful will govern the world for a thousand years with the Lord as His bride.[118] This is the 'paradise of the Millennial kingdom', as

---

116 Young San Yunguwon, *Ozungbokumkwa Samzungkuwonui Chukbok (Fivefold Gospel and the Blessing of Threefold Salvation)*, Seoul Logos, Seoul, 1991, 111.

117 Jang-Hyun Ryoo, *Young Sanui Zongmalone Kwanhan Bipanzok Gochal (A Critical Study of Dr. Yong-Gi Cho's Eschatology)*, 188.

Yong-Gi Cho says.

According to Yong-Gi Cho, the eternal paradise will come after the paradise of the Millennial kingdom. He also explains the situation after the Millennial kingdom, the final judgment, the New heaven and New earth. Namely, Yong-Gi Cho says that when the Millennial kingdom is over, Satan will be free from abyss for a while, at this time Satan will tempt so many people on earth. God will separate and filter again those people who have lived for a thousand years without being tempted by Satan, namely, those who will follow Christ and those who will follow Satan. Yong-Gi Cho explains that when the sheep and the goats will be clearly separated, the people who are not in the city will be disappeared by the fire that comes down from heaven, the Satan who was tempting them will be thrown into the lake of fire and brimstone (Rev 20:7-10) and will suffer forever. According to Yong-Gi Cho, subsequently there will be the final judgment (white throne judgment). Cho continue to say that, Jesus will sit on the white throne, and all the people who died without believing in the Lord will be resurrected to stand before this throne and be judged one by one. Everyone whose name is not written in the book of Life will be thrown into the lake of fire to suffer forever (Rev 20:11-12). But Yong-Gi Cho emphasizes that the people who follow the Lord will enter into the New heaven and New earth, the eternal world; the New Jerusalem as the capital of

---

118 Mun-Hong Choi, *Youn-San Cho Yong-Gi Moksawa Hananimui Nara (Young-San Rev. Yong-Gi Cho and the Kingdom of God)*, 190.

the New heaven and New earth, will come down from heaven, from God. And Yong-Gi Cho affirms that in the New Jerusalem there will be the throne of God and of the lamb; from this throne the river of the water of life flows; and there will be the tree of life on the left and right of this river; there will not be any more death and mourning, sickness and curse. Therefore, Yong-Gi Cho says, "A weak body will be transformed into a strong body, a physical body will be into a spiritual body, and an ugly body into a glorious body, and will live forever with Jesus." Yong-Gi Cho explains that this is the final paradise which we are expecting for.

According to the teaching of Yong-Gi Cho, when a faithful accepts Jesus as the Savior, paradise will be present in his heart (the paradise of heart); this faithful will enter the Millennial kingdom and the eternal paradise through the church paradise which is the gathering of the saints; he will live with Jesus and reign as king forever and ever.[119]

The rapture theories are divided into 'pre-tribulation rapture theory', 'mid-tribulation rapture theory', and 'post-tribulation rapture theory' in terms of time frame. Yong-Gi Cho supports 'pre-tribulation rapture theory.' According to this, the church will be raptured before the seven-year tribulation and will not experience the tribulation. The church will be raptured together with the resurrected dead faithful (First resurrection, Rev 20:4-5), at the Second

---

119 Mun-Hong Choi, *Youn-San Cho Yong-Gi Moksawa Hananimui Nara (Young-San Rev. Yong-Gi Cho and the Kingdom of God)*, 191-193.

Coming of Jesus in the air before the Tribulation. Formal believers cannot be raptured (John 3:5), and only those who are filled with the Holy Spirit and have prepared oil will be raptured. Therefore, Yong-Gi Cho follows the pre-tribulation rapture theory and says that the baptism in the Holy Spirit is a sure guarantee of the rapture.[120]

3) Jang-Hyun Ryoo's Evaluation of Yong-Gi Cho's Reign of God

Jang-Hyun Ryoo evaluates that Yong-Gi Cho has a tendency to emphasize the religious/existential function of the reign of God. Yong-Gi Cho affirms that through the suffering of Jesus Christ on the Cross, the fallen soul, the sick mind, the prodigal moral life and the sick body will be healed, and when God dwells in the human heart through the Holy Spirit, one becomes a child of God and a citizen of paradise. However, overemphasizing the religious and existential function of the reign of God may limit the reign of God to the human existential realm and weaken its social function, so Jang-Hyun Ryoo argues that religious and social functions should be emphasized at the same time. Because the reign of God is a new state in which not only the religious relationship in which God becomes the Father and human beings become his children, but also the social relationship in which human beings become brothers and

---

[120] Jang-Hyun Ryoo, *Young Sanui Zongmalone Kwanhan Bipanzok Gochal (A Critical Study of Dr. Yong-Gi Cho's Eschatology)*, 184-185.

sisters is properly formed. Jang-hyun Ryoo affirms that the missionary task of the Pentecostal movement in the 21st century is to proclaim both religious and social messages.[121]

Jang-Hyun Ryoo evaluates Yong-Gi Cho's eschatology as a dispensational eschatology that advocates premillennialism in terms of its overall theological tone. Therefore, according to Jang-Hyun Ryoo, the eschatology of Yong-Gi Cho shares the theological problem with dispensational eschatology that advocates the end times, such as literal interpretation of the Bible, historical determinism, and Christian fatalism. Jang-Hyun Ryoo insists that this is a theological task that must be overcome since the Pentecostal movement in 21st century will be developed as a proper spiritual movement. Therefore, he explains as follows, pointing out the three problems that should be deeply reflected upon theologically:

First, eschatology must be distinguished from 'theory of the end of the world.' Eschatology is not the 'theory of the end of the world', which refers to events that will occur at the end of the world and history, but is a study of the purpose of history and a statement about the nature of the reign of God and how the reign of God will be completed. In other words, as a turning point in history that speaks of a new beginning, it describes the complete disintegration of this generation and the arrival of a new order, that is, a New heaven and New earth. Therefore, eschatology implies belief in God's right-

---

[121] Jang-Hyun Ryoo, *Young Sanui Zongmalone Kwanhan Bipanzok Gochal (A Critical Study of Dr. Yong-Gi Cho's Eschatology)*, 173-174.

eous rule and the spirit of resistance and criticism against unrighteous forces in world reality. Jang-Hyun Ryoo affirms that an eschatology that lacks these two elements is unbiblical and becomes a pseudo-eschatology that deceives believers.

Secondly, Jang-Hyun Ryoo clearly expresses that the literal interpretation of the Bible is not the right method to understand eschatological symbols. The literal interpretation of the Bible understands the apocalyptic symbols (the seven-year tribulation, the rapture, the Second Coming of Jesus in the air and Second Coming of Jesus on earth, the appearance of the antichrist, the Armageddon war, the Millennial kingdom), as historical facts in the future, and believes also as a promise that will be fulfilled by the Second Coming of Jesus. But Jang-Hyun Ryoo insists that the eschatological symbols in the Bible should be understood as a message of warning and advice to be always awake for the imminent coming of the reign of God, saying that the reign of God will be completed through the fighting with the antichrist (Mt 25:13; Mk 13:32-33).

Third, the eschatology of dispensationalism limits the salvific activity of God within the rule of history. It insists that the character and finality of God's revelation are already determined by generation. Therefore according to Jang-Hyun Ryoo, this eschatology leads to historical determinism, which limits the completion of the reign of God within the historical regularity, and justifies the unrighteous events in the world as an inevitable event before the Second Coming of Jesus, based on the Christian fatalism.[122] The reign of God is a reign of freedom which will be completed according to the will of God. Therefore, Jang-Hyun Ryoo insists on recovering the proper eschatology with a strong experience of the Holy Spirit, so that the Pentecostal movement in Korea in the 21st century may handle the mission of the times delegated by God. And he affirms that it depends totally on how the junior scholars of Yong-Gi Cho are diligent in theological study to overcome his limitation, succeeding creatively the positive aspects of Yong-Gi Cho's eschatology.[123]

Although Yong-Gi Cho follows the 'theory of rapture before the tribulation', he divides the seven years into three and a half years before, and three and a half years after, and understands that the church will be raptured before 'seven-year tribulation', and especially, that the second half of the seven-year tribulation will be the real period of tribulation. Therefore, Yong-Gi Cho's interpretation is different from the traditional 'theory of rapture before the tribulation' or the 'theory of rapture during the tribulation.' According to Yong-Gi Cho, when the church will be raptured, the 144,000 faithful (Rev 7:14) will be left over to do a mission for three and a half years for those who are not raptured, and then they will be raptured too. Since Yong-Gi Cho understands that the second half of the seven-year tribulation is a real tribulation, and sees that only those who are filled with the Holy Spirit will be raptured, not all the faithful, Jang-Hyun Ryoo evaluates that Yong-Gi Cho follows the 'theory of

---

122 Jang-Hyun Ryoo, *Young Sanui Zongmalone Kwanhan Bipanzok Gochal (A Critical Study of Dr. Yong-Gi Cho's Eschatology)*, 192-193.
123 Jang-Hyun Ryoo, *Young Sanui Zongmalone Kwanhan Bipanzok Gochal (A Critical Study of Dr. Yong-Gi Cho's Eschatology)*, 194.

partial rapture', not the 'theory of total rapture.' Therefore, by pointing out that there is actually no concept of rapture in the Bible, even though the 'theory of seven years of tribulation', the 'theory of rapture' based on the literal interpretation of the Bible, Jang-Hyun Ryoo explains like this: 1 Thessalonians 4:14-17, which is often cited as a biblical base for the 'theory of rapture', is not the 'theory of rapture', but the word to comfort the suffering faithful and give them the assurance of resurrection. Moreover, the first resurrection in the Revelation is a symbol of the realistic restoration of the Israelite people, while the second resurrection concerns the eschatological personal resurrection. Jang-Hyun Ryoo says that in the Bible, the eschatological resurrection is only once. Moreover, since the 'theory of seven-year tribulation' sees the appearance of the antichrist's and the tribulation as an inevitable event before the Second Coming of Jesus, Ryoo criticizes it as a Christian fatalism that accepts the injustice in the world as a fateful event.[124]

4) The Ecclesiology of Yong-Gi Cho

The typical interpretation of Yong-Gi Cho on the reign of God is considering the church as the reign of God.[125]

---

124 Jang-Hyun Ryoo, *Young Sanui Zongmalone Kwanhan Bipanzok Gochal (A Critical Study of Dr. Yong-Gi Cho's Eschatology)*, 186-187.
125 Young-Mo Cho, *Young San Cho Yong-Gi Moksaui Hananim Nara Ihe (Dr. Yong-Gi Cho's Theology on the Kingdom of God with Reference to the NT)*, in Ministry & Theology of Young San, vol. 3, ed. Young San Theological Institute, Hansei

God certainly established a foundation of the reign of God in the world as the price of suffering of Jesus Christ on the Cross. That reign of God is the church where we gather to worship. Jesus established the foundation of the church and makes the church solid every day by sending the Holy Spirit who is the power of the reign of God.[126]

Yong-Gi Cho sees that the church is a possession of Jesus, and his earthly paradise, since Jesus is the head, the king, and the absolute sovereign of the church. Therefore, Jesus as a king directly administers and governs the church.[127] And according to Yong-Gi Cho, since there is a restoration and blessing in the reign of God, it is right to enjoy this blessing in the present church.[128] But Yong-Gi Cho insists on evangelizing to the end of the earth with eschatological hope, because for the faithful the present earthly life and the blessing are not everything.[129]

Yong-Gi Cho maintains that the church is the place where Jesus founded the paradise by destroying Satan and his reign on the Cross.

University Logos, Gunpo, 2008, 110.

126 Yong-Gi Cho, *Geui Narawa Geui Uiga Muosin-ga? (What is his kingdom and what is his righteousness?)* in *Sermon Collections*, vol. 17, 255-256.

127 Young-Mo Cho, *Young San Cho Yong-Gi Moksaui Hananim Nara Ihe (Dr. Yong-Gi Cho's Theology on the Kingdom of God with Reference to the NT)*, 96-97.

128 Pan-Ho Kim, *Ozungbokumkwa Samzung Chukbok Sasang-e Natanan Hananim Nara (The Kingdom of God Appeared in the Doctrines of Fivefold Gospel and Threefold Blessing)*, 243.

129 Pan-Ho Kim, *Ozungbokumkwa Samzung Chukbok Sasang-e Natanan Hananim Nara (The Kingdom of God Appeared in the Doctrines of Fivefold Gospel and Threefold Blessing)*, 245.

Therefore, Cho affirms that the present church should get the booty of war by defeating the devils and spirits in every place, because the church is the 'victorious reign of Jesus Christ.' Yong-Gi Cho says that the booty includes forgiveness, baptism in the Holy Spirit, healing, blessing and eternal life, he underlines that the today's 'living church' is precisely a church that practices sharing this booty wherever it goes. Considering that the church is the reign of Jesus, who rules it with the supremacy of a king, Yong-Gi Cho maintains that the church identifies itself with the reign of God. He emphasizes that the faithful should bear witness to the reign of God, because the Jesus's command to the disciples before his ascension is still valid today (Mk 16:15-18).[130]

5) Some Protestant Theologians' Interpretations of Yong-Gi Cho's Ecclesiology

Young-Mo Cho sees that Yong-Gi Cho consistently insists that earthly church is the reign of God. Therefore, Young-Mo Cho interprets that this aspect of Yong-Gi Cho is connected with the concept of his present blessing about the reign of God, rather than being influenced by any particular doctrine or theology. Because Young-Mo Cho notes that when Yong-Gi Cho presents the church as the reign of God, he always connects the church with the present

---

[130] Mun-Hong Choi, *Youn-San Cho Yong-Gi Moksawa Hananimui Nara (Young-San Rev. Yong-Gi Cho and the Kingdom of God)*, 198.

blessing of the reign of God. Young-Mo Cho presents an example: in 1997, when South Korea was facing a great economic crisis with the intervention of IMF (International Monetary Fund), Yong-Gi Cho presented the church as the reign of God in the sermon of 7 December 1997 entitled "The Wisdom of living the Economic Crisis." Here, Yong-Gi Cho underlined the method of extending the church, the reign of God: going to the church for Sunday worship; being faithful in offering the ten percent of one's income (tithe) to God; living the life of an evangelist. In the most difficult financial crisis for believers, by explaining logically that the church is the reign of God', Yong-Gi Cho proclaims the message of principle and method of blessing that can be enjoyed in that reign of God. Young-Mo Cho summarizes that for Yong-Gi Cho, the church is a community of faith of saved people who recognized the kingship of Jesus, and in this point there is a relationship between the reign of God and the church to have the same king and the same people. Therefore, Young-Mo Cho presumes that the growth power of YFGC (Yoido Full Gospel Church) is based on this theology of Yong-Gi Cho.[131]

According to Mun-Hong Choi, the miserable situation of Yong-Gi Cho's initial pastoral work led him to persistently spread the present aspect of the reign of God. Yong-Gi Cho affirms that the fruits of the Fivefold Gospel and of the Threefold Blessing that Jesus realized through the Cross, must be realized in the 'reign of the heart.'

---

131 Young-Mo Cho, *Young San Cho Yong-Gi Moksaui Hananim Nara Ihe (Dr. Yong-Gi Cho's Theology on the Kingdom of God with Reference to the NT)*, 97–99.

Especially Yong-Gi Cho emphasizes the need to rule the heart with four elements (thought, dream, faith, word) because the destiny of the faithful depends on how they rule their heart. Therefore, Mun-Hong Choi summarizes that the Fourth dimension spirituality, which is at the center of Yong-Gi Cho's theology, and his understanding on the reign of God, are closely related.[132]

6) The Catholic Church's Understanding of the Reign of God

The catechism of the Catholic Church[133] explains the Ascension of Christ, the reign of God and the Second Coming of Christ as follows:

Christ's Ascension into heaven signifies his participation, in his humanity, in God's power and authority. Jesus Christ is Lord, he possesses all power in heaven and on earth. He is "far above all rule and authority and power and dominion", for the Father "has put all things under his feet." (Eph 1:21-22) Being seated at the Father's right hand signifies the inauguration of the Messiah's kingdom, the fulfillment of the Prophet Daniel's vision concerning the Son of man.

Though already present in his Church, Christ's reign is nevertheless yet to be fulfilled "with power and great glory" (Lk 21:27)

---

[132] Mun-Hong Choi, *Youn-San Cho Yong-Gi Moksawa Hananimui Nara (Young-San Rev. Yong-Gi Cho and the Kingdom of God)*, 199-200.

[133] *Catechismus Catholicae Ecclesiale*, CBCK, 2003, #662-678.

by the King's return to earth. This reign is still under attack by the evil powers, even though they have been defeated definitively by Christ's Passover. Until everything is subject to him, until there be realized New heaven and New earth in which justice dwells, the pilgrim Church, takes her place among the creatures. Since the Ascension, Christ's Coming in glory has been imminent, even though "it is not for you to know the times or seasons which the Father has fixed by his own authority (Act 1:7)." But Catholic Church has rejected even modified forms of this falsification of the kingdom to come under the name of millenarianism, especially the "intrinsically perverse" political form of a secular messianism.

As Lord, Christ is also head of the Church, which is his body. Christ, taken up to heaven and glorified after he had thus fully accomplished his mission, dwells on earth in his Church. "The kingdom of Christ (is) already present in mystery." Therefore, the church became "on earth, the seed and the beginning of the kingdom." In heaven, Christ permanently exercises his priesthood. He "always lives to make intercession" for "those who draw near to God through him." (Heb 7:25) Jesus Christ, the head of the Church, precedes us into the Father's glorious kingdom so that we, the members of his Body, may live in the hope of one day being with him forever.

Before Christ's Second Coming the Church must pass through a final trial that will shake the faith of many believers. This persecution that accompanies her pilgrimage on earth will unveil the "mystery of iniquity" in the form of a religious deception. The supreme religious deception is that of the antichrist, a pseudo-messianism by which man glorifies himself in place of God and of his Messiah come in the flesh. On the Last Day Jesus will say: "Truly I say to you, whatever you did for one of these least brothers of mine, you did for me." (Mt 25:40)

The Profession of faith of Paul VI in 1968, explains the reign of God like this: It emphasizes the reign of God began in the Church of Christ, but is not of this world, and its growth consists in enthusiastic response to God's love and the spread of holiness among human beings. It also says that the real growth of the reign of God cannot be confused with the progress of civilization, science, and the development of human technology. And urges us to contribute for the good of the Ground country, to promote justice, peace and fraternity among men, especially to help the poor and the needy.[134]

The *Evangelii Nuntiandi* (8 Dec. 1975), the Apostolic Exhortation of Paul VI, affirms that the Church refuses to replace the proclamation of the kingdom of God with the proclamation of forms of human liberation. It even states that her contribution to liberation is incomplete, if she neglects to proclaim salvation in Jesus Christ.[135]

The *Redemptoris Missio* (7 Dec. 1990), the Encyclical of Pope John Paul II, says the relation between the reign of God, Church and Christ is described as follows. The kingdom of God cannot be detached

---

[134] J. Neuner, sj – J. Dupuis, sj, *La Fede Cristiana nei documenti dottrinali della Chiesa cattolica*, San Paolo, Milano, 2002, 29 (#39.20).

[135] Pope Paul VI, *Evangelii Nuntiandi: Apostolic Exhortation*, (Dec. 8, 1975), CBCK, 2009, #34.

either from Christ or from the Church. Christ not only proclaimed the kingdom, but in him the kingdom itself became present and fulfilled. The kingdom of God is not a concept, a doctrine, or a program that can be freely interpreted. But the kingdom of God is a person with the face and name of Jesus of Nazareth, the image of the invisible God. If the kingdom is separated from Jesus, it is no longer the kingdom of God which he revealed. One may not separate the kingdom of God from the Church. It is true that the Church is not an end unto herself, since she is ordered toward the kingdom of God of which she is the seed, sign and instrument. Since the Church's special connection with the kingdom of God and of Christ, the Church has "the mission of announcing and inaugurating among all peoples."[136]

Sang-Tai Shim, a catholic theologian,[137] explains traditional eschatology and contemporary eschatology as follows: Traditional eschatology, since about 15th century, understood the individual's life and the end of the world history as a kind of prior information revealed by God. It gave the impression of an advance notice of the real final state to come. Because it was attempted with speculative interpretation based on the ancient mythological worldview and the cosmological worldview of the Middle Ages, or it was at-

---

[136] John Paul II, *Redemptoris Missio: Encyclical on the permanent validity of the Church's missionary mandate* (Dec. 7, 1990), CBCK, 2014, #18.

[137] Sang-Tai Shim, disciple of Cardinal Walter Kasper, was a professor of dogmatic theology in the Suwon Catholic University in South Korea.

tempted with the literal interpretation of the biblical statement. Christian eschatology in early theology was interested in that: 'How will I be after death? Can I still live in the other life after my life in this world? How will life be like in the other world? Because after the Ascension of Christ, his Second coming was delayed, the Christian's attention was focused on the individual's future. Concentrating on the salvation of the individual soul, the interest in the final situation of all mankind and the world was left behind. And the traditional eschatology was teaching about death and judgment, paradise and hell from an individualistic point of view. The final state of the individual and the whole world could be described in this way:

Everyone will die because of original sin. After death, the soul, separated from the body, will be judged immediately before God. According to his deeds in life, God will judge the individual to send him to the eternal blessed paradise or to the eternal punishing hell or to the purgatory training. The Catholic Church teaches differently from the Orthodox Church and the Protestant Church, that the souls of those who died with little sins, will be in purgatory training to be perfectly purified to enter paradise. These souls in purgatory are helped by the faithful on earth through Mass, or prayer or charity. At the end of the world and history, there will be a cosmic cataclysm, Jesus will return, and the dead will be resurrected and publicly judged by Jesus. Through this judgment, the righteous persons will enjoy the eternal blessing, but the malefactors will receive eternal punishment. And the world will be completed, reaching its goal.[138]

The Protestant Reformers, like Martin Luther (1483~1546) and Jean Calvin (1509~1564), denied the traditional catechism on purgatory. So the Council of Trent (1545~1563), citing the teaching of the Council of Florence (1439~1445), reaffirmed the doctrine of purgatory as follows:

> The Catholic Church, inspired by the Holy Spirit, based on the Bible and the tradition of the Fathers, through many holy councils and, recently, through this holy universal Council, used to teach that purgatory is existing and the souls in purgatory can receive the help through the prayers of the faithful, especially through holy Mass. Therefore, this holy Council is ordering that the bishops will superintend with sincerity, the doctrine of purgatory, will be believed and preserved and taught and proclaimed in everywhere.[139]

Sang-Tai Shim summarizes the characteristic of the eschatological positions that have been generally settled in the theological world since the 1960s, but which differ from traditional eschatology. Firstly the most diffused insight is considering that the biblical statements about the eschatological event are a metaphor of Christian hope. And its dominant position is that this biblical metaphor of this hope should not be interpreted as objective information on the

---

138 Sang-Tai Shim, *2000 Nyundeui Hankug Kyohoi (Korean Church in 2000 Year [15])*, FSP, Seoul, 1993, 23-26.

139 Jun-Yang Park, *Jongmallon-Yungwonhan Sengmyungul Hyanghayo (Eschatology-Towards Eternal Life)*, Bible and Life, 2011, 104-105.

eschatological event. Therefore, they interpret that those statements related to man and the end of the world, are the expressions of promise and hope that are essentially part of faith. According to Sang-Tai Shim, today's eschatology has a general tendency that figures out the eschatological reality as a personal God himself, not stipulate as a place, materializing objectively. It emphasizes that the eschatological event that began with Christ has not yet completed for human beings, but there is a dominant insight that says that the eschatological event is already present as a beginning form. Therefore, according to Sang-Tai Shim, modern eschatology wants to see the question of individual's destiny in the salvation prospective of the whole world history, escaping from individualistic narrowness.[140]

Sang-Tai Shim says that even though there are several forms of today's eschatological positions, it can be generally divided into two current. Therefore, he explains as follows: The eschatology that concentrates on the individual's eschatological situational regulations, and the eschatology that gives importance to the relationship between the world and history. Firstly, there are types of eschatology that focus on the individual's eschatological situation and downplay the world and history itself and the individual's connection to this historical process. These include 'existential', 'transcendental' and 'personalistic' eschatologies. It was very popular among theologians until the 1950s. Unlike this, there are eschato-

---

[140] Sang-Tai Shim, *2000 Nyundeui Hankug Kyoboi (Korean Church in 2000 Year [15])*, 27-28.

logical forms that emphasize the relationship between the world and history rather than the situation of the individual: 'evolutionary revolutionary', 'political' and 'liberating' eschatology. According to Sang-Tai Shim, this has been a leading position among theologians since the 1960s. Sang-Tai Shim judges that it is desirable for these two forms have a mutual cooperation or a complementary relationship.[141]

Sang-Tai Shim summarizes roughly in this way, the basic content of the eschatological belief that is accepted as the orthodoxy and is widely spread among today's theologians. The eschatological hope of Christians will be realized on the basis of God's work, which is impossible to grasp. Therefore, a Christian is not a person who has more and just information about the eschatological future. Christian means a person who believes in God, who raised Jesus from the death, who is love itself, and a person who hopes that God will lead all events for good.

The reign of God that Christians hope, is already present in this world, not the world after death, which we can enter after death. Christians hope that the reign of God will come as a gift that makes man and the whole world complete. But Christian hope is not to wait passively for the reign of God to come. This hope must be put into action for the completion of the reign of God, which has not yet been fully realized in the historical world, with a commitment to realize freedom, equality and peace. The hope for the reign of

---

141 Sang-Tai Shim, *2000 Nyundeui Hankug Kyoboi (Korean Church in 2000 Year [15])*, 30-31.

God is a hope for the New heaven and New earth, that comes from the power of creative love.

This hope makes man free from the vicious cycle of the past, which produces evil and discord, and makes man forget the old things and forgive. And it makes man take an adventure together with others towards a new future.[142] The realization of the reign of God is achieved now and forever in history in every act of love performed by a single human being. Therefore, in love, the present and the future are linked together in love. Therefore, Sang-Tai Shim, affirms that this love is not separated from the present, but it is the beginning of the future and the dawn that occurs in the present.[143]

Sang-Tai Shim explains the contents of hell, purgatory and paradise as seen by majority of modern theologians: **Hell** is not a place, but it means the fixation on the criminal act. The biblical statements about hell should be understood as a warning against a way of life that rejects love for God and humanity and takes only self as the motivation and measure of action. Hell remains as a mystery that cannot be explained. When a person rejects his neighbor, rejects a community of love and becomes a slave to selfishness, we could say that hell is already happening in the present world. **Purgatory** is not half of hell, but it is a moment of encounter with God that occurs with death. Purgatory is a process of purification of a person,

---

[142] Sang-Tai Shim, *2000 Nyundeui Hankug Kyohoi (Korean Church in 2000 Year [15])*, 31-32.

[143] Sang-Tai Shim, *2000 Nyundeui Hankug Kyohoi (Korean Church in 2000 Year [15])*, 33.

after recognizing his unworthiness to be united perfectly with the loving God, encountering God with a feeling of shame and pain. Namely, man judges himself as a sinner who should be punished in front of God's pure love. While man opens himself more, God communicates Himself more strongly, purification is going on, and then man goes out towards perfect unity with God, being free from self-closing. Paradise is a perfected form of love and communication as a complete fullness of man's life. Man can reach self-fulfillment when he practices love getting out of oneself. This paradise already expands in reality, starting from the place where the personal egoism and group egoism are overcome, and when agape love is lived. Therefore, Sang-Tai Shim concludes that if extreme loneliness can be seen as an essential element of hell, the blessed human bonding or community character could be an essential element of paradise.[144]

4. Conclusion

1) Threefold Blessing

What has been said so far about the Threefold Blessing of Yong-Gi Cho can be summarized as follows. The main motivation of his pastoral ministry is to give extreme hope to those who are in extreme

---

[144] Sang-Tai Shim, *2000 Nyundeui Hankug Kyoboi (Korean Church in 2000 Year [15])*, 34-35.

despair situation. For Yong-Gi Cho, 3Jn 1:2 was the key to understanding the Bible. His Fivefold Gospel (Born again, Fullness of the Holy Spirit, Blessing, Divine healing, the Coming King) is theory and doctrine for faith, while the practical aspect to applying this doctrine is the Threefold Blessing (Blessing of soul, Blessing of life, Blessing of Physical health) in the dimension of holistic salvation of a person. According to Yong-Gi Cho, there is one priority: the blessing of the soul. Next comes the blessing of all things and the health of the body. This is achieved through prayer, study of the Word, and worship of God. In case of illness, the emphasis is on fasting vigil prayer for repentance of sin and disobedience and for healing.

Everyone has a desire to be saved, to be healthy, and to have everything go well. Therefore, the theology of the Threefold Blessing could be a message to give hope to many people, and it is true that this Threefold Blessing played a key role in making Yoido Full Gospel Church grow as the biggest congregation in the world. But having also the aspects to be more deepened, as it was observed earlier, among theologians, there is a positive evaluation group and a negative evaluation group on the blessing theology of Yong-Gi Cho.

Mun-Hong Choi evaluates positively the Threefold Blessing of Yong-Gi Cho. Saying that it is necessary to have personal communion with the Holy Spirit in order to enjoy more the Threefold Blessing, Mun-Hong Choi expects that the social salvation ministry related to the Threefold Blessing will not fail, it will not be like Minjung theology or Liberation theology.

Won-Suk Ma, evaluates Yong-Gi Cho's theology of blessing is with a soteriological motivation by Christ's atoning work and points out that further research on the Holy Spirit is needed. He also raises several questions about the unclear theological goal and intentions in Yong-Gi Cho's theology of blessing. In other words, "What is the blessing for? Does it serve man himself or the kingdom of God? How does the Christian concept of blessing differ from shamanic or secular concepts of blessing?" Wong-Suk Ma also notes the importance of discussing Pentecostal concepts of social service, arguing that social and communal contexts cannot be ignored in favor of individualism in blessing theology.

Yong-Sub Chung points out that Yong-Gi Cho's claim that a good faith in Jesus brings the so-called Threefold Blessing is a lie, and that Cho's preaching encourages people to focus on their wealth, health, and success rather than on their personal salvation.

Won-Kun Park, saying that the well-known pastors of prosperity theology have the common negative aspects, asks a question, "For whom is church growth?"

Ki-Suk Yun criticizes that the cupidity of material possession of Yong-Gi Cho and his family expresses the corruption of the Korean Protestant Church, and affirms that if a pastor lives without moral sense, he is no longer a pastor.

In addition to these questions, I would like to ask a question: "How does the theology of the Threefold Blessing teach about a mutual balanced life between the blessing of soul, the blessing of health and the blessing of material?" Because the expansion of material blessing could be a center of the Threefold Blessing as one of the temptations that human being can easily fall into, rather than having a balance between these three aspects.

And I also wonder how the faithful are taught to use the money "for where and how", in the individual and the church dimension. We can see the answer to the question, "For whom is church growth?", when we look at the future of Yoido Full Gospel Church after Yong-Gi Cho's death (14 September 2021). The theology of blessing gives the impression that God created the universe only for those who live the theology of blessing today. So how can we explain the relation between the lives of the exemplary Christians before us and the Threefold Blessing? For example, I wonder how it can explain the lives of St. Peter and St. Paul, who were not so much blessed in material life as two great evangelists of the church. And he needs to explain: "If the faithful follow the Threefold Blessing, pray for the material richness and enjoy it, when they can be satisfied saying that they are already so rich?"

Although Yong-Gi Cho underlines human-centered material blessing, his theology is not shamanistic. Asking the material blessing is a common aspect of any religion. Because, Yong-Gi Cho follows the Scripture believing in Trinity, God Father, Son, and the Holy Spirit, praising and giving glory to God. Firstly, because, he was not a fortune-teller like a shaman, or asked for healing, blessings in the name of gods, spirits of Shamanism.

2) Divine healing

Yong-Gi Cho defines the Divine healing as a supernatural healing involving the power and providence of God, not by ordinary medical practice. He emphasizes that the Divine healing is a gift from God which should be certainly testified, being included in the atonement of Jesus Christ. Yong-Gi Cho uses the Bible in this context: "By his wounds you have been healed." (1Pt 2:24) According to Yong-Gi Cho, since forgiveness of sin and sickness coexist like the two sides of a coin, Jesus on the Cross who solved sin, which is the man's fundamental problem, also solved the problem of sickness. Yong-Gi Cho underlines that, because Jesus is the same forever, the Christ's healing ministry of 2000 years ago could be repeated today. Therefore, if Jesus is present among us through the Holy Spirit, he is working now in the same way. Based on this, Yong-Gi Cho was sure of the possibility of miraculous healing, and he urged the faithful to participate in this experience. But if Yong-Gi Cho insists that Christ shed the ransom blood for healing, there will never exist the real meaning of Divine healing for non-Christian, because the presupposition of the healing is to accept Christ as the healer.

The Catholic Church tries to find an answer to the question of why sickness comes also to the righteous in the New Testament by explaining the healing in this way. Namely, Jesus met the sick people continuously during his public life, and he cured so many people through miraculous healing as a characteristic of his ministry. These healings are the signs of his mission as a Messiah (Lk 7:20-23), it symbolizes the victory of God's reign and holistic healing (Body and soul). Therefore, the Catholic Church sees that these healings testify the Jesus' authority to forgive sin (Mk 2:1-12).[145]

The Catholic Church also says that the victory of Messiah on sickness like human's other suffering, comes not only through the healing miracle, but also through the voluntary and innocent passion of Christ. And the church explains that through the passion of Christ, he gave everybody the opportunity to unite one's suffering with the suffering of the Lord. Christ, who accomplished the work of salvation through suffering, also elevated human suffering to the level of salvation. In this way, each person, in his or her own suffering, becomes a participant in the redemptive suffering of Christ.[146]

In the Catholic Church, sickness is seen as an instrument for the unity with Christ and spiritual purification. It is also considered as an opportunity to practice love for those who are with the patient. And it is a time for prayer especially. Because, that they ask a grace to accept that sickness as the will of God, or they pray earnestly for healing.[147] Anyway, the Church says that sickness has a meaning

---

[145] Erminio Lora ed., *Enchiridion Vaticanum*, vol. 19, EDB, Bologna, 2004, 761-763; Catholic Bishops' Conference of Korea, Chiyu Gidoekwanhan Hunlyung (Instructions on Healing Prayer), in the Teachings of the Catholic Church, vol. 18, 2001, 161.

[146] Erminio Lora ed., *Enchiridion Vaticanum*, vol. 19, 763-765; Catholic Bishops' Conference of Korea, Chiyu Gidoekwanhan Hunlyung (Instructions on Healing Prayer), 162-163.

[147] Erminio Lora ed., *Enchiridion Vaticanum*, vol. 19, 757; Catholic Bishops' Conference

in the mystery of salvation.[148]

In the Catholic Church there is not only a personal prayer for healing, but also for a patient and for the dying there is the Anointing of the sick. And prayer for the recovery of health encourages an effective natural healing method and medical treatment without refusal.[149]

The Church received from the Lord the mission to take care of the sick (Mt 10:8). Therefore, as part of her mission, the Church is trying hard to take care of the sick and pray for them.[150] That's why the Catholic Church has the 'Anointing of the sick' among the seven sacraments, especially to strengthen those who are suffering from illness.[151]

The Catholic Church explains the effect of the Anointing of the sick in four aspects: First, the sick receives grace, a special gift of the Holy Spirit. This is the grace of consolation, peace and courage to overcome the difficulty associated with the state of serious illness

---

of Korea, Chiyu Gidoekwanhan Hunlyung (Instructions on Healing Prayer), 158.

148 Erminio Lora ed., *Enchiridion Vaticanum*, vol. 4, EDB, Bologna, 1978, 1173; Catholic Bishops' Conference of Korea, Byungza Songsa Yesik (Rite of the Anointing of the Sick), Committee for Liturgy of CBCK, 2018, #1.

149 Erminio Lora ed., *Enchiridion Vaticanum*, vol. 19, 769; Erminio Lora, ed., Enchiridion Vaticanum, vol. 7, EDB, Bologna, 1982, 349; Catholic Bishops' Conference of Korea, Chiyu Gidoekwanhan Hunlyung (Instructions on Healing Prayer), 165; Catholic Bishops' Conference of Korea, Byungza Songsa Yesik (Rite of the Anointing of the Sick), #4.

150 *Catechismus Catholicae Ecclesiale*, #1509.

151 *Catechismus Catholicae Ecclesiale*, #1511.

or old age. This sacrament also helps them not to be shaken by the temptations of the evil one to fall into fear and frustration in the face of death. It is for the forgiveness of sins and for the spiritual healing, and also, if it is God's will, to have physical healing. Second, there is union with the passion of Christ. Namely, by the grace of this sacrament, the sick person receives the strength and the gift of being closely united to the passion of Christ. Suffering, the result of original sin, takes on a new meaning. Namely, suffering becomes a participation in the saving work of Jesus. Thirdly, the sick person who receives this sacrament, contributes to the good of the people of God. The sick for his part, through the grace of this sacrament, contributes to the sanctification of the Church and to the good of all people. By celebrating this sacrament the Church, in the communion of saints, intercedes for the benefit of the sick. Four, it is a preparation for the final journey. The Anointing of the Sick is for the sick, especially those who are about to leave this life. There is the holy anointing which is different from the anointing of the other sacraments: that of Baptism, which sealed the new life in us, and that of Confirmation, which strengthened us for the combat of this life. This last anointing fortifies the end of our earthly life like a solid rampart for the final struggles before entering the Father's house.[152]

The Catholic Church, giving the Anointing of the sick, offers the Eucharist as viaticum to those who are about to leave this life. Communion in the body and blood of Christ, received at this mo-

---

152 *Catechismus Catholicae Ecclesiale*, #1520-1523.

ment of "passing over" to the Father, has a particular significance and importance. Namely, it is the seed of eternal life and the power of resurrection, and it is the sacrament of passing from death to life, from this world to the Father.[153]

Yong-Gi Cho is convinced that only the precious blood of Christ is the perfect righteousness of man, and that Jesus who solved sin, which is the man's fundamental problem, on the Cross, also healed the problem of sickness. Remembering this point, we will see how a catholic theologian, Francis A. Sullivan thinks about healing.

According to Francis A. Sullivan, if death came into the world because of sin (Rm 5:12), then in the state of justification, there should be no sickness or death. Therefore, if the salvation means restoration to the original state of justification, then the saved should be free from sickness. But it is not correct to say that the salvation is to returning to the original state of justification. Since we still have to die, those who were healed and saved from death by Jesus, died like all of us.[154]

Francis A. Sullivan presents a healing theory which is different from that of Yong-Gi Cho. According to Sullivan, how can we understand the relation between healing and salvation, if we cannot accept the principle that Christ makes us free from our sickness in the same way with that he frees us from our sins? Francis A. Sullivan agrees

---

153 *Catechismus Catholicae Ecclesiale,* #1524.
154 Francis A. Sullivan, *Carismi e Rinnovamento Carismatico, Ancora,* Milano, 1983, 182-183.

with the theory of David Stanley. Namely, the evangelists understood those healings done by Jesus as a part of his fight against the evil's power on the humanity.[155]

David Stanley explains how Mark, Matthew, and Luck understood the healing done by Jesus like this:

According to Mark, the healing ministered by Jesus constitutes the first frontal attack against the reign of Satan. Jesus came to establish the reign of God in human history. He had to begin by breaking the rule of evil on earth, and making people free from the bondage of the 'strong man', namely from Satan.[156]

Matthew is with the opinion of Mark, saying that the healing ministry of Jesus is an important element of the fighting to destroy the reign of Satan on earth.[157] According to Luck, Jesus sees in these healings the beginning of the defeat of evil.[158]

Furthermore, David Stanley describes the healings of Jesus as an 'initial' movement against the reign of Satan; the preliminary defeat of evil. The healings do not represent the whole and perfect victory over death, which will come suddenly.

Therefore, Francis A. Sullivan affirms that the key to understanding the meaning of the healings of Jesus is in the fact that they are indications of the future total victory over the power of death

---

[155] Francis A. Sullivan, *Carismi e Rinnovamento Carismatico*, 184.
[156] David Stanley, "*S. I. Salvation and Healing,*" The Way 10 (1970), 307-308.
[157] David Stanley, "*S. I. Salvation and Healing,*" 311.
[158] David Stanley, "*S. I. Salvation and Healing,*" 314.

before humanity. The healing of Jesus is an "'indication' of his future Lordship over the universe", but the Lordship of Jesus is not yet absolute or certain.

Because his enemies are still active and powerful, these enemies will not be completely destroyed until his final coming, when there will be no more death (Rev 21:4).

Francis A. Sullivan explains that if we start with this principle, we can understand why Jesus did not only spend much of his public life healing people, but also sent his disciples out into the world with the power to heal. And it can be understood, why the Holy Spirit has continued to distribute the gift of healing throughout the Church history. Namely, the Church, as the body and bride of Christ, participates in the fight against Satan. Francis A. Sullivan understands that the healings obtained through the prayer and sacraments of the Church, are the sign of the triumph of death through his resurrection, and also the sign of his triumph over death, the final enemy to be defeated at his Second coming.

Furthermore, according to Sullivan, for healing to truly be a sign of salvation, it is not necessary that the saved ones need to be healed from all sickness. Healing is a sign of our physical salvation. But it does not indicate that this salvation is fully realized. However, Sullivan considers that the healing is a worthy and effective sign, despite we cannot be sure that it will be granted in every case.[159]

Francis A. Sullivan considers charismatic healing as a sign that

---

159 Francis A. Sullivan, *Carismi e Rinnovamento Carismatico*, 185-186.

indicates a triumph over death that is yet to come. This point help us to accept the fact that some people are healed through prayer, while others no. Every charismatic healing is a totally free anticipation of physical salvation, which will be verified in the future. Therefore, Sullivan underlines, since we are still subject to death, we have no right before God to be free from any cause of death such as sickness and disease. Because charismatic healing depends on God's free will to give it 'when and where.' And it is also anticipating the resurrection of the body that will take place at Jesus' second coming, as sign of his power to raise the dead to eternal life.[160]

According to Francis A. Sullivan, we cannot get the final triumph on earth, but every healing and every progress in medical science is a victory against the power of death over all mankind. He affirms therefore, because God wants us to seek medical help when we are sick, refusing medical help could be a sign of pride, a failure to believe in God's power as a healer. And refusing the medical help, and only relying on prayer, is a way of forcing God to perform a miracle. This is not a truly religious attitude, but is an attempt to manipulate God.[161] Francis A. Sullivan emphasizes that when we pray for healing, we should not ask God to answer our prayer in the way we want. According to him, we should pray with certitude that God cares for the sick person, but we must also humbly recognize that we cannot know precisely like Martha and Mary who did

---

160 Francis A. Sullivan, *Carismi e Rinnovamento Carismatico*, 187.
161 Francis A. Sullivan, *Carismi e Rinnovamento Carismatico*, 188-189.

not know what kind of triumph over death could happen for a greater glory of God.[162]

All the contents seen before can be compared in this way: Firstly, the healing explained by Yong-Gi Cho and by the Catholic Church has some differences. Yong-Gi Cho defines that Divine healing means a supernatural healing involved by the power and the providence of God, not through the ordinary medical practice. But the Catholic Church does not define especially a word of healing, seeing that God cures not only through prayer, but also through the Anointing of the sick, medical care, and natural healing. Yong-Gi Cho affirms that Divine healing should be testified as a gift of God, being included in the atonement of Jesus Christ. And he encourages believers to participate in this experience, because the forgiveness of sin and healing are like the two sides of the coin, and because the healing ministry of Christ can be repeated now also, since Jesus Christ is the same forever.

The Catholic Church encourages active efforts to restore health in several ways: the healings in the public life of Jesus are a sign of his mission as Messiah; these healings testify that Jesus has the power to forgive sin. Furthermore, the Catholic Church understands that the individual person in his suffering can participate in the redemptive suffering of Christ, and sickness could be an instrument to unite with Christ and an instrument of spiritual purification. Firstly,

---

162 Francis A. Sullivan, *Carismi e Rinnovamento Carismatico*, 191.

in the Catholic Church, it is characteristic to interpret that sickness has a meaning in the mystery of salvation.

3) The Reign of God

According to Jang-Hyun Ryoo, the reign of God that Yong-Gi Cho talks about is 'the place where God's sovereignty is exercised' or 'a place where the dominion and mighty rule of the living God is fully present.' Yong-Gi Cho explains the paradise in different forms with several terms: the paradise after death, the New heaven and New earth, the heart of human being, the eternal paradise, the immanent paradise on earth, the spiritual paradise, and the paradise of the church. Yong-Gi Cho especially emphasizes that the Church is the reign of God, because he persistently spread the presentness of the reign of God, connecting directly to the situation of his early pastoral ministry.

The Catholic Church speaks of paradise, purgatory and hell differently from Yong-Gi Cho, and emphasizes the communion of the Church on earth and the Church in heaven. Namely, the Catholic Church believes in the communion of all Christ's faithful, those who are pilgrims on earth, the dead who are being purified, and the blessed in heaven, all together forming one Church. And the Catholic Church believes that in this communion, the merciful love of God and his saints is always attentive to our prayers.[163]

---

163 *Catechismus Catholicae Ecclesiale*, #962.

The Catholic Church says that the reign of God and the Church cannot be separated. For the Church is ordered toward the God's kingdom, of which she is the seed, sign and instrument. Therefore, it teaches that the Church has the mission to proclaim God and the reign of Christ, and also to establish this reign among all peoples. Yong-Gi Cho emphasizes the Church's growth, enjoying the blessing of the reign of God and sharing booty with eschatological hope. The Catholic Church affirms that the reign of God began in the Church of Christ, but it is not of this world; its growth consists in responding always more passionately to God's love and in spreading holiness among people. And the Catholic Church encourages Christians to contribute to the welfare of the earthly state, to promote justice, peace and fraternity, specially to help the poorest and most needy.

Yong-Gi Cho insists on the Millennial kingdom theory and supports the pretribulation rapture theory. He says, interpreting Daniel 9:24-27 literally, that at the end of time there will be the tribulation for seven years after completion of the church era, and at that time, the church or the faithful will be raptured. About this, Jang-Hyun Ryoo, evaluating that the eschatology of Yong-Gi Cho is Dispensationalism which goes with premillennialism, says that this kind of eschatology should be overcome so that the Pentecostal movement may be developed as a true spiritual movement. Jang-Hyun Ryoo points out that this is a theological task to overcome.

The Catholic Church rejects even modified forms of this falsification of the kingdom to come under the name of millennialism. In particular, it rejects the political form of secularized messianic faith as 'inherently evil.' And it teaches that only God the Father knows that time. So there is a big difference in the attitude of faith to millennialism between the Catholic Church and the theology of Yong-Gi Cho.

In the soteriology, there is a clear distance between the theology of Yong-Gi Cho and the catholic theology. Yong-Gi Cho says that those who participate physically as a formal believer cannot be raptured, but only those who prepare the oil and are filled with the Holy Spirit will be raptured. According to Yong-Gi Cho the baptism in the Holy Spirit is the sure guarantee for this rapture. But the Catholic Church is more open to the ecumenical movement and interreligious dialogue, being more comprehensive for the salvation of other religions' faithful, than the theology of Yong-Gi Cho, which insists that only the Pentecostal believers who received the baptism of the Holy Spirit, will be raptured. There are so many Christians without the baptism of the Holy Spirit. Therefore, the theology of Yong-Gi Cho needs to explain more theologically for these Christians. The Catholic Church believes that the souls in purgatory can enter paradise through Mass, prayer, charity, mentioning the 'private judgment' and 'public judgment'. Also, she emphasizes the agape life to overcome personal selfishness and group selfishness.

Yong-Gi Cho mentions the attribute of the reign of God: a reign without sin; a reign that heals the sick; a reign that drives out the devils; a reign of abundance. But Yong-Gi Cho got the prison sentence with the money problem related to Yoido Full Gospel Church, and because of this, there was a big infighting in the church. I wonder how his theology which gives special importance to the Church as the reign of God sees this point. And Yong-Gi Cho says that eternal paradise is eternal heaven, and immanent paradise is paradise on earth. He was supposed to lead his followers and also his family members to eternal paradise. But the last part of his life was so embarrassed, helping his family members to enjoy earthly pleasures. It makes us think, "What was the growth of the Church for?"

Yong-Gi Cho affirms that believers should fight against Satan and spirits by relying on the Holy Spirit. According to Yong-Gi Cho, Jesus has won the war against Satan, and it is already 'finished war' on the Cross, so the believers should possess the kingdom of heaven and get the booty of Fivefold Gospel and Threefold Blessing. Therefore, Yong-Gi Cho teaches that it is very important to know that the believers are in the middle of the spiritual war with Satan. Yong-Gi Cho emphasizes that to be a 'living church' is to be a church that practices the sharing of this booty everywhere.

While Yongi-Gi Cho focuses on the booty called the Fivefold Gospel and Threefold Blessing when he mentions spiritual war, the direction of the spiritual war of the Catholic Church is different. The *Gaudete et Exsultate* (Pope Francis, 19 March 2018) explains spiritual war as follows.

Pope Francis underlines that the Christian life is a constant battle, and we need strength and courage to withstand the temptations of the devil and to proclaim the Gospel. He affirms that this battle cannot be reduced to the struggle against our human weaknesses and proclivities (Laziness, Lust, Envy, Jealousy or any other), and that it is also a constant struggle against the devil, the prince of evil.

> The Christian life is a constant battle. We need strength and courage to withstand the temptations of the devil and to proclaim the Gospel. This battle is sweet, for it allows us to rejoice each time the Lord triumphs in our lives.
> We are not dealing merely with a battle against the world and a worldly mentality that would deceive us and leave us dull and mediocre, lacking in enthusiasm and joy. Nor can this battle be reduced to the struggle against our human weaknesses and proclivities (Laziness, Lust, Envy, Jealousy or any others). It is also a constant struggle against the devil, the prince of evil. ... He rejoiced when his disciples made progress in preaching the Gospel and overcoming the opposition of the evil one.[164]

Apostolic exhortation makes it clear that evil one is a personal being who assails us, not evil in the abstract one. And it gives a concrete example, that in leaving us the Our Father, Jesus wanted us to conclude by asking the Father to "deliver us from evil." Jesus also taught us to ask that the evil power will not prevail over us.

---

164 Pope Francis, *Gaudete et Exsultate: Apostolic Exhortation on the Call to Holiness in Today's World* (March 19, 2018), #158-159.

We will not admit the existence of the devil if we insist on regarding life by empirical standards alone, without a supernatural understanding. It is precisely the conviction that this malign power is present in our midst that enables us to understand how evil can at times have so much destructive force. ... He is present in the very first pages of the Scriptures, which end with God's victory over the devil. Indeed, in leaving us the Our Father, Jesus wanted us to conclude by asking the Father to "deliver us from evil." That final word does not refer to evil in the abstract; a more exact translation would be "the evil one." It indicates a personal being who assails us. Jesus taught us to ask daily for deliverance from him, lest his power prevail over us.[165]

Pope Francis emphasizes that we should not think of the devil as a myth, a representation, a symbol, a figure of speech or an idea. And the Pope says that we should not let down our guard because he poisons us with the venom of hatred, desolation, envy and vice. And since our path towards holiness is a constant battle, we can count on the powerful weapons: faith-filled prayer, meditation on the word of God, the celebration of Mass, Eucharistic adoration, sacramental Reconciliation, community life, works of charity, missionary outreach.

Hence, we should not think of the devil as a myth, a representation, a symbol, a figure of speech or an idea. ... He poisons us with the venom

---

165 Pope Francis, *Gaudete et Exsultate*, #160.

> of hatred, desolation, envy and vice. When we let down our guard, he takes advantage of it to destroy our lives, our families and our communities. "Like a roaring lion, he prowls around, looking for someone to devour." (1 Pet 5:8)
>
> ...These expressions are not melodramatic, precisely because our path towards holiness is a constant battle. ... For this spiritual combat, we can count on the powerful weapons that the Lord has given us: faith-filled prayer, meditation on the word of God, the celebration of Mass, Eucharistic adoration, sacramental Reconciliation, works of charity, community life, missionary outreach.[166]

Pope Francis presents three ways for the best counterbalance to evil, namely, the cultivation of all that is good, progress in the spiritual life and growth in love. And he affirms that we need to raise the banner of the cross to fight with aggressive tenderness against the assaults of evil.

> Along this journey, the cultivation of all that is good, progress in the spiritual life and growth in love are the best counterbalance to evil. Those who choose to remain neutral, who are satisfied with little, who renounce the ideal of giving themselves generously to the Lord, will never hold out. Even less if they fall into defeatism, for "if we start without confidence, we have already lost half the battle and we bury our talents. Christian triumph is always a cross, yet a cross which is at the same

---

[166] Pope FRANCIS, *Gaudete et Exsultate*, #161-162.

time a victorious banner, borne with aggressive tenderness against the assaults of evil."[167]

Pope Francis advices to ask always the Holy Spirit what Jesus expects from us at every moment of our life and in every decision we must make.[168] And he affirms that the path of holiness is a source of peace and joy, given to us by the Holy Spirit. The Pope advices to keep awake, to abstain from every form of evil, seeing that spiritual corruption is a comfortable and self-satisfied form of blindness. Because even Satan disguises himself as an angel of light. Likewise, Pope Francis emphasizes the path of holiness in the spiritual war, while Yong-Gi Cho emphasizes the booty.

> The path of holiness is a source of peace and joy, given to us by the Spirit. ... "Abstain from every form of evil." (1 Thess 5:22) "Keep awake." (Mt 24:42; Mk 13:35) "Let us not fall asleep." (1 Thess 5:6) ...
> Spiritual corruption is worse than the fall of a sinner, for it is a comfortable and self-satisfied form of blindness. Everything then appears acceptable: deception, slander, egotism and other subtle forms of self-centeredness, for "even Satan disguises himself as an angel of light." (2 Cor 11:14) Jesus warned us against this self-deception that easily leads to corruption. He spoke of a person freed from the devil who, convinced that his life was now in order, ended up being possessed by seven other

---

167 Pope FRANCIS, *Gaudete et Exsultate*, #163.
168 Pope FRANCIS, *Gaudete et Exsultate*, #23.

evil spirits. (Lk 11:24-26)[169]

---

169 Pope FRANCIS, *Gaudete et Exsultate*, #164-165.

PART III

Pastoral Challenge

The Church growth of Yoido Full Gospel Church is basically the fruit of Yong-Gi Cho's preaching, Cell Group System, Fourth dimension theory, and Pentecostal worship style. Therefore, in order to observe the pastoral area of Yong-Gi Cho, we will first look at the Fourth dimension theory, and then the preaching method and the Cell Group System. For the sermon, presenting the way suggested by Yong-Gi Cho and by Pope Francis will be observed the common aspect and the unique character of protestant and the Catholic Church. Will be presented also the Cell Group System, Guyuk Yebe (Cell group worship) of Yoido Full Gospel Church, and the Small Community of Catholic Archdiocese of Seoul will also be presented. This study is to reflect the pastoral renewal and the way of spiritual growth of the faithful.

1. Anthropology and the Fourth Dimension spirituality of Yong-Gi Cho

The Fourth dimension theory is essential to the spirituality of Yong-Gi Cho. Dimension is a concept to express the degree of expansion of space or shape. Euclid of Alexandria, father of geometry, defined point, line, plane, solid like this: "a point is that which has no part", "a line is a length without width." "A plane is that which has only length and width, a solid is that which has length, width and height."

Yong-Gi Cho explains the basic theory of his Fourth dimension spirituality with the concept of point, length, plane and solid like this: Namely, geometry says that when two points are connected, it becomes a line, and this is called as the One dimension. But Yong-Gi Cho says that the One dimension here is an imaginary line. Because the line of the One dimension should not have thickness and width. For example, when we draw a line with a pencil, in reality, the thickness appears as high as the pencil lead. That is why Yong-Gi Cho says that at the moment of drawing a line, to be precise, that line is the Two dimension because it already appears as thickness. Therefore, the One dimension that we are expressing and drawing is fatefully sucked into the Two dimension at the moment of drawing, will be dominated by the Two dimension.

He explains the Two dimension with the same principle. The Two dimension is a plane, but because at the moment of drawing that plane, thickness already appears. Therefore, although according to our mathematical understanding it is the Two dimension, in reality it becomes Three dimensional solid. Consequently, Yong-Gi Cho says that the Two dimension includes the Three dimension, and it is dominated by the Three dimension. According to the same principle, the Three dimension is a solid made of plane. But because space enters at the moment of solidification, it includes the Fourth dimension, and it is dominated by the Fourth dimension. Namely, the Three dimension becomes a Three dimension that includes the Fourth dimension. Consequently, the Three dimension includes space-time; space contains infinity, and time contains eternity. Therefore, Yong-Gi Cho explains that the Fourth dimension is a world of space-time, which is the addition of time to space of the Three dimension; it is a world of soul and also spiritual world beyond the sensory world. And he affirms that the owner of eternity and infinity is God, and God himself is eternal and infinite.

> Geometry says that when the two points are connected, it becomes a line. This is the One dimension.[1] The One dimension draws a line between two points, but it should have neither thickness nor width. Because the One dimension has neither thickness nor width, it is an imaginary line. ... If we draw a line with a pencil, the thickness appears as high as the pencil lead. Then, at the moment of making a line, this line is not already the One dimension. Because thickness has already

---

[1] Dr. Paul Yong-Gi Cho, *The Fourth Dimension, vol. 1, Rhema Publication Ministry*, 1979, 38.

appeared, to be precise, it becomes the Two dimension. That is why the One dimension that we are expressing and drawing is fatefully sucked into the Two dimension at the moment of drawing, will be dominated by the Two dimension. ...

According to the same principle, the Two dimension is plane, but because at the moment of drawing this plane, the thickness already appears in the One dimensional line, although according to our mathematical understanding it is the two dimensional, in reality, it becomes Three dimensional solid. ... Likewise, the One dimension, the plane of the Two dimension, is also in reality an imaginary one. For the plane without thickness at all is the Two dimension. Then, the Two dimension also fatefully belongs to Three dimension and will be dominated by it, whether it likes it or not. From a Two dimensional point of view, it is the Two dimension that contains the Three dimension.

The Three dimension is a solid made of planes, but because space enters at the moment of solidification, it is not a complete Three dimension. The concept of the Three dimensional solid is also an imaginary one. Therefore, the Three dimension is fatefully dominated by the Fourth dimension, and it includes space-time of the Fourth dimension. Namely, the Three dimension becomes a Three dimension that includes the Fourth dimension. Consequently, the Three dimension is solid, namely, it includes space-time, and at the moment of appearance of space-time, space already belongs to infinite, time belongs to eternity. ... Space contains infinity, and time contains eternity. Consequently, it could be told that the Fourth dimension is the world of space-time, which is the addition of time to space of the Three dimension. It is a world of the soul and also a spiritual world beyond the sensory world. The owner of eternity and infinity is God. God is eternal and infinite.[2]

In order to understand Yong-Gi Cho's Fourth dimension, it is important to remember that the higher dimension includes and dominates the lower dimension. He links this to the relationship between God and his creature.

According to Young-Gi Cho, because man is a cubic existence that belongs to the Three dimensional world, this Three dimensional existence, at the moment of existence, belongs to the Fourth dimension and is dominated by the Fourth dimension. Therefore, Yong-Gi Cho understands that all human being is created as an existence to be occupied by the infinite and the eternity, and the human being is to be occupied by God, whether sitting down, asleep or awake. Consequently, he understands that God, the eternal and infinite existence, rules the whole world below the Three dimension. Yong-Gi Cho insists that this principle is an important clue to recognize God, and it is a very scientific reason that the higher dimension includes and dominates the lower dimension.

Man is a cubic existence who belongs to the Three dimensional world. Because man belongs to the Three dimensional world, and as soon as the Three dimension happens, he fatefully belongs to the Fourth di-

---

[2] Yong-Gi Cho, *4 Chwonui Yungsung (4th Dimension of Spirituality)*, Church Growth Institute, 2010, 63–65.

mension, and man is created as an existence dominated by the Fourth dimension. Therefore, because man is a cubic existence, when space, the Three dimension happens, infinity comes into us, when time happens eternity comes into us. This is a principle that is contained in everyone, Christian, or non-Christian. Namely, every human being, the Three dimensional cubic, is created as an existence occupied by the infinity and the eternity. Therefore, we are destined to be occupied by God, whether we are sitting, sleeping or awake. This principle is an important clue for recognizing God. It is a very scientific reason that the higher dimension includes and dominates the lower dimension. Consequently, God, the eternal and infinite existence, dominates the whole world below the Three dimension.[3]

Yong-Gi Cho says that since human being is a spiritual existence who has a soul, being in the Three dimension, belongs to the Fourth dimension. And seeing the relationship between the soul and the body of a human being, Cho affirms that the human being's spirit dominates the Three dimensional body, if the spirit is well, the body is healthy.

Since human being is a spiritual existence who has a soul, being in the Three dimension, he belongs to the Fourth dimension. ... Although human body returns to earth, soul exists forever even if he goes to heaven or goes to hell. If we see this in the Fourth dimensional sense, human

---

3 Yong-Gi Cho, *4 Chwonui Yungsung (4^b Dimension of Spirituality)*, 66.

being is a living existence forever. The human spirit dominates the body of the Three dimension. If that spirit is damaged, the body gets sick, if that spirit is well, the body is healthy.[4]

Yong-Gi Cho explains the Fourth dimensional existence with God, man and Satan. But he says that man is the lowest of the Fourth dimension, Satan is in the middle and God is the highest of the Fourth dimension. He develops the Fourth dimension theory emphasizing that Satan of the Fourth dimension, wants to dominate human being and the Three dimension which is the inferior dimension.

> The Fourth dimensional existence is God, man, and Satan. Now, we are the lowest of the Fourth dimension, Satan is in the middle and God is in the highest of the Fourth dimension. Because the Fourth dimension dominates the Three dimension, human being dominates the Three dimensional world. And since we human being is spiritual existence, through invention and discovery, we can change the Three dimension. Satan belongs to the Fourth dimensional existence. Therefore, he wants to dominate human being and the Three dimension which is the inferior dimension.[5]

Yong-Gi Cho, affirms that the spiritual war with Satan is inevitable in this earth, thinking that Satan rules the Three dimensional world,

---

4 Yong-Gi Cho, *4 Chwonui Yungsung (4th Dimension of Spirituality)*, 68.
5 Yong-Gi Cho, *4 Chwonui Yungsung (4th Dimension of Spirituality)*, 69.

where we belong. If we win in the spiritual war, Satan cannot influence the Three dimensional world. He emphasizes the reason why we must win in the spiritual war, because if we give in Satan, from that moment on, Satan begins to dominate and influence our Three dimension.[6]

Yong-Gi Cho says that the saved man obtains the eternal life through the Fourth-dimension of God. And he continues to affirm that his spirit, heart, and mind will be filled with the Fourth dimension of God, if, believing this fact, proclaiming the victory in the spiritual war that is going on every day, the Three dimensional world will be completely ruled by the God's sovereignty.[7] And then he emphasizes the necessity of discipline to win in the spiritual war. Even though God has displaced us to the Fourth dimension, we need to discipline the spirit of the Fourth dimension to dominate Satan and the Three dimensional world, because we are still living in the lower dimensional life.

> God gave us the key to paradise. God moved us to the Fourth dimension where God belongs. But we are still living in the lower dimensional life. Although God gave us the authority to rule the Three dimension and Satan, we still volunteer to have a life tied by it.
> We are saved by believing in Jesus, displaced to the holy Fourth dimensional world. Now staying there we should be able to govern Satan and

---

6 Yong-Gi Cho, *4 Chwonui Yungsung (4th Dimension of Spirituality)*, 70.
7 Yong-Gi Cho, *4 Chwonui Yungsung (4th Dimension of Spirituality)*, 71.

the Three dimensional world. Remembering that our body belongs to the Three dimension, but spirit belongs to the holy Fourth dimension of God, we must make this of mine. This is the reason why we have to discipline the Fourth dimensional spirit.[8]

Yong-Gi Cho also insists that in order to change the Three dimensional life, we have to change the Fourth dimension; this change of the Fourth dimension depends on how we handle the four elements (thought, faith, dream, word) which compose the Fourth dimension, namely depends on how we do the programming. Because this is how the Fourth dimensional spirit works.

This means that if the Fourth dimension changes ultimately, the life of the Three dimension changes. The change of the Fourth dimension depends on how we deal with the four elements (thought, faith, dream, word) which compose the Fourth dimension. We need to change these elements. We have to do the programming of the thought, faith, dream, word which are in us, with the thought, faith, dream, word of the Fourth dimension. To do programming is to give the command so that the computer can work. When we do the programming within us, the thought, the faith, the dream, the word of the Fourth dimension, the Fourth dimensional spirit works. Through this process our life can be changed.[9]

---

8 Yong-Gi Cho, *4 Chwonui Yungsung (4th Dimension of Spirituality)*, 72-73.
9 Yong-Gi Cho, *4 Chwonui Yungsung (4th Dimension of Spirituality)*, 76-77.

It is necessary to first reflect the Pneumatological anthropology of Yong-Gi Cho, in order to better understand Cho's theory.

1) The Pneumatological anthropology of Yong-Gi Cho

Yong-Gi Cho thinks that human beings are created in the image of God and are made up of spirit, soul and body. Linking this to the Triune God, he compares it to three different containers and explains its characteristics. Namely, the spirit is a bowl to receive God. The soul is a bowl to put oneself, and it has knowledge, sentiments, will and personality. The body is a bowl to put the world, this body can know everything that happens around us through the five sense organs.

> As God is the Father, the Son and the Holy Spirit in the Trinity, he created man with spirit, soul and body. As each position of the Father, the Son, and the Holy Spirit is different, he created the position of spirit, soul, body differently. The spirit is a bowl to receive God. Therefore, it is impossible to know God except through the spirit. The reason why today's people do not know God, is because their spirit is separated from God. The soul is a bowl to put oneself. It has knowledge, sentiments, will and personality. A man with strong soul, has strong self-will, a man with weak soul, has a weak ego. Finally, the body is a bowl to put the world. We can know everything that happens around us through the five sense organs.[10]

Yong-Gi Cho says that man is created in the image of God by the God's sovereignty, man is a spiritual man created by the Holy Spirit. Namely, according to Gen 2:7, man became a 'living spirit' differently from other animals, because God blew into his nostrils the breath of life. Therefore, man, made of God's spirit, could participate not only in the material world of the Three dimension, but also in the spiritual world of the Fourth dimension.[11] Cho affirms that man belongs to the Fourth dimension as a spiritual existence, but he has fallen as a servant of Satan because he has lost his free will through corruption. Yong-Gi Cho is convinced that the man of absolute hopelessness can only be transformed into the man of absolute hope by God's absolute sovereign grace through Jesus Christ. And Yong-Gi Cho affirms that when we go forward with full trust and depending on the God's absolute sovereignty, we can apply the spiritual rule of the Fourth dimension in our lives.[12]

Yong-Gi Cho, teaches us how to do this, and encourages us to recognize a clear goal in our minds that does not go against the wish of the Holy Spirit, and to draw a realistic picture of our goal

---

10 Yong-Gi Cho, *Sunbokumui Jinli (Trouth of Full Gospel)*, vol. 2, Seoul Logos, 1979, 258; Mun-Chul Shin, Young Sanui Songnyung-nonzok Ingannon (Pneumatological Anthropology of Young San), in Journal of Young San theology, vol.4, Young San Theological Institute of Hansei University, Gunpo, 2007, 99.

11 Mun-Chul Shin, *4 Chawonui Yungsong-edehan Sinhkzok Gochal (A Theological Appraisal of the Spirituality of the Fourth Dimension)*, in Journal of Young San Theology, vol. 13, Young San Theological Institute of Hansei University, Gunpo, 2008, 222.

12 Mun-Chul Shin, *4 Chawonui Yungsong-edehan Sinhkzok Gochal (A Theological Appraisal of the Spirituality of the Fourth Dimension)*, 220-221.

in our minds and pray fervently. But he makes sure that it should not be confused with the 'mind control', 'mind expansion', 'yoga', and 'transcendental meditation.' According to Yong-Gi Cho these consciousness belong only to the field of Satan to develop the human's mental world (soul's potentiality).

> First, recognise a clear objective in your heart that is not against the wish of the Holy Spirit. And then, having drawn the picture in the heart vividly and realistically for that objective, pray hard until the perfect response comes. But do not confuse this with 'mind control', 'mind expansion', 'yoga' or 'transcendental meditation.' These consciousnesses belong only to the field of Satan to develop the human's mental world (soul's potentiality). Please stand up and perform the miracles of the almighty God more clearly than any magician of Egypt.[13]

Therefore, the Fourth dimension spirituality, Yong-Gi Cho says, is not obtained through 'mind control', or human mental discipline, but it is clearly possible in the absolute sovereignty of God. In reality he confesses that in the beginning of his pastoral ministry he emphasized human free will for the growth of the church influenced by Arminianism, but later on his concept of God is with the idea of God's absolute sovereignty.[14]

---

13 Yong-Gi Cho, *4 Chawonui Yungzokseghe (The Fourth Dimension)*, Seoul Logos, 2010, 85.
14 Mun-Chul Shin, *4 Chawonui Yungsong-edehan Sinhkzok Gochal (A Theological Appraisal of the Spirituality of the Fourth Dimension)*, 219.

Yong-Gi Cho explains the role of the Holy Spirit in relation to human beings, who have spirit, soul and body, and says that through the Holy Spirit, the Spirit of God, human beings can restore the image of God, govern all things and secure the original position of human beings. Namely, Yong-Gi Cho says that the Holy Spirit establishes a spiritual relationship with man through man's spirit; gives man reason and will to seek truth and goodness through man's soul; gives grace so that man will live according to the word of God through the body. Therefore, Mun-Chul Shin affirms that the pneumatological anthropology of Yong-Gi Cho can provide the answer to how fallen man can recover the original image of God between God's grace and human free will, and how man can live a life as a desirable image of God.[15] In the pneumatological anthropology of Yong-Gi Cho, he can say that man's will is indispensable condition, in that the man's will collaborates with the Holy Spirit.[16] Yong-Gi Cho advices us to pray, saying that "God puts the will to do His will through the Holy Spirit, and gives us wish in our heart." Namely, we will pray, "Lord, send me now the desire to follow your will." And then we have to wait patiently before the Lord with an open heart, until only the wish of God given by the Holy Spirit, becomes more and more evident.

---

15 Mun-Chul Shin, *Young Sanui Songnyung-nonzok Ingannon (Pneumatological Anthropology of Young San)*, 100.

16 Mun-Chul Shin, *Young Sanui Songnyung-nonzok Ingannon (Pneumatological Anthropology of Young San)*, 102.

After praying, "Lord, send me now the wish to follow your will", you will wait till God gives the holy wish. When you pray, the holy wishes given by God overflow in your heart. But when you pray, you must wait while the God's wish takes place. After praying a little, do not stand up and go out in a hurry, telling, "Oh, I got all the answers." ... Because the wish sometimes comes from the thought brought by Satan strangely, or comes from your own thinking. ... Therefore, you must wait the will of the Lord before him with an open heart. Then, only one wish will appear with great peace over other thinking. If you wait patiently your own wish and Satan's wish will fade and only the wish given by the Holy Spirit becomes more and more evident.[17]

Mun-Chul Shin, saying that we can derive the pneumatological anthropology from the Fourth dimension of Yong-Gi Cho, summarizes it as follows. Namely, the Holy Spirit gives man dream and vision, which are the spiritual language of the Fourth dimension, and makes man creatively govern the material world of the Three dimension. And when the Holy Spirit hatches dream and vision in the saved man, in the Three dimension, man can have the ability to use God's thinking, God's dream, God's faith, and God's word, which is the spiritual principle of the Fourth dimension. At this time, totally depending on the God's grace, through the help of the Holy Spirit, when man's will becomes new in Christ, he can be transformed into a creative man. Mun-Chul Shin also says that we can

---

17 Yong-Gi Cho, *4 Chawonui Yungzokseghe (The Fourth Dimension)*, 128.

understand that the pneumatological anthropology is the work of the Holy Spirit which is active in the soul of man.[18]

Yong-Gi Cho says that we learn the language of the Holy Spirit through the Bible. And Cho advises us to ask the Holy Spirit to teach us dream and vision that are his language leaning on the Holy Spirit, to keep these visions and to obey how the Holy Spirit leads our lives.

> The Bible is the divine Word about the spiritual world of the Fourth dimension, not the Three dimension. ... Through the Bible, we learn the language of the Holy Spirit. And we can know how the Holy Spirit makes your vision and dream grow and come true. Entrust all to the Holy Spirit. Let the Holy Spirit come to you and makes the Word, which you read, have a life. And then keep your wish in your heart according to the word of God. You have the responsibility to make many people see the God's miracle and give glory to God. Therefore, ask the Holy Spirit to teach you dream and vision, which are the language of the Holy Spirit. Keep these visions well. Lean on the Holy Spirit. Obey how the Holy Spirit leads your life.[19]

Yong-Gi Cho explains God's will for us to connect with creation in this way. Namely, after God created everything, God created Adam and Eve, that the seventh day was the first day of Adam. He

---

18 Mun-Chul Shin, *4 Chawonui Yungsong-edehan Sinhkzok Gochal (A Theological Appraisal of the Spirituality of the Fourth Dimension)*, 223.
19 Yong-Gi Cho, *4 Chawonui Yungzokseghe (The Fourth Dimension)*, 84-85.

says that God carried out the plan that Adam would begin his life on God's Sabbath day. According to Yong-Gi Cho, Adam is not created to work but to live for the glory of God, and to rest in God.

> God created Adam and Eve after creating all things. ... Please imagine that Adam and Eve came to God and said like this, "God, this day is the first day of our life. Everything is so beautiful, but is there anything to help you?" Maybe God could answer like this, "No. I have already done everything for you. ... I have carried out the plan that you would begin your life on the Sabbath day. You are not created to work, but to live for my glory. Now, you rest in me."[20]

Yong-Gi Cho understands that the God's purpose in creating man is for fellowship and communion with man; to make man enjoy the abundant glory of God.[21] And he summarizes the salvation and the role of the believer this way. Namely, man does not need to do anything to be saved. Because God's plan to save us in Jesus Christ was completely fulfilled on the Cross of Calvary 2,000 years ago. Therefore, although man is very sinful, if he comes to God by believing in Jesus, he will receive the perfect salvation given by God as a gift. Yong-Gi Cho emphasizes that the salvation is by the grace of God, but we do not receive it through human action. Yong-Gi Cho insists that the role of today's believer is to work, pray, and

---

20 Yong-Gi Cho, *4 Chawonui Yungzokseghe (The Fourth Dimension)*, 227-228.
21 Yong-Gi Cho, *4 Chawonui Yungzokseghe (The Fourth Dimension)*, 230.

listen to the sermon every day to enter into the God's rest.

> One man goes to God, asking "God, what can I do to be saved?" That time, God answers: "Son, no need to do anything. Because I have done everything for you, there is nothing more to do! Live in my rest. I finished the work. Now I invite you to a new spiritual life that I have prepared for you. What you will do is only to believe in me. Worship me. Just follow me. Come to me and rest. My son, you are saved by my grace." If you want to be saved by your own good works, you disturb God's authority. Because the salvation work belongs to God. ... No human religion can save our soul. But if you come to God by believing in Jesus, you receive the perfect salvation given by God as a gift, despite you are miserable and sinful. The salvation is by the grace of God, we do not receive it through human action. ... The plan that God wanted to save in Jesus Christ from eternity was perfectly realized on the Cross of Calvary 2,000 years ago.
> God has finished everything and rested, what is your role as a believer today? ... For one reason only, we work and pray, listen to the sermon every day. It is because we are going to enter into God's rest.[22]

Thus, for Yong-Gi Cho, the relationship between God's rest and man is very important. Therefore, he explains how the cow learns to work with the yoke, how we need to carry our own yoke like this. First, he gives an example of a calf and a mother cow. A calf

---

22 Yong-Gi Cho, *4 Chawonui Yungzokseghe (The Fourth Dimension)*, 234-235.

was tied to the yoke together with the mother cow. But in reality, because the mother cow carried the heavy yoke, the calf learned how to plow without being tied to the reins. And then Yong-Gi Cho explains the connection between our own work and the yoke of Jesus. He understands that Jesus did not say that we should carry our own yoke alone, but rather that Jesus said, "Take my yoke and learn from me", "Come under my yoke and rest." And then he emphasizes that we are invited to bear the yoke of Jesus, which is easy and light. Connecting the work and the yoke, Yong-Gi Cho insists that we must come before Jesus and live in the enjoyment of God's rest, because the work is not ours but God's.

> Long ago in Palestine, when a farmer was training a calf to plow the field he put the calf under the yoke. But in reality the yoke was on the mother cow's neck. In the beginning, the calf hesitated to be tied to the yoke with the mother cow, but afterward he must have been interesting and happy. Because the calf was not carrying a heavy yoke, but the mother cow was. The calf just followed how the mother cow does. In this way the calf learned how to plow without being tied to the reins by sharing the yoke with the mother cow.
> Jesus did not say that we should carry our own yoke alone. Jesus tells us clearly: "Take my yoke, and learn from me." ... "When I carried the Cross, I also carried your burden. You have not paid for your sins on your own. You did not suffer for your sins. You have paid nothing. Only I bear the heavy burden of your sins, and suffer in the shedding of blood. Come under my yoke and rest." You are invited to carry the

yoke of Jesus. The yoke of Jesus is easy and light. The work is not yours but of God's. Therefore, we must come before Jesus and live in the enjoyment of God's rest. What a great blessing it is to live in the rest of God.[23]

According to Yong-Gi Cho, although Jesus wants to carry our burden regardless what kind of burden we have today, the problem is with us. Because we are too self-centered and independent, sometimes it takes time to unload a heavy yoke. He emphasizes that if we follow the Lord's teaching, all the problems will be solved and we can gain strength.[24] Resting in God is a very strong aspect of the anthropology of Yong-Gi Cho. He shares his experience in this way, convinced that the Holy Spirit told him: Son, why do you want to carry all these burdens for yourself? It is too heavy for you; that church is not your church, but mine; the answer is with me; you live only in my grace and rest in me.

> "Son, why do you want to carry all these burdens for yourself? It is too heavy for you. The pastoral ministry which I delegated you, and your own work belong to me. That church is not your church but mine. You must live in my rest. Because I know the method of planning and execution for my church, the answer is with me. You live only in my grace and rest in me." The word given by God in my heart changed my life completely. And I felt that the heavy burden that had been on my should-

---

23 Yong-Gi Cho, *4 Chawonui Yungzokseghe (The Fourth Dimension)*, 238.
24 Yong-Gi Cho, *4 Chawonui Yungzokseghe (The Fourth Dimension)*, 240.

ers disappeared.[25]

2) Thought

Yong-Gi Cho explains that thought is infinite and eternal, saying about thought as the first element that belongs to the spiritual world of the Fourth dimension. It is because thought belongs to the Fourth dimension but cannot be seen, or calculated in the Three dimension; it has neither thickness nor width. He emphasizes that what we need to remember is that thought can change and lead the Three dimensional world. Yong-Gi Cho gives an example: if a man has negative thought of the Fourth dimension, all the elements of his Three dimensional world will appear negatively.[26] He affirms that thought also affects action. Namely, according to the degree of positive thought, the possibility of success will be different. Because if a man thinks that it won't work, his action will be passive and the probability of being neglected will be high; if a person thinks that it will work, his action will be accelerated and he will run actively. And thought also affects body's reaction. Because when we imagine the scene described in the video or text, our body reacts as it is. If we remember a pleasant scene, our body becomes light and active. Imagining a frightening situation makes our heart beat faster.[27]

---

25 Yong-Gi Cho, *4 Chawonui Yungzokseghe (The Fourth Dimension)*, 239.
26 Mun-Chul Shin, *4 Chawonui Yungsong-edehan Sinhkzok Gochal (A Theological Appraisal of the Spirituality of the Fourth Dimension)*, 207.
27 Yong-Gi Cho, *4 Chwonui Yungsung (4^b Dimension of Spirituality)*, 96-97.

Therefore, Yong-Gi Cho insists that before changing the action, we must first change the thought, affirming that if we change the Fourth dimensional thought, the Three dimensional action will be different.[28]

Thoughts influence emotions, actions, and body reactions. But Yong-Gi Cho affirms that unconditional optimism is the human thought and it does not solve all the problems in life. Because it is a human thought of the Fourth dimension. Yong-Gi Cho advices to resemble God's thought through meditation of the Word. He underlines that in dialogue with God, we need to have the thought that is in the God's sovereignty, not our own thought; to practice this, we need to check, examine, and repent of our thought.[29]

He also says that when the God's thought is present in our spirit through our way of thinking, the faith appears. For this, we must first listen to the Word, because the word of God enters in our thinking through listening.

> First, you must listen to the Word. By listening, the word of God enters in your thinking. Through your way of thinking, the thought of God is present in your spirit and the faith appears. And through this faith your life will be transformed into a Christian life.[30]

Yong-Gi Cho advices us to read the Bible regularly so that our

---

[28] Yong-Gi Cho, *4 Chawonui Yungsung – Silchonpyun (4th Dimension of Spirituality-Practice)*, Church Growth Institute, 2010, 38.
[29] Yong-Gi Cho, *4 Chwonui Yungsung (4th Dimension of Spirituality)*, 98–99.
[30] Yong-Gi Cho, *4 Chawonui Yungzokseghe (The Fourth Dimension)*, 141.

thoughts are filled with the word of God. When we read the Bible it is important to have an attitude to receive spiritual food that nourishes our heart and thought, and with which the Holy Spirit refreshes our way of thinking.

> You need to read regularly the Bible which is food of life. But do not read it as a way to find a new principle of life before God formally. And also do not read the Bible only for the purpose of historical study. Instead of these, read the Bible to nourish your heart, thought, and to become an ingredient, namely, to become the spiritual food with which the Holy Spirit refreshes your way of thinking. Make your thought be filled with the word of God. Meditate the Word deeply. Then you can walk and communicate with God in a new dimension.[31]

Yong-Gi Cho says that according to how we think of God, "Who is God?", our life changes very differently. Namely, when we think of God who scolds, judges, and fears, our life is without vitality and joy; but when we recognize that the "good God" is in us, we can live happily thanks to God's ability.[32]

Comparing our body with a kind of the Fourth dimensional computer, Yong-Gi Cho says that those who create the program with positive thinking say that a positive story always happens in their Three dimension. Therefore, he introduces the persuasive way of

---

31 Yong-Gi Cho, *4 Chawonui Yungzokseghe (The Fourth Dimension)*, 171.
32 Yong-Gi Cho, *4 Chwonui Yungsung – Silchonpyun (4ᵗʰ Dimension of Spirituality-Practice)*, 39.

thinking ("I can do it")³³ and the active thinking ("Think bigger and think wider"). Active thinking means thinking to put into action with the spirit of "Never give up" (even if he falls down seven times, he will get up without giving up)³⁴. To mention the size here is to say that the size of thought makes the reality. That is to say, if the seeing and thinking is small, there is a high possibility of bearing small fruit of reality, but the big thought bears big fruits.

But Yong-Gi Cho confesses that looking back his 53 years of pastoral ministry, he did not have only big thoughts, but there was also continuous bloody prayer and dedication, study and effort to realize those thoughts. Because effort and dedication are necessary to make thought grow into reality.³⁵

3) Faith

Faith is one of the words which are used most often in the church. Yong-Gi Cho, defining that true faith is 'to believe in God who is a miracle worker', affirms that when we go to God, we must keep in mind in our heart that "God is a miracle worker."³⁶ When we are in a situation of darkness without hope, how do we do? It is

---

33 Yong-Gi Cho, *4 Chwonui Yungsung (4ᵗʰ Dimension of Spirituality)*, 111.
34 Yong-Gi Cho, *4 Chwonui Yungsung – Silchonpyun (4ᵗʰ Dimension of Spirituality-Practice)*, 40.
35 Yong-Gi Cho, *4 Chwonui Yungsung (4ᵗʰ Dimension of Spirituality)*, 109-110.
36 Yong-Gi Cho, *Naui Kyohoi Songzang Iyaki (My Church Growth Stories)*, Seoul Logos, Seoul, 2005, 335.

difficult to keep the faith even though we have a strong faith, because all the visible things of the Three dimension shake our thought and heart in confusion negatively. According to Yong-Gi Cho, the more times like this, we must think and rely on God of the Fourth dimension, and then the Lord gives us the strength to overcome that situation and also works miracles.[37]

Yong-Gi Cho also defines faith as a substance of mind which cannot be seen, and as the ability to realize the will and the heart of God. He emphasizes that faith is an absolute condition in the relationship with God, and although God wants to give us good things, if we don't believe, everything is in vain. Yong-Gi Cho especially emphasizes the importance of seeing a reality of what we cannot see with the eyes of faith, as if it is present, and then becoming a winner in life by learning how to live with faith, because faith is a substance of what we cannot see.

> Faith is a substance of mind that cannot be seen. Moreover, in our relationship with God, faith is an absolute condition. ... Although God wants to give a good thing, if we don't believe, everything is in vain. Faith is the ability to realize the will and the heart of God. ...
> The world of God must see everything with faith. Because faith is a reality of what we can't see, with the eyes of faith we should see as if it is present. Likewise, when we look at the grace of God, these will appear as a reality in our lives. ... You who have learned, like this, to

---

37 Yong-Gi Cho, *4 Chwonui Yungsung (4th Dimension of Spirituality)*, 126.

live with faith, will always be a winner in life.[38]

Emphasizing that in order to have true faith we must have the heart of God, Yong-Gi Cho explains the method using the Fourth dimensional world as follows. That is, human being is limited by time and space, which are the past, present, and future. However, since God is not limited by these, God can see and call what will be realized in the future, considering that it has already been realized in the present. Yong-Gi Cho clearly affirms that when we enter the Fourth dimensional world of God's dream and fantasy, we can also call like God what does not exist, as if it exists, but it is not as an auto-suggestion.

He insists that faith is accepting. That is, although the body is still uncomfortable and painful, we must accept with faith in our hearts that the body is already healed. And for Yong-Gi Cho, to believe in the God of healing is to believe that God has already cured and restored us. Yong-Gi Cho insists that Jesus was crucified carrying all our faults and sicknesses. And Cho is sure that God sees us who is already healed and restored through the Cross.

> Man is limited by time and space, which are the past, present, and future. Therefore, we expect our present desires to be fulfilled in the future. But God is not limited by time and space. God can see and call what will be realized in the future, considering that it has already been realized

---

[38] Yong-Gi Cho, *4 Chwonui Yungsung (4^b Dimension of Spirituality)*, 128-129.

in the present. Therefore, in order to have true faith, we must first have the heart of God. If you have the heart of God, we can also call what does not exist. Then, how can you call what does not exist as if it exists like God by crossing the barrier of time and space? You should enter the Fourth dimensional world of dream and fantasy. ... When you enter the Fourth dimensional world of dream and fantasy, time and space can no longer confine you. I don't say that you will do auto-suggestion: "Now, what I want has already come true." You must enter into the dream and fantasy of God. ...

Faith is not something we earn by trying harder. Faith is accepting. Although the body is still uncomfortable and painful, it is to accept with faith in the heart that the body is already healed. The Bible clearly says, "Therefore I say to you, all that you ask for in prayer, believe that you will receive it and it shall be yours." (Mk11:24) Jesus was crucified, carrying all of our faults and sicknesses. God never sees us as an existence overburdened with the physical sickness and pain of life. God sees us already healed and restored through the Cross. If we also see ourselves through the Cross of Jesus Christ we can see our figure that is already healed and become healthy. If so, we no longer need to pray God for healing. Rather, thanksgiving and praise will overflow. When we see ourselves as a victorious figure, there is no reason to suffer. To believe in the God of healing is not just to believe that God has a healing power. Beyond this, it is to believe that God has already cured and restored us. Therefore, faith is very practical and concrete.[39]

---

39 Yong-Gi Cho, *Naui Kyohoi Songzang Iyaki (My Church Growth Stories)*, 336-338.

Yong-Gi Cho affirms that if we believe in God who is now working in our life, God will really accompany our life together. For Yong-Gi Cho, it is therefore very important to have a present confession of faith: "I believe now." Yong-Gi Cho points out that although some Christians who are struggling with sickness, poverty and despair, do not ask God's work to overturn that reality. He considers that it is due to the idea that we can only be forgiven of sin and saved in the present, by interpreting faith as faith in the future. According to him, this is the attitude that denies the present faith for the working of the living God. Yong-Gi Cho says that faith is always now, present. Therefore, according to him, if we don't believe that God is working in the present, God does not save our present, and we cannot say that this faith is a real faith.[40] He emphasizes that since God is eternal, God does not exist only in the past and in the future, but for God, there is always only the present.[41]

When Yong-Gi Cho began his pastoral ministry, he thought that true faith is believing that good things will happen in the future. Namely, Yong-Gi Cho will say, "I believe that what I pray for today will be fulfilled tomorrow. I believe that what I prayed for this month will be fulfilled next month. I believe that what I prayed for this year will certainly be fulfilled next year." But he said that when he prayed like this, nothing was realized. After several repeated mistakes, he learned that the real faith is not in believing what will be

---

40 Yong-Gi Cho, *4 Chwonui Yungsung – Silchonpyun (4th Dimension of Spirituality-Practice)*, 70.
41 Yong-Gi Cho, *Naui Kyohoi Songzang Iyaki (My Church Growth Stories)*, 342.

realized in the future, but it is to believe that his wish is already realized. He confesses that after learning this, when he brought the future into the present through dream and fantasy, his wishes began to be fulfilled in the present. He then gives the specific example of the pregnant twins he experienced by constructing Kukmin Daily and the Kangnam branch sanctuary (Kangnam Zisungzon), with the conviction that we must conceive dream and fantasy as a woman conceives a baby.

> I am pregnant with Kukmin Daily (Kukmin-ilbo) inside me right now. It is not to believe that the newspaper will come out in the future. Kukmin Daily is already a part of my life through dream and fantasy. Also, I am pregnant with the branch sanctuary which is under construction in Kangnam. I don't dream that in the future the church construction will be finished, and the faithful will worship there. I am watching the scene of the church being already completed and so many believers worshiping and receiving the grace.
> Now, in me, the twins are growing up fast. One is called Kukmin Daily, and the other Kangnam Zisungzon. They move, kick and play inside my body. I can feel my children. ... They are a part of my life. While I live and breathe, the dream and the vision also live on in me. But when I die, they die too. We are one.[42]

According to Mun-Chul Shin, Yong-Gi Cho sees faith in two ways.

---

42 Yong-Gi Cho, *Naui Kyohoi Songzang Iyaki (My Church Growth Stories)*, 338-341.

One is the human belief that happens in the Three dimensional world, and the other is the God's faith that comes from the Fourth dimensional world. The faith of Fourth dimension emphasized by Yong-Gi Cho is not the belief erupted from ourselves, but the God's faith that comes from God.[43]

Yong-Gi Cho explains that the 'written Word' and the 'proclaimed Word' related to faith in this way. He clearly says that the word of God given to us is the eternal and unchanging absolute truth. But he insists that even though we can get knowledge and understanding of God by reading the 'written Word', does not appear faith in all the written Words of the Bible. Namely, we cannot obtain the faith from God to realize a special work. In other word, Yong-Gi Cho interprets Rm 10:17 (Thus faith comes from what is heard, and what is heard comes through the word of Christ) to say that the ingredient to build faith is more than just reading the word of God.[44] For example, according to Yong-Gi Cho, the Word, "Come." given to Peter by Jesus in the storm is a 'proclaimed Word' of Jesus, the eternal Word, as especial Word. Yong-Gi Cho affirms that this 'proclaimed Word' brings faith, and faith comes from hearing. Therefore, Yong-Gi Cho interprets that Peter did not only walk on the water with the intellectual faith in God, but he could walk on the water with the faith by receiving the especial Word that was spoken by Jesus at that time.[45]

---

43 Mun-Chul Shin, *4 Ciawonui Yungsong-edehan Sinhkzok Gochal (A Theological Appraisal of the Spirituality of the Fourth Dimension)*, 213.
44 Yong-Gi Cho, *4 Chawonui Yungzokseghe (The Fourth Dimension)*, 112.

Yong-Gi Cho explains more about the 'written Word', the 'proclaimed Word' and the role of the Holy Spirit. He insists that the 'proclaimed Word' comes from the 'written Word.' When we hear the word of God and study the Bible, when the Holy Spirit inspires that word or applies that word to our particular circumstances, that word becomes the 'proclaimed Word.' But Yong-Gi Cho clearly says that the 'proclaimed Word' to a particular person is not commonly given to everyone. He says the importance of waiting, because the 'proclaimed Word' is given to the people who wait, relying on the Lord until the Holy Spirit makes the 'written Word' revive as the 'proclaimed Word.'

> The 'Proclaimed Word' comes from the 'written Word'. The 'written Word' is like the pool of Bethesda. You hear the word of God and study the Bible. But when the Holy Spirit inspires that word or applies that word to your special circumstances, the 'written Word' becomes the 'proclaimed Word.'
>
> The 'written Word' is given to everybody. ... It lets the world know about God. But the 'proclaimed Word' for a particular person in a particular situation is not commonly given to everyone. The 'proclaimed Word' is given to those who wait, who trust in the Lord, until the Holy Spirit makes the 'written Word' revive as the 'proclaimed Word.'[46]

---

45 Yong-Gi Cho, *4 Chawonui Yungzokseghe (The Fourth Dimension)*, 115.
46 Yong-Gi Cho, *4 Chawonui Yungzokseghe (The Fourth Dimension)*, 117.

Yong-Gi Cho worries today's pastors by saying that if there is no time at all to wait for the Holy Spirit makes a 'written Word' revive as a 'proclaimed Word', the Lord will not revive the necessary verses in our heart. According to Yong-Gi Cho, pastors are too busy with other things than preparing the sermon. Namely, they spend time as conductors, treasurers, architects, and directors of so many works. And then they are too tired, so they do not have time to serve the Lord, no time to eat the green grass of the Word and turn it into milk. Therefore, the faithful of that church only eat the grass, they are not supplied with the milk of the Word. Yong-Gi Cho points out that this is a great mistake, and suggests that pastors should devote themselves, like apostles, to prayer and spreading of the Word, and that other works of the church should be shared with deacons and laity.[47]

It is easy to say "I believe", but it is not easy to really believe without any doubt in the heart. Therefore Yong-Gi Cho explains Mk 11. Namely, it says: "Have a faith in God. Amen, I say to you, whoever says to his mountain, 'Be lifted up and thrown into the sea', and does not doubt in his heart but believes that what he says will happen, it shall be done for him. Therefore I tell you, all that you ask for in prayer, believe that you will receive it and it shall be yours." (Mk 11:22-24) Some Greek scholars translate "Have a faith in God" into "Have a faith in God", others translate into "Have a faith of God." Yong-Gi Cho insists that since both of these are all correct, we must

---

[47] Yong-Gi Cho, *4 Chawonui Yungzokseghe (The Fourth Dimension)*, 118-119.

put the two meanings together. We must believe in God and also have a faith of God in us.[48] And Yong-Gi Cho says that when we receive the 'proclaimed Word', this faith is not our own, but a faith given to us by God. He affirms that after receiving this faith we can command that the mountain be lifted up and thrown, but without receiving the faith of God we cannot do this work.[49]

Yong-Gi Cho teaches that in order to have the faith of God, we must rely completely on Jesus Christ. Because we receive it "through faith in Christ." In other word, he says that "Christ saves us through faith, and the saving power is not in faith itself. He argues that the faith of God, given through Jesus Christ, is given through the Bible, the word of God. Therefore, Yong-Gi Cho teaches that by reading and meditating on the word of God every day, we can have greater faith and do God's miracle in the Three dimensional world. He says that "If faith does not rely on the word of God, there is a danger of falling into the blind faith, so we must beware of the danger of having faith without the foundation of the Word. According to Mun-Chul Shin, for Yong-Gi Cho, faith and the word of God always appear together.[50]

Yong-Gi Cho says that the conviction a Christian should have is "a belief that we are saved by believing in Jesus Christ and that

---

48 Yong-Gi Cho, *4 Chawonui Yungzokseghe (The Fourth Dimension)*, 172-173.
49 Yong-Gi Cho, *4 Chawonui Yungzokseghe (The Fourth Dimension)*, 133.
50 Mun-Chul Shin, *4 Ciawonui Yungsong-edehan Sinhkzok Gochal (A Theological Appraisal of the Spirituality of the Fourth Dimension)*, 214-215.

God is leading our lives, staying always with us."[51] And to put this faith into practice, he says it is necessary to live a life of believing and following the 'Word's working power.' As a first step, he explains *Rhema* and Logos like this, in order to discover the word of *Rhema*. Namely, Logos is a word of God in general, but *Rhema* is a Word that when we read the Bible, a verse suddenly hits us in the chest and starts a fire, and gives us strong faith.

> Logos is a word of God in general, and to make this Word become a Word given specially to an individual, the voice of God must be heard. The voice of God speaks specially in our heart through the Holy Spirit; when we have faith through this Word, we hear this voice. The Word that produces this kind of faith is called '*Rhema*' in Greek. When we read the Bible, a verse suddenly hits in the chest and starts a fire, and gives us strong faith, that Word is '*Rhema*'.[52]

Yong-Gi Cho explains how to gain faith of God by using Mk 2: 1-5, the healing event where the friends of a paralyzed man tore off the roof and made a hole and brought him to Jesus. In the first step of faith, although that paralyzed man had faith, nothing happened. Nevertheless, he went on to the second step and put into practice his desire to be healed by meeting Jesus directly.

---

51 Yong-Gi Cho, *4 Chwonui Yungsung – Silchonpyun (4^b Dimension of Spirituality-Practice)*, 66.

52 Yong-Gi Cho, *4 Chwonui Yungsung – Silchonpyun (4^b Dimension of Spirituality-Practice)*, 67.

Yong-Gi Cho interprets the miracle because Jesus saw the paralyzed man's faith and added the faith of God to his faith, and he could experience this miracle. With this point, Yong-Gi Cho says one principle. Namely, it is a principle that God adds the faith of God to our faith. No matter how small our faith is, if we put into practice, it will grow and increase. Finally, we can get the faith of God to experience the miracle. And Yong-Gi Cho, mentioning pastor Oral Roberts, explains the 'Seed of faith', which is to show our living faith to God, because there is life in the seed.

> In the first step of faith, that paralyzed man had faith. Although he really believed, nothing happened. Nevertheless, he went on to the second step and put into the practice his desire to meet Jesus directly and be healed. Jesus knew his wish and his decision to come before Jesus. And Jesus knew that he was doing his best to put his wish and decision into action. ... Jesus, seeing the faith of the paralyzed man, added the faith of God to his faith. At that moment, the paralyzed man had experienced the miracle of moving a mountain. There is a very important principle here. It is that God puts the faith of God on our faith. ... Therefore, no matter how small our faith is, if we put into practice, it will grow and increase. Finally, we can have the faith of God that makes us experience the miracle of moving a mountain. The faith of God works on our faith. ... Pastor Oral Roberts taught the 'Seed of faith' as an important principle to receive the faith of God, that makes a miracle. The 'Seed of faith' is to show to God our living faith because there is life in the seed.[53]

Yong-Gi Cho explains the difference between the faith that man tries to believe and the faith of God, and the attitude to receive the faith of God like this. According to him, firstly, faith starts from the human aspect, and this is a kind of striving faith. Because the faith of God is given by the Holy Spirit, and in order to receive this faith, we need to have the faith that starts from our side. Therefore, Yong-Gi Cho says that it is necessary to plant the seed of faith by doing everything we can so that God will see the faith we have. Because God gives God's faith to the seed of our faith, no matter how small it is by seeing that seed planted and its sprout. Yong-Gi Cho gives importance to waiting for God's time with prayer based on the word of God after planting the seed. Because in his time, he will give his faith on our prepared faith.

> There is a clear difference between the faith that man tries to believe and the faith of God. First, faith begins from the human aspect, and this is a kind of striving faith. (Of course, even this faith is a God's gift) ... If we have the faith that comes from our side, we can receive the God's faith given by the Holy Spirit. Then, how can we receive the faith of God? Do everything you can to make God see the faith you have. Namely, plant the seed of faith through action, and then pray standing on the word of God. When you plant the seed of living faith, it will be the foundation on which God will make his faith take root. ... After planting the seed, you have to wait with prayer. The waiting period

---

53 Yong-Gi Cho, *4 Chawonui Yungzokseghe (The Fourth Dimension)*, 174-175.

is very important. Do not rush the work only with your own faith without waiting. Believe in God. Worship God. In God's time, he will show the faith of God on your prepared faith.[54]

Yong-Gi Cho teaches that the almighty God, who has absolute sovereignty, gives faith to all of us according to our amount, and wants us to actively use the faith we receive. He explains the growth step for our faith to grow and be used perfectly and effectively, namely the basic four steps that are in the hatching process of our faith's awakening.

First, Yong-Gi Cho says that we need to clearly picture the 'object of faith' in our mind. Because faith is a 'real images of what we desire (Concrete things)', there should be a clear goal of our desire in faith: "Faith is the realization of what is hoped for and evidence of things not seen." (Heb 11:1) Yong-Gi Cho sees that if we only think without a clear goal, that prayer will not reach God.[55] For example, if you need a desk and chair, don't ask vaguely for a desk and chair, be specific about the type of desk and chair you want to have.[56]

Second, we will have ardent desires. Namely, we will have a vivid image in our heart, and then we will have an ardent desire for the goal. Yong-Gi Cho, when he began his pastoral ministry in 1958, he had an ardent desire to serve in the biggest church in Korea. And then he lived by concentrating on that desire only when he

---

54 Yong-Gi Cho, *4 Chawonui Yungzokseghe (The Fourth Dimension)*, 184-185.
55 Yong-Gi Cho, *4 Chawonui Yungzokseghe (The Fourth Dimension)*, 24-25.
56 Yong-Gi Cho, *4 Chawonui Yungzokseghe (The Fourth Dimension)*, 28.

was asleep or awake. He confesses that as a result, his church is known as the largest church in the world.

Third, he advises that when an ardent desire refloat, kneel down and pray until to have conviction and peace. For example, at the moment of prayer, if peace and conviction given by God appear in our heart, according to him, we do not need to pray anymore for that problem. To have conviction can sometimes it might take 20 minutes, two hours, two weeks, or two years. But Yong-Gi Cho insists on praying until he attains the true image of faith, no matter how long it takes.[57]

Fourth, he says that we will transmit the word of God. It means that after having the conviction, we must show the proof of faith. Yong-Gi Cho interprets Rom 4:17 by saying that the Bible writes that God raises the dead, this word means the God of miracle who calls what does not yet exist as if it exists. And he also gives an example with Genesis (Gen 17:1-5; 18:14): "Abram, you will no longer be called Abram, but you will be called the father of many nations. Your name will be called Abraham, not Abram. And as for Sarai, your wife, do not call her Sarai, but call her Sarah, which means the mother of a multitude of nations." Yong-Gi Cho explains how it shows the proof of faith. Namely, according to him, Abraham and Sarah called each other 'Abraham' and 'Sarah', and as sure as they gave birth 'Isaac', which means 'laugh.'[58]

---

57 Yong-Gi Cho, *4 Chawonui Yungzokseghe (The Fourth Dimension)*, 40-42.
58 Yong-Gi Cho, *4 Chawonui Yungzokseghe (The Fourth Dimension)*, 45-47.

Yong-Gi Cho teaches that there is a time to pray and there is a time to command. According to him, first, we will pray in the prayer room, and when we finish praying and step out into the spiritual battlefield, we must command with authority in the creative word to make it happen. For Yong-Gi Cho it is very important that in the Bible, Jesus always commanded, prayed all night, commanded with the Word to heal the sick in the places where they lived. He emphasizes that God is telling us to heal the sick by commanding with the word of faith, and of course it is to heal through Christ who is in us. Therefore, Yong-Gi Cho says that he also proclaims courageously the word of Divine healing in the pastoral field, the sick are healed through the work of the Holy Spirit in his congregation.[59] Yong-Gi Cho affirms that a grace he has received is just 'bold faith in Christ.' It means that when we proclaim boldly, the Holy Spirit works.[60] He emphasizes that as it takes time for a mother conceive and give birth to a child, it takes time for the things we long for and pray for to be answered and come to pass. He shares his experience of receiving the answer to prayer with this principle: Praise the Lord who will give him the things he has earnestly asked for, and confess with his lips that he has already received them, believing and thanking Him. According to Yong-Gi Cho, in His time, God responded exactly as he prayed.[61]

---

[59] Yong-Gi Cho, *4 Chawonui Yungzokseghe (he Fourth Dimension)*, 49–50.
[60] Yong-Gi Cho, *4 Chawonui Yungzokseghe (he Fourth Dimension)*, 53.
[61] Yong-Gi Cho, *4 Chawonui Yungzokseghe (he Fourth Dimension)*, 33.

4) Dream

Yong-Gi Cho expresses that dream is a spiritual language of the Holy Spirit, saying about dream and vision as one of the elements that belong to the Fourth dimensional spiritual world. According to him, the Holy Spirit gives dream and fantasy to the faithful; he leads them to live a creative life; through the word of God he teaches us dream and vision.[62] Yong-Gi Cho emphasizes that if there is no dream, namely if the Fourth dimension is not programmed with dreams, there is no hope also in the Three dimension.[63]

Yong-Gi Cho explains the four processes to make dream and vision come to fruition: First, the Holy Spirit breathes several dreams and visions into our hearts and continues to speak through them; Second, when we concretely dream the goal relying on God, we can hatch our own future; Third, through never-ending efforts, we can finally get a good result; Fourth, all of this belongs to God's sovereignty, so we dream in the Holy Spirit, but we must develop our dreams with the desire to be used preciously by God.[64]

Yong-Gi Cho notes that dream and vision are very different from ambition and personal greed, which appear in the Three dimensional material world. Because personal ambition or greed could

---

[62] Mun-Chul Shin, *4 Ciawonui Yungsong-edehan Sinhkzok Gochal (A Theological Appraisal of the Spirituality of the Fourth Dimension)*, 210.
[63] Yong-Gi Cho, *4 Chwonui Yungsung (4th Dimension of Spirituality)*, 82.
[64] Yong-Gi Cho, *4 Chawonui Yungzokseghe (The Fourth Dimension)*, 62.

be influenced by Satan or be a dream created by man's soul. He emphasises that the dream of God is a distinct dream from these.[65]

Yong-Gi Cho compares the difference between right dream and greed. Namely, dream has hope for tomorrow, no need to commit sin, but greed can be fulfilled by breaking everything and committing sin. He considers that no matter how good the dream or idea are, if God is not with it, it is just human ambition and greed. And then he gives the example of Abraham, Moses and Joseph.

> In dreams, there is hope for tomorrow. There is no need to break the law or sin. But greed can be fulfilled by breaking everything and committing sin. There is a reason why Moses failed to save people when he was young. Because with only young blood he dreamed according to his own thoughts. No matter how good the dream and idea are, if God is not with it, it will remain only human ambition and greed. On the other hand, Abraham and Joseph won in tribulation. Because they dreamed together with God.[66]

And Yong-Gi Cho says that we will pray strongly with God's hope and live a life of sharing hope.

When we look, believe, dream, and pray in God, he makes everything come true. Pray strongly with God's hope. We are all chosen noble peo-

---

[65] Mun-Chul Shin, *4 Ciawonui Yungsong-edehan Sinhkzok Gochal (A Theological Appraisal of the Spirituality of the Fourth Dimension)*, 212.
[66] Yong-Gi Cho, *4 Chwonui Yungsung (4^h Dimension of Spirituality)*, 154-155.

ple of God. No need to be disappointed because we cannot see right now. Please wait. Meditate on the suffering of the Cross. And live a life of sharing hope.[67]

Yong-Gi Cho insists that "to look is to possess." For example, in the Book of Genesis, God said to Abram, "Look about you, and from where you are, gaze to the north and south, east and west; all the land that you see I will give to you and your descendants forever." (Gen 13:14-15) According to Yong-Gi Cho, Abraham looked at that land and when he returned to the tent, he lied down and dreamed of possessing that land. And he also considers that the Holy Spirit began to rule using the spiritual world language of the Fourth dimension. And he explains that when Abraham was 100 years old, Sarah was 90 years old, gave birth to a son, Isaac.[68]

Yong-Gi Cho also believes that "looking with the mind's eye" plays an important role in the spiritual world of the Fourth dimension. Therefore, Cho says that animals can never exercise the ability to imagine, because imagination is a spiritual activity. Yong-Gi Cho explains how Jacob received his wages in his relationship with his uncle Laban in the book of Genesis 30: 32-41, using the Words of Genesis and the role of looking. In the Book of Genesis, we read that Jacob agreed to take only the cattle that were stained as his wages, and only took care of the white animals that Laban

---

67 Yong-Gi Cho, *4 Chwonui Yungsung (4th Dimension of Spirituality)*, 183.
68 Yong-Gi Cho, *4 Chawonui Yungzokseghe (The Fourth Dimension)*, 64.

had left behind. Jacob built a fence of speckled branches and set it up in front of the water trough where the strong sheep drank. There the sheep drank water and mated. Yong-Gi Cho believes that Jacob stood there every day and watched in faith as he painted a picture of the birth of the stained lambs. And God created a vision and a dream in the heart of Jacob, as a result, according to the Jacob's faith, as he saw it, the sheep gave birth to many stained lambs.[69]

> Uncle, from now on, I will work under the following conditions. Please pick out the stained, the spotted, and the black from uncle's flock that I am shepherding. I will only take care of the white sheep. And if the white sheep give birth to spotted or stained or black lambs, give them all as my wages. ...
> Laban separated from his sheep and goats all the spotted, the stained and the black, and put them in a place three days' distance away. Jacob ended up shepherding only the white cattle that his uncle Laban had left behind. Jacob went to the mountains and cut down willows, apricots, and cypresses, and then he stripped the bark with his knife and made it white, spotted and stained. So he made a fence out of the branches and placed it in front of the water trough where the strong sheep drank. There the sheep drank water and mated.
> Day after day, Jacob stood there and watched in faith as he painted a picture of the birth of the speckled, spotted lambs. God created a vision and a dream in the heart of Jacob. ... Every time Jacob saw the branches,

---

[69] Yong-Gi Cho, *4 Chawonui Yungzokseghe (The Fourth Dimension)*, 70-71.

God helped him to see and dream of God's promises with the eyes of faith. ... Even in his sleep, he would have dreamed of sheep giving birth to speckled lambs. As a result, according to Jacob's belief, as he saw it, the sheep gave birth to many stained, spotted, and black lambs.

Yong-Gi Cho says that after a long time since Jacob had lived, God put up another wood, namely the Cross on the hill of Calvary. This is not stained wood peeled with a knife, but stained with the blood of the life of God's only Son. Therefore, Yong-Gi Cho insists that whoever looks at this wood of Cross stained by the precious blood of Jesus, can be changed and receive a new life and a new self-portrait, a new dream and vision through the power of the Holy Spirit.

> After a long time since Jacob had lived, God put up another wood. This time he put up the Cross on the hill of Calvary. This wood is not stained wood peeled with a knife, but stained with the blood of the life of God's only Son. Whoever looks at this wood of the Cross, stained with the precious blood of Jesus, can be changed and receive a new life and a new self-portrait, a new dream and vision through the power of the Holy Spirit.[70]

For Yong-Gi Cho, the goal of the dream, which is the Fourth dimensional element, should be specific. Because the real situations

---

70 Yong-Gi Cho, *4 Chawonui Yungzokseghe (The Fourth Dimension)*, 72.

that will appear in the Three dimension are very real, and we need to set detailed and tangible goals while looking towards the real thing. Yong-Gi Cho suggests that to achieve this goal we must pray a lot, especially he suggests fasting prayer. Fasting prayer is to make the Fourth dimensional world clear and to make dream clear. He emphasized that we will only look at God by cutting off the energy source through fasting, giving up the self that says, "I can do it on my own." In this way, when the self is changed, the Fourth dimensional world is changed, and we can know the details of the dream shown by God.[71]

Yong-Gi Cho emphasizes that looking at the Cross of Jesus Christ we must accept in our hearts the goal of the concrete dream of becoming healthy from the sickness of soul, body and life. And he affirms: No matter what the situation of the present body, heart and life is, we shouldn't dwell on it; if we accept the dream of Jesus through the Cross, at that time we can see the power of God.

> Looking at the Cross of Jesus Christ, we must accept in our hearts the goal of the concrete dream of becoming healthy from the sickness of soul, body and life. No matter what the situation of the present body, heart and life is, we shouldn't dwell on it. We should accept the dream of Jesus through the Cross. At that time our mental disorder will be removed, and be healed, and we can see the power of God. Yes. We must look at the goal of the dream, which is in Jesus Christ through

---

[71] Yong-Gi Cho, *4 Chwonui Yungsung (4ᵗʰ Dimension of Spirituality)*, 170.

the Cross. Through this, we can remove the mental disorder of curses and poverty, and accept the blessing and prosperity of Abraham through Christ. This is the dream which Christ has towards us.[72]

Yong-Gi Cho gives two examples related to the method of using dream. First, it is what he taught during the seminar for pastors who want to see the church growth. He said that the Holy Spirit will work, if they concretely write on the paper the appearance and the goal of the church in two years that they have seen in their prayer, and pray day and night looking at it which was attached to their church office. He emphasizes having a dream in our heart and says that when we look at such a dream, the dream will produce faith, and the Holy Spirit will work. Because according to Yong-Gi Cho, exactly that dream in the heart becomes the hand of God who creates the future.

> Please prepare a piece of paper and a pencil. Write on the paper the appearance and goals for your church in two years that you have seen in prayer, and how many members you dream your church to have in two years. ... Attach the paper written the goal in your church office, and pray day and night looking at it, and drawing this vision in your heart. The Holy Spirit will work.[73]

---

72 Yong-Gi Cho, *4 Chwonui Yungsung (4th Dimension of Spirituality)*, 171.
73 Yong-Gi Cho, *4 Chwonui Yungsung (4th Dimension of Spirituality)*, 167-168.

The other example is the story of pastor Cabre from South America who helped a child without an ear. Pastor Cabre prayed earnestly with the laying on of hands, imagining a scene that God is making a wonderful ear for the child and gluing it on. First, a small nodule appeared, and the parents also looked at the child and patted him, saying every morning, "Our baby, your ear is so beautiful!" thinking that as if there was an ear that did not exist. As a result of the constant prayer of pastor Cabre and the parents, a miracle happened: a small nodule spread out like a fan. Yong-Gi Cho explains this case: when we first picture, dream, and imagine by faith in the Holy Spirit what we desire, it will manifest according to that picture.

> A mother came to receive the laying on of hands, carrying a child who had no ear. Pastor Cabre, while he was praying, he imagined a scene that God is making a wonderful ear for the child and gluing it on. And he prayed fervently, laying hands on his heart. And then, not long after the prayer, a small nodule was arisen for this child, not ear. Although he thought it was strange, he prayed very hard. When they came back to receive the prayer, he did the same laying on of hands prayer as before, imagining the dream and drawing the picture of the ear appearing. According to him, he continued to pray in this way. He asked the parents of a child, thinking that this child had an ear, to look at the child and stroke it, saying every morning, "Our baby, your ear is so beautiful!" One day, after some time has passed without especial thing happened in prayer, he also made a prayer of laying on of hands, thinking that as if there was an ear that did not exist. And then according to him when

he opened his eyes, that small nodule spread out like a fan. This is impossible unless it is a miracle of the Lord. In this way, when we first picture, dream, and imagine by faith in the Holy Spirit what we desire, it will manifest according to that picture.74

Yong-Gi Cho says that dream and wishes do not come true by themselves, but it is necessary to pass through the tunnel of hardship. Because when we go through the tunnel, our ego is broken, we believe in God more, obey to him.75 He suggests that we program our heart with a holy dream through the Holy Spirit, because the dream is given by the Holy Spirit. According to him, the future of man can be known by observing how he speaks of his dream. And even though reality is so difficult, if there is a dream in the heart, that dream will occupy the Three dimension and change it. According to Yong-Gi Cho, since the change comes from the Fourth dimensional world, even though the present life is so difficult and empty, if we have the right dream and take care of it in incubator, it will be changed with it.76 Yong-Gi Cho suggests that we start with small things first to realize this dream, emphasizing that the ultimate goal of believers does not remain on this earth, but there is an eternal goal related to the eternal reign.77

---

74 Yong-Gi Cho, *4 Chwonui Yungsung (4th Dimension of Spirituality)*, 169-170.
75 Yong-Gi Cho, *4 Chwonui Yungsung (4th Dimension of Spirituality)*, 181.
76 Yong-Gi Cho, *4 Chwonui Yungsung (4th Dimension of Spirituality)*, 83.
77 Yong-Gi Cho, *4 Chwonui Yungsung (4th Dimension of Spirituality)*, 172.

5) Word

According to Yong-Gi Cho, a word, which belongs to the Fourth dimensional world, although it cannot be seen, has a great creative power to change destiny and environment. He says that God created the world with the Word, and we are created in the image and likeness of God, but what makes us different from other creature is that we can speak. And believing that our word creates our own destiny, he explains that we can receive the powerful word that can change our lives, if the Holy Spirit is with us, and if we always meditate on the Word and pray.[78]

The Bible says, "Death and life are in the power of the tongue, those who choose one shall eat its fruit." (Proverbs 18:21) Death and life are in the Three dimension, but the tongue is in the Fourth dimension. Yong-Gi Cho, saying that when he hears other person's word, he can guess to some extent about that person's life, explains it like this. Namely, those who are successful say that their desire have already come true, while those who fail say that they have already failed. He thinks it is in vain to say ruin in the Fourth dimension, and expect success in the Three dimension. Because negative words programme his Fourth dimension negatively and influence the Three dimension. And he affirms that those who criticize and curse others also program their own Fourth dimension, so it will return to their

---

[78] Yong-Gi Cho, *4 Chwonui Yungsung – Silchonpyun (4^h Dimension of Spirituality-Practice)*, 126.

own Three dimension with the curse.⁷⁹ According to him, it is because, even though the word is directed to the other person, at the moment we spit it out, we also hear it and recommend it to our own Three dimensional world.⁸⁰ Like this, it is very important, because the word that comes out of our mouth influences the other person and also influences ourselves.⁸¹ Therefore, Yong-Gi Cho suggests that those who use the word of Fourth dimension will try to praise the positive aspects of others, rather than pointing out the shortcomings and making others feel discouraged.⁸²

Yong-Gi Cho believes that the word of Fourth dimension is the word that is dominated by the Holy Spirit, because it is the word that is proclaimed with thought, faith and dream in the heart. He affirms that we will proclaim the word of Fourth dimension believing that what we say will come true, because it is the word of Fourth dimension that has power and authority.⁸³ According to him, because those who use the word of Fourth dimension speak creative language,⁸⁴ and the power to overcome the environment that appears to fail is in the words that come from the lips.⁸⁵

---

79 Yong-Gi Cho, *4 Chwonui Yungsung (4ᵗʰ Dimension of Spirituality)*, 85–86.
80 Yong-Gi Cho, *4 Chwonui Yungsung (4ᵗʰ Dimension of Spirituality)*, 218.
81 Yong-Gi Cho, *4 Chwonui Yungsung (4ᵗʰ Dimension of Spirituality)*, 200.
82 Yong-Gi Cho, *4 Chwonui Yungsung – Silchonpyun (4ᵗʰ Dimension of Spirituality-Practice)*, 129.
83 Yong-Gi Cho, *4 Chwonui Yungsung – Silchonpyun (4ᵗʰ Dimension of Spirituality-Practice)*, 134.
84 Yong-Gi Cho, *4 Chwonui Yungsung – Silchonpyun (4ᵗʰ Dimension of Spirituality-Practice)*, 130.

Yong-Gi Cho also emphasizes that a word can kill or save people, since a person's word has the power to come true as it is. So he suggests that we try to speak a creative word, even a word that brings emotion and joy to others, that brings success.[86] Yong-Gi Cho insists that we make a creative lip confession to God, who makes possible what does not exist, and also makes possible what seems impossible in the dark. But he points out that the creative lip confession without true loving language will be in vain.[87]

Yong-Gi Cho encourages us to be captured by the power and word of the Holy Spirit. Because word is power, it needs to be managed and controlled, and the best master is the Holy Spirit. He also suggests that we will be helped by the Holy Spirit how to respond sensitively and how to speak and what to speak in an important time to reduce speaking mistakes. According to him, the habit of speech that pleases God is to speak words that save people, to speak words of blessing and praise. And he explains that the powerful word is a word of the Fourth dimension that is in God, and we can get it with the Holy Spirit, the Word and prayer.[88]

Yong-Gi Cho believes that the word is an important tool in the spiritual war to win the environment. Therefore, he gives an example saying that if we release our faith through words and if we keep

---

85 Yong-Gi Cho, *4 Chwonui Yungsung (4th Dimension of Spirituality)*, 215.
86 Yong-Gi Cho, *4 Chwonui Yungsung (4th Dimension of Spirituality)*, 213.
87 Yong-Gi Cho, *4 Chwonui Yungsung – Silchonpyun (4th Dimension of Spirituality-Practice)*, 131.
88 Yong-Gi Cho, *4 Chwonui Yungsung (4th Dimension of Spirituality)*, 201.

repeating it with our lips and admit it, there will be an amazing change in the environment. There is a story about an 89 years old missionary who suffered a stroke that left him language obstacle and paralyzed. It says that the missionary was completely healed by the power of the word that the people around him proclaimed: "I commend you in the name of Jesus of Nazareth, get up and walk." Namely, the sick reality of the Three dimension was transformed by the word which is the element of the Fourth dimension.

> Pastor Stanley Jones, a missionary in India, is well known as a man of positive faith. ... When he was almost 89 years old, he suddenly collapsed from a stroke. For several months, he couldn't stand up and couldn't speak. He asked a nurse for a favor. Whenever she saw him, morning or night, she would tell him this: "Get up and walk in the name of Jesus of Nazareth." Because his whole body was paralyzed, he could not freely say what he wanted to say. So he asked a nurse for this word of faith. That's why, whenever the nurses saw him, they proclaimed: "I commend you in the name of Jesus of Nazareth, to get up and walk." The pastor replied, "Amen!" People around him laughed at the foolishness. But pastor Jones knew how great is the power of word of mouth. ... One day, as time passed in this way, pastor Jones, 89 years old man, finally overcame the stroke completely. It was the power of the confession of the lips. It was possible because he released his faith through words. Finally, he changed the Three dimensional reality through the word, which is the element of the Fourth dimension.[89]

According to Yong-Gi Cho, the difference between a believer and an unbeliever is that we can fight with death. He thinks that the unbeliever has no weapon to fight with, but for the believer, the word of God is just that weapon. The word of God becomes the knife of the Holy Spirit. Yong-Gi Cho presents a concrete way: if we accept the will of God and the word of God in our heart and fight by confessing with our lips, we will win. For example, when we think that we have the assurance of an answer while we pray for a long time with a prayer topic, and think that we already received, we must speak as if what does not exist is present. Therefore, we must confess: "God Father, thank you for the healing already." And then we must commend: "Sickness, go away!" Because according to Yong-Gi Cho, the time when the work finally happens is the time of commending.

> When we think that we have an assurance of answer while we pray for a long time with a prayer topic, we must speak as if what does not exist is present. "God Father, thank you for healing already. Please heal all. Thank you for healing me already. Because my family members are already saved, please save them quickly." ... In this way, faith comes into our heart, and if we can speak as if what does not exist is present, we must now commend toward a mountain. "Tai-San, go away!" "Sickness, go away!" "Unbelief, go away!" "Curse, go away!" "Poverty, go away!" The time when the work finally happens is the time of

---

89 Yong-Gi Cho, *4 Chwonui Yungsung (4th Dimension of Spirituality)*, 206-207.

commending. ... Jesus always accomplished his final work through commending. "Take your bed and go back", "Demon, go out!", "Lazarus, come out!" etc. Through commending the creative work was done.[90]

Yong-Gi Cho says, as we saw earlier, that there may be a time difference between the moment of believing and the moment of appearing in reality. But he insists that those who believe, admit what they believe, and commend beyond time and space, their desire must come true. And he invites us to win in the spiritual war by declaring the word of the Lord directly with our mouth, because we are fighting a powerful spiritual war every day, every moment, even if it is not seen now.[91]

Yong-Gi Cho says to apply the Word of the Bible to the word of the Fourth dimension: "To the one who has, more will be given; from the one who has not, even what he has will be taken away." (Mk 4:25) And he interprets that if we admit with our mouths that we do not have it, God will take away what we have, but if we think of what we have, thank God and praise Him, God will fill us with something better. Yong-Gi Cho concludes that words are the last of the spiritual elements of the Fourth dimension because it reveals a person's thought, faith, and dream, and that word is subject to God's judgment.[92]

---

[90] Yong-Gi Cho, *4 Chwonui Yungsung (4th Dimension of Spirituality)*, 210-211.
[91] Yong-Gi Cho, *4 Chwonui Yungsung (4th Dimension of Spirituality)*, 212-213.
[92] Yong-Gi Cho, *4 Chwonui Yungsung (4th Dimension of Spirituality)*, 219-220.

2. Preaching

1) Yong-Gi Cho's preaching method

Yong-Gi Cho's preaching is very famous because it transmits hope and encouragement to his poor believers. He defines preaching as follows: "Preaching is the transmission of the Gospel of Christ to believers and non-Christians, receiving the word of God as his messenger. The purpose of preaching is to do pastoral work and revival, teaching and counseling."

Yong-Gi Cho also presents five such characteristics of preaching. First, he sees that the most important thing in preaching is to transmit the message of God. Therefore, he affirms that if preaching is without the word of God, that preaching is a human word, it cannot be the word of God. Secondly, Yong-Gi Cho believes that it is very important in preaching to transmit the message of Christ in words that are easy for the listeners to understand. Because Yong-Gi Cho sees that preaching with the words that the listeners can easily understand is better than preaching with difficult theological terminology or intellectual contents. Thirdly, he emphasizes that the preacher transmits only the word of God, receiving a clear message of God from the Bible. He affirms that the preacher is not the one who teaches philosophy or tells ethics or morals. Fourth, he insists on remembering that preaching is the great commission of Jesus and to practice it. Fifth, he affirms that preaching must produce results. Because he believes that preaching must lead unbelievers to conversion and salvation, and the transformation of Christian's life.

> First, the most important thing in preaching is to transmit the message of God. That's why you should not leave the revelation of God given from Genesis to the Book of Revelation. If the preaching is without the word of God, that preaching is the human word, it cannot be the word of God. Secondly, preaching is to transmit the message of Christ in words that are easy for the listener to understand. ... Preaching with the word that is easy for the listener to understand is better than preaching with difficult theological terminology or intellectual contents. ... Thirdly, preaching means that a preacher transmits the word of God by receiving the power of the Holy Spirit. The preacher is not a person who teaches philosophy or tells ethics or morals, so he must receive a clear message of God from the Bible. ... The preacher should transmit only the word of God. Fourthly, ... preaching the Gospel is the great commission of Jesus. ... Jesus said, "Go, therefore, and make disciples of all nations, baptizing them in the name of the Father, and of the Son, and of the Holy Spirit, teaching them to observe all that I have commanded you. I am with you always, until the end of the age." (Mt 28:18-20) Fifth, preaching should produce results. Preaching leads unbelievers to conversion and salvation. As a result, believers also go to a deeper place of faith, and they will love, dedicate, volunteer, and be transformed into a positive attitude towards life, being formed into a Christ-like personality.[93]

---

93 Yong-Gi Cho, *Nanun Iroke Solkyohanda (I preach like this)*, 23-25.

Yong-Gi Cho insists that it is necessary to have a goal with clear focus for effective and powerful preaching. He says that in the way of effort for the time of miracle through God's work, first, we need to set a goal and draw a picture of ourselves who has reached the goal in our mind and then, do our best to achieve it. Evaluating the reason for the failure of most preachers today, which is the neglect of this simple regularity, Yong-Gi Cho affirms that preaching grows through long tearful prayer, pulpits, and training.[94]

According to him, the ultimate goal of man is not "how to live well", but "how to die well before God", therefore he insists that the goal of preaching is to boldly proclaim the reality after death and lead people towards the eternal way relying on the word of God.[95] Therefore, according to him, the first duty of a preacher is to inform what the true purpose of life is, and the next is to teach how to live it. Our Lord wants us to live abundantly and happily, not only in the next life, but also in the present life. But he says that there is a condition by which our Lord solves problems and blesses us. Namely, after firmly solving the problem of eternal life, he will be responsible for that person's whole life: "But seek first the kingdom (of God) and his righteousness, and all these things will be given to you besides." (Mt 6:33) Pointing out that some people believe in Jesus with the motivation to heal the sick, to receive the material blessing, consolation and encouragement, Yong-Gi Cho

---

94 Yong-Gi Cho, *Nanun Iroke Solkyohanda (I preach like this)*, 216-217.
95 Yong-Gi Cho, *Nanun Iroke Solkyohanda (I preach like this)*, 219.

says clearly, this is a dangerous view of faith.[96]

He remembers the reaction of the listeners early in his ministry when he preached a sermon that was far from the attention of a poor, sick, and suffering audience. They were not interested in preaching ethics or morality, about paradise and hell, and they thought that such things were nothing more than ornaments and luxuries suitable only for those who were full and comfortable.

> At that time most of my sermons were about Christian ethics or morality, paradise and hell. And I also talked only about spiritual blessings and grace. But the church members, or those to whom I preached, were all apathetic about these things. Because they were so poor, sick, and caught up in their lives, that ethics and morality, heaven and hell, were matters of no interest. They felt that these arguments were nothing but an ornament or a luxury, suitable only for those who were full and comfortable.[97]

Yong-Gi Cho confesses that he used to preach a sermon that lacks connection with the listeners, as a result, the church did not grow; but along the way, his pastoral philosophy began to emerge. Therefore, Yong-Gi Cho drew a conclusion that he should testify about the living God who is now and here in the reality of life, by solving the problem of food, clothing and shelter. Because if the

---

96 Yong-Gi Cho, *Nanun Iroke Solkyohanda (I preach like this)*, 220.
97 Yong-Gi Cho, *Nanun Iroke Solkyohanda (I preach like this)*, 398.

sermon is connected to the listener's heart, they will come to church with interest. He read the Bible again from the beginning with an attitude as if he had never read it before. As a result, Yong-Gi Cho saw that the pastoral ministry of Jesus was a pastoral ministry to solve the problem of this earthly life, and doing so, he spread the Gospel: "Repent, for the kingdom of heaven is at hand." (Mt 4:17). He discovered that the Apostles also like Jesus preached the Gospel together with the solution to the problem. They healed the lame (Acts 3:6-9), healed the demon-possessed (Acts 16:16-18), and solved real human suffering directly through God's great power.[98]

Yong-Gi Cho explains two principles of preaching that he practices to give a powerful message, namely counseling form of preaching, and message-centered preaching to solve the problem. First, he tells about counseling form. When people come to church for the first time, they come with a big problem, like family problems, business failure, sickness, and so on. The preaching should respond to people's needs. It is to help them to solve their difficult problem by listening to the preaching. Here, Yong-Gi Cho says the difference between the Christian's asking blessing and Shamanism. Namely, Christianity is fundamentally different from Shamanism: Christians ask for blessing in the name of Jesus with the promised Word after repenting of sin before God the Father, while Shamanism's faith for blessing asks for blessing without believing in God the Creator.

---

98 Yong-Gi Cho, *Nanun Iroke Solkyohanda (I preach like this)*, 400.

Actually, the purpose of Christianity is to give man the blessing of enjoying eternal life and glorifying God. Therefore, it is completely different from the Shamanism's simple faith for blessings. We, the believers in Jesus, don't bow down to the spirits, but repent of our sins before God the Father, Creator of heaven and earth, and then ask for blessings in the name of Jesus with the promised Word. Therefore, it is basically different from Shamanism, which unconditionally asks for blessings without believing in God the Creator.[99]

As the second principle of preaching, Yong-Gi Cho explains message-centered preaching to solve the problem. He shares that in the front line of pastoral ministry, when we look at the people of the world, we can see many who are suffering, such as those with a broken family, a cancer patient, those who are Jobless and hungry, drunkards, and those who need help with spiritual, mental, physical, or social problems. Yong-Gi Cho believes that pastors are the captains of poor and suffering people. Therefore, Yong-Gi Cho confesses that as a captain, he prepares the preaching by focusing on how he can solve the problem of those who are suffering with the word of God, and how the faithful can learn to believe well in God and become the people of paradise, and at the same time, how they can live and receive blessings in this world. Therefore, Yong-Gi Cho says that the root of his message in preaching is to transmit the blessing of the Threefold salvation.[100]

---

99 Yong-Gi Cho, *Nanun Iroke Solkyohanda (I preach like this)*, 401.

Yong-Gi Cho emphasizes giving the message that gives dream and hope for effective and useful preaching.[101] And in seeking green pastures for the sheep in the Bible, he emphasizes that if it is profitable, the preacher should eat and digest it first before feeding it to the flock. He provides the specific details to envision creatively risking one's life, to prepare thoroughly the preaching, and to proclaim the Fivefold Gospel and the Threefold Blessing. He says that the preacher will boldly proclaim Divine healing because Jesus always healed the sick, and God is working for healing today.

① The preacher must go around the pasture (from Genesis to Revelation) day and night to find a pasture where there is plenty of green grass and overflowing clean water. If it is profitable, the preacher should eat and digest it first before feeding it to the flock.[102]

② He must envision creatively risking his life, and thoroughly prepare. Envisioning means that the preacher tries to picture in his heart the preaching that he is going to deliver. For this he must pray before God and become a dreamer with a humble heart. Because only those who can look at the future with dream in the grace of God, can create. And he must also immerse himself in researching the Bible risking his life, and all the preaching must be prepared with prayer and finished with prayer. The main

---

100 Yong-Gi Cho, *Nanun Iroke Solkyohanda (I preach like this)*, 402-403.
101 Yong-Gi Cho, *Solkyonun Naui Inseng (Preaching is my life)*, Seoul Logos, 2009, 22.
102 Yong-Gi Cho, *Nanun Iroke Solkyohanda (I preach like this)*, 222.

text of the preaching must be studied thoroughly, and when he finds an example or data, he must practice it just like in real life.[103]

③ At the center of the Cross of Jesus Christ, proclaim the power of the precious blood and spread the Fivefold Gospel and the Threefold Blessing. The joy and peace in Christ is the biggest treasure of human life, therefore the preaching in Christ must not be inclined to the worldly ethics and morals. Proclaim that the precious blood shed on the Cross has the power to save us, heal us, and bring God's blessings. Propagate the Gospel of being born again through the Cross of Jesus Christ, the Gospel of Fullness of the Holy Spirit, the Gospel of Divine healing, and the Gospel of Blessing, the Gospel of Christ as the Coming King. Propagate that if we believe in Jesus, the soul will be blessed, everything will go well, and the spirit, soul and body will be healthy.[104]

④ Boldly proclaim Divine healing. Because we can find in the Gospel that Jesus always healed the sick, God is also working for healing today. I boldly proclaim the Divine healing message in every preaching. And Jesus said that casting out demons and healing the sick is the proof that paradise is among us.[105]

The preacher must have the power to touch people's heart and lead them to God. For this, Yong-Gi Cho suggests that we will have

---

[103] Yong-Gi Cho, *Solkyonun Naui Inseng (Preaching is my life)*, 305.
[104] Yong-Gi Cho, *Solkyonun Naui Inseng (Preaching is my life)*, 87.
[105] Yong-Gi Cho, *Solkyonun Naui Inseng (Preaching is my life)*, 117.

a personal meeting with the Holy Spirit, be anointed by the Holy Spirit, relying on his guidance and praying earnestly. Because he believes that when we acknowledge, invite, and communion with the personal Holy Spirit, there is an amazing manifestation of the Holy Spirit's work in the preaching.[106] He distinguishes these two, Logos and *Rhema*, and makes sure that the preacher must give a message based on '*Rhema*.' Namely, he says that Logos indicates the 'written Word', while '*Rhema*' indicates the 'proclaimed Word' that particularly touches the heart. The 'proclaimed Word' is the Word of God's response to me today. He makes clear it that these are all the same word of God, but it is noticeably different. Namely, the Bible says, "Thus faith comes from what is heard, and what is heard comes through the word of Christ." (Rm 10:17) Here, "what is heard comes through the word of Christ" is the 'proclaimed Word.'[107] According to Yong-Gi Cho, true preaching is to transmit the prophetic word of God, without adding or subtracting. Because the preacher is a communicator who receives the word of God and delivers it as it is. Therefore, he insists that it cannot include any human thought or opinion.[108]

Yong-Gi Cho says there are two criteria for judging whether a preaching is effective. Namely, the content of what we speak, and the way we communicate.[109] He compares preaching to cooking

---

106 Yong-Gi Cho, *Solkyonun Naui Inseng (Preaching is my life)*, 206.
107 Yong-Gi Cho, *Solkyonun Naui Inseng (Preaching is my life)*, 146.
108 Yong-Gi Cho, *Solkyonun Naui Inseng (Preaching is my life)*, 233.

'Gom-guk' (a Thick beef soup) or 'Hanyak-tang' (Herbal medicine soup). He prepares preaching by taking the title with prayer inspired by the Holy Spirit in life, putting it into the herbal medicine bowl and boiling it for a long time with deep meditation and prayer. He confesses that his whole life as a pastor is preparation for preaching, because the center of pastoral ministry is preaching.[110] Yong-Gi Cho first emphasises that the key to the whole preaching should be simple and clear so that everyone can easily understand it. This can be compared to an architectural drawing and the framework of the whole structure in the construction. He believes that once the Bible text and theme of the preaching have been determined, the next question is how to create the structure of the preaching.[111]

Yong-Gi Cho insists on envisioning as the starting point of preaching, and specially the necessity to have a creative conception. He gives the example of a sculptor with a large stone, and affirms the Bible as the most important material and continuous prayer. Firstly, like a sculptor who puts a large stone in front of him and draws in his mind the finished appearance of a work to be sculpted, the preacher must try a new concept to arouse fresh interest although it is what everyone knows. Yong-Gi Cho believes that for a preacher, the message research is a lifelong task. Therefore, he affirms that it is necessary to read many books for preaching, but the most important one is the Bible. Because a preacher without the Word of

---

109 Yong-Gi Cho, *Nanun Iroke Solkyohanda (I preach like this)*, 352.
110 Yong-Gi Cho, *Solkyonun Naui Inseng (Preaching is my life)*, 285.
111 Yong-Gi Cho, *Solkyonun Naui Inseng (Preaching is my life)*, 307.

the Bible he cannot even think. And Yong-Gi Cho says that the preacher should pray constantly and take notes without missing the moment of sparkling inspiration; the most important thing is to endlessly ask for the help from the Holy Spirit.

> Envisioning is the first step in preparing a preaching, it is trying to picture in our minds the preaching we will deliver. We need to envision what topics we are going to preach on, what we are going to say, what examples we are going to give, and how this argument will be developed. It is like a sculptor who places a large stone in front of him and draws in his mind the finished appearance of a work to be sculpted. ... The preacher must try a new concept to arouse fresh interest, although it is what everyone knows. ... First, set a clear goal of the preaching in the work of the Holy Spirit, and look at the finished appearance through dream and fantasy. And then, it is only when we keep our thoughts in the depths of our hearts and constantly pray, praise and give thanks in faith, that we are able to do creative things. To be a creative person, we must pray deeply before God, humble our hearts and become a dreaming person. ... No need to say to read the books that are necessary for the church and for preaching. For a preacher, researching the message is a lifelong task. There are no altitudes that say that's enough. Just as the pearl-digging woman desperately digs pearls, fighting with all the dangers of waves and sea, the steps of the preacher who is looking for a good message, should not stop. The most important one among the materials for a preaching is the Bible. The Bible is the absolute element for the pastoral work of the preacher. We cannot even think of

a preacher without the Word of the Bible, ... There is a moment of sparkling inspiration for everyone. This inspiration will disappear like lightning, if we do not write it down promptly. We must keep a notebook and pencil by our bedside even at home. When inspiration moves us like the water of Bethesda pond, we should not miss it and catch it. The most important thing is to pray constantly to the Holy Spirit.[112]

Yong-Gi Cho says that while preparing the preaching, all preaching should be prepared with prayer and concluded with prayer, and choose the topic and text that meet the needs of the audience. He compares that preaching is like a house, the example is like the window of that house; the text of the preaching is like the gear, the example is like the oil. He believes that an appropriate example is that of the preaching as a seasoning that gives flavor to food. He explains all the detailed description of these things in this way: suggesting to practice the prepared manuscript repeatedly; if necessary, to check our own preaching by recording it with a small recorder; try to preach directly in front of a mirror for effective preparation.

The preacher should be a praying person. All the preaching should be prepared with prayer and concluded with prayer. It is better for the preacher to write down the topic or the text that came up during prayer, and choose the topic and text that fit the needs of the audience by observing them. The title should not only include the contents of the preaching,

---

[112] Yong-Gi Cho, *Solkyonun Naui Inseng (Preaching is my life)*, 289-293.

but also be specific, and it is desirable that it convey the exact meaning. ... An appropriate example is that of the sermon as a seasoning that gives flavor to food.

Spurgeon, the famous English preacher, explained sermons and examples: "If I compare preaching with a house built by a builder, the example is like the window of that house. If there is no window at all in that house, that house is like a dark and gloomy jail, if there are too many windows, it loses the coziness of the room."

These words of Spurgeon have been so helpful to me. The mental structure of a man cannot bear hard theory for a long time. ... If I compare the text of the preaching with the gear, the example is like the oil. According to my experience, if one preaching has two examples it will be good enough, but no more than three. ... If the example is realistic and concrete, it has stronger influence. It is more effective if an example is a fact that everyone knows in real life surroundings, rather than a story from long ago. Among the examples, the preacher's faith testimony which has been directly experienced, has a charm that captures the listener's heart. ...

Then write a manuscript with the prepared material, and after writing a manuscript, practice repeatedly not to be awkward in communication. Try to record with a small recorder to check one's own preaching and also try to preach directly in front of a mirror is an effective way of preparation.[113]

---

113 Yong-Gi Cho, *Solkyonun Naui Inseng (Preaching is my life)*, 298-300.

Yong-Gi Cho believes that no matter how a preacher delivers a good word, if that word does not remain in the memory of the believers, that preaching has failed. Therefore, he presents six elements of the preaching composition. He explains them in detail as follows: faithfulness to the biblical text, unity, simple composition, order, overall balance, progressiveness.

> First, I am faithful to the biblical text. The biblical text we are preaching on is the primary goal we want to communicate. ... Because preaching is to communicate the biblical word as it is, it is never to reveal the preacher's human thoughts.
> Secondly, it must have unity. Even though when we usually speak with three or four subtopics when we preach, it must be focused on one topic. ... No matter how a good word is delivered, if that word does not remain in the memory of the believers, that preaching has failed.
> Thirdly, make a simple composition. In order to achieve the unity mentioned earlier, the composition of the preaching must be simple. To communicate an important fact, the preacher presents some subtopics, but if their relationship is so complicated or too professional, it will be very difficult and boring for the listeners. It is undesirable to deal with a difficult theological argument or philosophical issue in the preaching.
> Fourth, put it in order. In preaching, it is necessary to have an order like a human body: the head is on top, the body is in the middle, and the legs are below. Each organ of the body has its role with interrelationship, preaching is the same. ... Each subtopic must maintain its role in relation to the main topic.

Fifth, think of an overall balance. Keep in mind that if one subtopic stands out too much among the subtopics, other parts will be relatively neglected. ...

Sixth, it must be progressive. The preaching should have a content that can attract the attention of the listeners from the beginning, and it should be developed gradually towards the climax. In this way, the preacher should lead the audiences so that they can easily come to the conclusion that the preacher intended.[114]

Eight principles of expression

The way a sermon is presented can have a huge impact on how it is understood. Therefore Yong-Gi Cho presents eight principles with examples. Namely, 1) Express precisely, because each person has a different standard in many aspects; 2) Use a simple and easy word that even an ignorant person could understand; 3) Use the sensual expression because people always understand by painting a picture in their minds; 4) Use the modifier in many ways for a quick understanding; 5) Use dramatic contrast to explain a fact so that the preacher can motivate the audience to overcome their own situation; 6) Describe many aspects one by one to give a holistic and comprehensive meaning by looking at several examples; 7) Express the development of the situation in the present progressive tense as if the preacher and the audience are present in that place together; 8) Give a realistic feeling by using a conversational ex-

---

114 Yong-Gi Cho, *Solkyonun Naui Inseng (Preaching is my life)*, 308-309.

pression to invite the audience to be a person who is listening to the conversation next to the preacher and can have an opportunity to think about it in their own way. The preacher's word should be expressed with confidence, but avoid using words full of assumption or suspicion.

> First, express precisely. Among the words we use, there are many that do not have clear meaning. When it comes to expensive things, each person has a different standard of 'expensive.' Therefore, preacher must use a specific and precise expression.
> Second, use a simple and easy word. ... The preaching is not for the preacher, but for the audience. Keep in mind that Jesus used the simple word that even an ignorant person could understand.
> Third, use the sensual expression. It means to draw with the word. ... People always understand by drawing a picture in their minds. ... For example, it will have a much better effect if we use the expression: "Jacob limped and limped along because his thigh was dislocated" rather than saying, "Jacob's thigh was dislocated." This sensuous expression makes the audiences go back to that situation as if they were looking at the picture and makes them feel empathetic. Draw a picture by thinking of people's minds as a canvas and your lips as a brush.
> Fourth, use the modifier in many ways for quick understanding. For example, expressing the modifier in many ways to modify various diseases, gives the opportunity to the audience to pay attention to their own sickness: "People came to Jesus with spiritual sickness, mental sickness, physical sickness."

Fifth, use dramatic contrast to explain a fact. For example, it's like this: Zacchaeus, who was wealthy from a human perspective, supposed to be happier and more joyful than everyone else. But he was sick in his heart, which others could not know. This contrast adds certainty of target and value, and motivates the audiences to overcome their own situation.

Sixth, describe many aspects one by one. For example, "There is no person, as happy as a person who lives according to one's own talent and vocation. A man who thinks that his job is given to him by God is the happiest, even if he is a pastor as pastor, if he is a teacher as teacher, if he is a worker as worker, or if he is in any other profession." This expression gives a holistic and comprehensive meaning by looking at several examples in the enumeration. ...

Seventh, express the development of the situation using the present progressive tense. For example, when we say biblical story, we express as if the situation has just happened now, or as if the preacher or the audience are present in that place together.

Eighth, gives it a realistic feeling using conversational expression. Then, the audience becomes a person who is listening to the conversation next to the preacher and can have the opportunity to think about it in their own way. ... It is better that when a preacher talks about the problem of sin or human inadequacy, he expresses it including not only the audience but also the preacher himself. For example, when a preacher says, "You are sinners", he is sitting in an arrogant place even in the moment he is not aware of it. Therefore, at this moment he must express, "I and you, we are all sinners." And the preacher's word should be expressed with confidence. Should avoid using words full of assumption or suspicion. Namely, to keep the facts in mind, that this kind of expression is absolutely forbidden: "We could even say that we are saved. I am not sure that the grace of Jesus will be upon you."[115]

Yong-Gi Cho says that there can be no Gospel witness in isolation from real-world issues, insists on preaching in the context of the times. Because the Gospel does not change, but a means of spreading the Gospel must be changed according to the time and the situation. He emphasizes that we must apply the message properly according to the audience: to witness to the Gospel, "to rural people with a Gospel suitable for rural people, to merchants with a Gospel suitable for merchants, and to intellectuals with a Gospel suitable for intellectuals."[116]

Yong-Gi Cho says that the content of the preaching should be communicated clearly and simply. He sees the preaching as divided into an introduction, a main theme and a conclusion; the shorter the introduction and the shorter the conclusion, the more effective it will be. He emphasized that three or four subtopics of the main topic are suitable, and when the first subtopic goes into the second subtopic, the preacher will make the audience feel that they remember the whole preaching by reminding them of the first subtopic again. And Yong-Gi Cho gives importance to these two things in order to get the attention of the audience. He affirms that first, preach-

---

115 Yong-Gi Cho, *Solkyonun Naui Inseng (Preaching is my life)*, 310-312.
116 Yong-Gi Cho, *Solkyonun Naui Inseng (Preaching is my life)*, 314-315.

er will remember that the audience wants to hear the story that is directly related to their own lives, and second, the preacher will communicate empirically what he was deeply enlightened while preparing the preaching. He is convinced that the preaching which could not change the preacher himself will be easily ignored.[117]

Yong-Gi Cho suggests that in order to respond effectively to the needs of the audience, the preacher must analyze information about the audience's situation and change his preaching attitude accordingly. Before the preaching, he must prepare himself by looking at their job, preferences, and personality. During the preaching, he must interpret the audience's reaction and deliver the message again in response to this reaction in order to achieve greater persuasiveness. And after the preaching, he suggests better preparation for the next preaching by observing the audience's thoughts and reactions to the preaching in various ways.

> First, analyze the audience before preaching. ... For example, if the audiences are factory workers, the preacher must take a look at their lives and preferences. In detail, he should analyze their age, sex, occupation, income, education, and discover the personality of the audience. And the preacher's attitude must be changed according to the audience, whether they are introverted or extroverted.
> Second, analyze the audience in the place of preaching. The attitude of the audience can be changed according to the preacher's message.

---

[117] Yong-Gi Cho, *Solkyonun Naui Inseng (Preaching is my life)*, 328-329.

... In order to preach effectively, the preacher interprets the audience's reaction quickly and accurately, and delivers the message again in response to this reaction to give higher persuasive power. And if the audience's attitude shows that they are bored or have lost interest, the preacher must make them pay attention by changing the topic.

Third, take a look at the reaction of the audience after the preaching. The preacher must use various methods to observe the audience's thoughts and reaction to his preaching. By doing so, he can change his own shortcomings and prepare the message that is suitable for the audience for the next time.[118]

Yong-Gi Cho says that the preacher must not forget the fact that he is communicating the word of God the moment he steps up to the pulpit, and he has to pay attention to every aspect. Yong-Gi Cho especially emphasizes that the preacher's dress, footstep, gaze, facial expression, gesture and voice must be focused on the effective communication of the preacher's message. Since the first impression of a preacher is greatly influenced by his appearance, he suggests that the preacher should dress plainly but with dignity. Cho suggests that the preacher's look at the audience must be fair, because every audience hopes to get the preacher's attention. He believes that the preacher's gentle facial expression puts the audience at ease, so that the content of the preaching can be delivered without resistance. Yong-Gi Cho says that gestures with body and hand must

---

118 Yong-Gi Cho, *Solkyonun Naui Inseng (Preaching is my life)*, 316-317.

PART III _ Pastoral Challenge **219**

be expressed spontaneously and confidently from the inner side of the preacher, and especially gesture must be varied and performed at appropriate time to suit the situation. He emphasizes that the voice of the preacher needs continual training and refinement, as well as proper breathing, a good vocalization and clear pronunciation.

Appearance

The preacher must not forget the fact that he is communicating the word of God. The moment he steps into the pulpit, all his human inadequacies are covered with God's authority. Because of this, the preacher who steps up to the pulpit has to pay attention to every aspect.

The first impression of the preacher is very much influenced by the appearance. No matter how great the content of the preaching is, if the preacher's first impression is not good, his preaching cannot achieve great results. ... The preacher should dress plainly but with dignity. If the preacher is overly fashionable or unusual in his dress, the audiences will be more interested in his clothing than his message. His clothing should be neat and free of wrinkles, avoiding bright colors. His hair should always be neat, and also keep the mouth clean.[119]

Attitude

First, the preacher must be natural in every way, with a stable consistent attitude. ... When the preacher steps on the pulpit, he should not walk too quickly or walking too slowly, making it looks unnatural. The

---

119 Yong-Gi Cho, *Solkyonun Naui Inseng (Preaching is my life)*, 320.

preacher's step should be elegant and confident. On the pulpit, the preacher must look at the audience with a straight posture.

Second, the preacher's look at the audience must be fair. A preacher stares at one place from beginning to the end of the preaching, but this attitude is undesirable. It should be remembered that every audience hopes to get the preacher's attention, and the preaching of the preacher will be for herself. ... Spreading one's gaze evenly is the effective way to increase persuasiveness and to obtain a good response for the preaching.

Thirdly, the preacher's facial expression must be peaceful. ... When the heart of the audience is at ease with the gentle facial expression of the preacher, the preaching will be delivered without resistance.

Body Language

Preaching is the delivery of words. But between words there is also body language. What we say with our bodies is called action. Action includes facial expression, posture and gesture. Action could be more effective in communicating our preaching than word. ... First, movement must be spontaneous. Gestures of body and hand should not be awkward as if they were deliberately decorated. The gesture must be expressed spontaneously and confidently from the inner side of the preacher. ... Second, gesture must be expressed at the right time according to the situation. ... Thirdly, the gesture must be changed in variety.

Voice

The voice of the preacher should be trained and be constantly refined.

When we speak we need to pay attention to these four aspects. First, proper breathing. Second, good pronunciation (Vocalization). When we are nervous, we make anxious sounds that are higher than our own voice. Therefore we must try hard to know the most suitable level of our usual voice. Third, we should avoid the nasal voice. It makes the preacher's word seem less serious. Fourth, the pronunciation should be clear. If the pronunciation is not clear, it is difficult to deliver the contents of the preaching accurately.[120]

Prayer after preaching

Yong-Gi Cho believes that preparing the preaching thoroughly and finishing it in the pulpit is not the end. Because keeping in mind that all the previous process was only possible with the help of the Holy Spirit, the preacher should check whether there was any human element, and he should pray for the fruit of the seeds sown. Then he insists that the prayer after the preaching is the beginning of the preparation for the next preaching, and suggests that the preacher pray with reference to the four necessary elements. Namely the honest self-exposure and the prayer of self-surrender, the positive prayer, and the acceptance with faith. Yong-Gi Cho says that one should develop exactly what is necessary for oneself and surrender oneself thoroughly to God. And Yong-Gi Cho suggests that if we prayed with positive thought, picturing in mind God fills us with the power of powerful preaching, we must accept it

---

120 Yong-Gi Cho, *Solkyonun Naui Inseng (Preaching is my life)*, 321-324.

with faith.

Firstly, what is necessary in prayer is honest self-exposure. ... "I am a sinner", "I am worse than a worm", "My preaching is insignificant." This kind of prayers makes your mind negative. When you pray to God, you should unfold exactly what you need. ... If you pray negatively your preaching will be according to this word. ... Therefore, through honest self-exposure, you should first find out which ghost makes you negative, destroys you, and you must cast out that ghost. In order to cast out the ghost you must know its identity. That ghost is the seven ghosts of egotism, greed, lying, hate, fear, inferiority and guilt. After casting out these ghosts, it is necessary to do the self-exposure to God in thorough repentance and supplication.

Second, a prayer of self-surrender is necessary. You must surrender yourself completely to God. When we give our whole life to the Lord, He will occupy us and lead us to live according to His will.

Thirdly, it must be a positive prayer. Even though we think positively, very often we say "I am an insignificant preacher." It seems to be a very humble prayer, but this kind of prayer makes us negative. You must draw a picture in your mind that God fills the power of powerful preaching.

Fourthly, the preacher must accept it with faith. ... When you prayed once with positive thinking, the preacher should immediately accept it with faith. After prayer, you should confess verbally, saying that "God, thank you for responding to me!" Dear preachers! If you pray according to the effective prayer rules of these four steps, the seeds of your preaching will bear amazing fruit.[121]

2) Pope Francis' recommended method for delivering homilies

Here we will see the contents about preaching mentioned in Evangelii Gaudium, the Apostolic Exhortation of Pope Francis. According to Pope Francis, a homily is the touchstone for judging a pastor's closeness and ability to communicate with his people. And the homily can actually be an intense and happy experience of the Holy Spirit, a consoling encounter with God's word.[122] He stresses that the liturgical proclamation of the word of God, especially in the Eucharistic assembly, is a dialogue between God and his people. The preacher must therefore know the heart of his community in order to realize where its desire for God is alive and ardent, as well as where that dialogue, once loving, has been thwarted and is now barren.

It is worth remembering that "the liturgical proclamation of the word of God, especially in the eucharistic assembly, is not so much a time for meditation and catechesis as a dialogue between God and his people, a dialogue in which the great deeds of salvation are proclaimed and

---

121 Yong-Gi Cho, *Solkyonun Naui Inseng (Preaching is my life)*, 302-304.
122 Pope Francis, *Evangelii Gaudium: Apostolic Exhortation to the Bishops, Clergy, Consecrated Persons, and the Lay Faithful on the Proclamation of the Gospel in Today's World* (2015), #135.

the demands of the covenant are continually restated". The homily has special importance due to its Eucharistic context: It surpasses all forms of catechesis as the supreme moment in the dialogue between God and his people which lead up to sacramental communion. The homily takes up once more the dialogue which the Lord has already established with his people. The preacher must know the heart of his community, in order to realize where its desire for God is alive and ardent, as well as where that dialogue, once loving, has been thwarted and is now barren.[123]

Pope Francis affirms that since the homily of the Catholic Church is situated within the framework of a liturgical celebration, it should be brief. If the homily goes on too long, it will affect two characteristic elements of the liturgical celebration: its balance and its rhythm. And the words of the preacher must be measured so that the Lord, more than his minister, will be the center of attention.

> The homily is a distinctive genre, since it is preaching situated within the framework of a liturgical celebration; hence it should be brief and avoid taking on the semblance of a speech or a lecture. A preacher may be able to hold the attention of his listeners for a whole hour, but in this case his words become more important than the celebration of faith. If the homily goes on too long, it will affect two characteristic elements of the liturgical celebration: its balance and its rhythm. When preaching

---

123 Pope Francis, *Evangelii Gaudium*, #137.

takes place within the context of the liturgy, it is part of the offering made to the Father and a mediation of the grace which Christ pours out during the celebration. This context demands that preaching should guide the assembly, and the preacher, to a life-changing communion with Christ in the Eucharist. This means that the words of the preacher must be measured, so that the Lord, more than his minister, will be the center of attention.[124]

The Pope suggests that the preacher will give a homily in the same way that a mother speaks to her child. Therefore, the preacher of the maternal church listens to their concerns and learns from them, with the closeness of the preacher, the warmth of his tone of voice, the unpretentiousness of his manner of speaking, the joy of his gestures.[125]

Pope Francis, emphasizing the "Words which set hearts on fire", says that the homily is far from dealing with abstract truths or cold syllogisms. And he points out that a preaching which would be purely moralistic or doctrinaire, or one which turns into a lecture on biblical exegesis, detracts from this heart—to—heart communication which takes place in the homily. And he says clearly that the challenge of an enculturated preaching consists in proclaiming a Gospel message, not ideas or detached values. He also emphasizes that what the preacher is proclaiming is not himself but the Lord

---

124 Pope Francis, *Evangelii Gaudium*, #138.
125 Pope Francis, *Evangelii Gaudium*, #139-140.

Jesus Christ.126

The Pope suggests that a homily should be thoroughly prepared. And he says that in order to have pastoral creativity, the preacher should devote a long time to study, prayer and reflection. Even if less time has to be given to other important activities, the Pope asks that a sufficient portion of personal and community time be dedicated to this task as instruments of God. Because he sees that a preacher who does not prepare is not "spiritual"; he is dishonest and irresponsible with the gifts he has received.

> Preparation for preaching is so important a task that a prolonged time of study, prayer, reflection and pastoral creativity should be devoted to it. With great affection I wish to stop for a moment and offer a method of preparing homilies. ... Some pastors argue that such preparation is not possible given the vast number of tasks which they must perform; nonetheless, I presume to ask that each week a sufficient portion of personal and community time be dedicated to this task, even if less time has to be given to other important activities. Trust in the Holy Spirit who is at work during the homily is not merely passive but active and creative. It demands that we offer ourselves and all our abilities as instruments (Rom 12:1) which God can use. A preacher who does not prepare is not "spiritual"; he is dishonest and irresponsible with the gifts he has received.127

---

126 Pope Francis, *Evangelii Gaudium*, #142-143.
127 Pope Francis, *Evangelii Gaudium*, #145.

Pope Francis suggests the first step in the preparation of homily like this. First, invoke the Holy Spirit in prayer. And then give our entire attention to the biblical text, which needs to be the basis of the preaching. Because to interpret a biblical text, we need to be patient, to put aside all other concerns and to give it our time, interest and undivided attention. He emphasizes that preparation for preaching requires a loving attitude: "Speak, Lord, for your servant is listening."

> The first step, after calling upon the Holy Spirit in prayer, is to give our entire attention to the biblical text, which needs to be the basis of our preaching. Whenever we stop and attempt to understand the message of a particular text, we are practicing "reverence for the truth." This is the humility of heart which recognizes that the word is always beyond us, that "we are neither its masters nor owners, but its guardians, heralds and servants." ... To interpret a biblical text, we need to be patient, to put aside all other concerns, and to give it our time, interest and undivided attention. We must leave aside any other pressing concerns and create an environment of serene concentration. It is useless to attempt to read a biblical text if all we are looking for are quick, easy and immediate results. Preparation for preaching requires love. ... "Speak, Lord, for your servant is listening." (1 Sam 3:9)[128]

The Pope presents the various means of literature analysis: atten-

---

128 Pope Francis, *Evangelii Gaudium*, #146.

tion to words that are repeated or emphasized, recognition of the structure and specific movement of a text, consideration of the role played by the various characters, and so on. But he emphasizes that our most important goal is to discover its principal message, not to understand every little detail of a text. According to the Pope, the central message is what the author primarily wanted to communicate; this calls for recognizing not only the author's ideas, but also the effect he wanted to produce. For example, if a text was written as an exhortation, it should not be used to teach doctrine; if it was written to teach something about God, it should not be used to expound various theological opinions.[129]

Pope Francis sees that even today, people prefer to listen to witnesses: they "thirst for authenticity" and "call for evangelizers to speak of a God they themselves know and are familiar with, as if they were seeing him." For this reason, the Pope stresses that whoever wants to preach must be the first to let the word of God move him deeply and become incarnate in his daily life. In this way preaching will consist in that activity, so intense and fruitful. He sees that "out of the abundance of the heart, the mouth speaks", and the Sunday readings will resonate in all their brilliance in the hearts of the faithful, if they have first done so in the heart of their pastor. Therefore, he suggests that the preacher ought firstly to develop a great personal familiarity with the word of God with a docile and prayerful heart.

---

129 Pope Francis, *Evangelii Gaudium*, #147.

The preacher "ought firstly of all to develop a great personal familiarity with the word of God. ... He needs to approach the word with a docile and prayerful heart so that it may deeply penetrate his thoughts and feelings and bring about a new outlook in him." It is good for us to renew our fervor each day and every Sunday as we prepare the homily, examining ourselves to see if we have grown in love for the word which we preach. Nor should we forget that "the greater or lesser degree of the holiness of the minister has a real effect on the proclamation of the word." ... For "out of the abundance of the heart, the mouth speaks." (Mt 12:34) The Sunday readings will resonate in all their brilliance in the hearts of the faithful if they have first done so in the heart of their pastor.

Whoever wants to preach must be the first to let the word of God move him deeply and become incarnate in his daily life. In this way preaching will consist in that activity, so intense and fruitful, which is "communicating to others what one has contemplated." For all these reasons, before preparing what we will actually say when preaching, we need to let ourselves be penetrated by that word which will also penetrate others, for it is a living and active word, like a sword "which pierces to the division of soul and spirit, of joints and marrow, and discerns the thoughts and intentions of the heart." (Heb 4:12) This has great pastoral importance. Today too, people prefer to listen to witnesses: they "thirst for authenticity" and "call for evangelizers to speak of a God whom they themselves know and are familiar with, as if they were seeing him."[130]

---

130 Pope Francis, *Evangelii Gaudium*, #149-150.

Pope Francis suggests the use of *Lectio Divina* in the preparation of preaching, saying the following. He explains that the spiritual reading of a text must begin with its literal sense, and it is a study to understand the central message of the text. He emphasizes that it should begin with that study and then go on to discern how that same message speaks to his own life. Otherwise, we can easily make the text say what we think is convenient, useful for confirming us in our previous decisions, suited to our own patterns of thought. The Pope suggests that we will ask many questions, feeling the presence of God, as we meditate on the Word of the Bible. For example, "Lord, what does this text say to me? What is it about my life that you want to change by this text? What troubles me about this text?" The Pope says that when we make an effort to listen to the Lord, temptations usually arise, and he gives some examples that could be helpful in discerning the temptation. Namely, one of them is simply to feel troubled or burdened and to turn away. Another common temptation is to think about what the text means for other people and so avoid applying it to our own life. It can also happen that we look for excuses to water down the clear meaning of the text. Or we can wonder if God is demanding too much of us, asking for a decision which we are not yet prepared to make. According to the Pope, this leads many people to stop taking pleasure in the encounter with God's word. Therefore, the Pope emphasizes that sometimes "even Satan disguises himself as an angel of light." Doing so, the Pope says that God the Father asks that we sincerely look at our own life and present ourselves honestly before him, and that we be willing to continue to grow, asking from him what we ourselves cannot as yet achieve.

There is one particular way of listening to what the Lord wishes to tell us in his word and of letting ourselves be transformed by the Spirit. It is what we call *Lectio Divina*. It consists of reading God's word in a moment of prayer and allowing it to enlighten and renew us. This prayerful reading of the Bible is not something separate from the study undertaken by the preacher to ascertain the central message of the text; on the contrary, it should begin with that study and then go on to discern how that same message speaks to his own life. The spiritual reading of a text must start with its literal sense. Otherwise, we can easily make the text say what we think is convenient, useful for confirming us in our previous decisions, suited to our own patterns of thought. Ultimately this would be tantamount to using something sacred for our own benefit and then passing on this confusion to God's people. We must never forget that sometimes "even Satan disguises himself as an angel of light." (2 Cor 11:14)

In the presence of God, during a recollected reading of the text, it is good to ask, for example: "Lord, what does this text say to me? What is it about my life that you want to change by this text? What troubles me about this text? Why am I not interested in this? Or perhaps: What do I find pleasant in this text? What is it about this word that moves me? What attracts me? Why does it attract me?" When we make an effort to listen to the Lord, temptations usually arise. One of them is simply to feel troubled or burdened, and to turn away. Another common temptation is to think about what the text means for other people, and so avoid applying it to our own life. It can also happen that we look for excuses to water down the clear meaning of the text. Or we can wonder if God is demanding too much of us, asking for a decision which we are not yet prepared to make. This leads many people to stop taking pleasure in the encounter with God's word; but this would mean forgetting that no one is more patient than God our Father, that no one is more understanding and willing to wait. He always invites us to take a step forward, but does not demand a full response if we are not yet ready. He simply asks that we sincerely look at our life and present ourselves honestly before him, and that we be willing to continue to grow, asking from him what we ourselves cannot as yet achieve.[131]

According to Pope Francis, a preacher is a contemplative of the Word and also of his people. In this way he learns "of the aspirations, of riches and limitations, of ways of praying, of loving, of looking at life and the world, which distinguish this or that human gathering." And because it is attentive to "the actual people of the proclamation of the Gospel", and can "take into account their language, their signs and symbols, and respond to their questions." For the Pope, this interest is profoundly religious and pastoral.[132]

The Pope says that a good homily should have "an idea, a sentiment, an image." Because an attractive image makes the message

---

[131] Pope Francis, *Evangelii Gaudium,DVGaudium*, #152-153.
[132] Pope Francis, *Evangelii Gaudium*, #154.

seem familiar, close to home, practical and related to everyday life. And because a successful image can make people savor the message, awaken a desire and move the will towards the Gospel. And he quotes the words of Paul VI: "if the homily is simple, clear, direct, well-adapted, the faithful expect much from preaching, and will greatly benefit from it." Pope Francis emphasizes that the importance of using the language which people can understand. Therefore, Pope Francis points out that preacher's words learned in certain situations are not part of the ordinary language of their listeners. According to him, if we want to adapt to people's language and to reach them with God's word, we must listen to them, share in their lives and pay loving attention to them. He suggests preacher to prepare the homily that has thematic unity, a clear order and correlation between sentences, so that the people can easily follow the preacher and grasp his line of argument. The Pope also says that a characteristic of a good homily is to use positive language. Because positive preaching always offers hope, and points to the future.

> Simply using a few examples, let us recall some practical resources which can enrich our preaching and make it more attractive. One of the most important things is to learn how to use images in preaching, how to appeal to imagery. Sometimes examples are used to clarify a certain point, but these examples usually appeal only to the mind; images, on the other hand, help people better to appreciate and accept the message we wish to communicate. An attractive image makes the message seem familiar, close to home, practical and related to everyday

life. A successful image can make people savor the message, awaken a desire and move the will towards the Gospel. A good homily, an old teacher once told me, should have "an idea, a sentiment, an image." Paul VI said that "the faithful expect much from preaching, and will greatly benefit from it, provided that it is simple, clear, direct, well-adapted." Simplicity has to do with the language we use. It must be one that people understand, lest we risk speaking to a void. Preachers often use words learned during their studies and in specialized settings which are not part of the ordinary language of their hearers. ... The greatest risk for a preacher is that he becomes so accustomed to his own language that he thinks that everyone else naturally understands and uses it. If we wish to adapt to people's language and to reach them with God's word, we need to listen to the people, to share in their lives and pay loving attention to them. Simplicity and clarity are two different things. Our language may be simple but our preaching is not very clear. It can end up being incomprehensible because it is disorganized, lacks logical progression or tries to deal with too many things at one time. We need to ensure, then, that the homily has thematic unity, clear order and correlation between sentences, so that people can follow the preacher easily and grasp his line of argument.

Another feature of a good homily is that it is positive. It is not so much concerned with pointing out what shouldn't be done, but with suggesting what we can do better. In any case, if it does draw attention to something negative, it will also attempt to point to a positive and attractive value, lest it remain mired in complaints, laments, criticisms and reproaches. Positive preaching always offers hope, points to the future, does not leave us trapped in negativity. How good it is when priests, deacons and the laity gather periodically to discover resources which can make preaching more attractive![133]

3. The Cell system as a pastoral strategy

1) The Cell system of Yoido Full Gospel Church

According to pastor Yong-Gi Chos' successor, pastor Young-Hoon Lee in YFGC (Yoido Full Gospel Church), one of the principle foundations of the explosive growth of the Pentecostal movement lies in the *house church movement*. Young-Hoon Lee says that this movement has its root in Christian community of the early church. (Act 2:42-47) He sees that the early Christians cultivated fellowship, Bible study and the Lord's Supper through small-group house meetings. Saying that they may also have shared an agape meal, although the evidence for this is not clear, Young-Hoon Lee insists that Yong-Gi Cho reorganized the structure of the small-group house meetings of the early church into a Cell system.[134]

Yong-Gi Cho considers that the Guyuk system (Cell group system, Cell church) is the treasure found in pastoral ministry.[135] YFGC

---

133 Pope Francis, *Evangelii Gaudium*, #157-159.
134 Young-Hoon Lee, *The Holy Spirit Movement in Korea*, 105-106.
135 Yong-Gi Cho, *Himang Mokhwe 45 Nyun: Guyuk Sogrup Buheung Iyaki (45 years of Hope Ministries: Cell Group Revival Stories)*, Church Growth Institute, 2006, 71.

evangelizes through the Guyuk system, saying that each Guyuk is like the core of the church revival in that place. Because Guyuk is seen as a place where vitality is discovered.[136] Sung-Hoon Myung, a disciple of Yong-Gi Cho, says that the Guyuk Yebe system (Cell group worship system) is the registered trademark of YFGC. Namely, Guyuk Yebe is the system that leads forward the YFGC. The Guyuk has a concept of a certain place. And Guyuk Yebe (Cell group worship) designates the small faith community where the believers, with the Cell leader appointed by Yong-Gi Cho, gather together in a certain place, share fellowship with the Word, and worship. Gwi-Sam Cho considers that pastors and leaders from all over the world have copied Guyuk Yebe system of Yong-Gi Cho in the name of *Home Cell Groups or Cell church*.[137] After introducing Guyuk Yebe (Cell group worship), the church of Yong-Gi Cho grew day by day. In 1980 there were 150,000 believers with 10,000 Guyuks. Gwi-Sam Cho insists that the principle of Guyuk Yebe is an exclusive language of YFGC and the opportunity to spread it throughout the world also began with the word, "*Successful Home Cell Group*" written by Yong-Gi Cho in 1978.[138]

---

136 Yong-Gi Cho, *Himang Mokhwe 45 Nyun: Guyuk Sogrup Buheung Iyaki (45 years of Hope Ministries: Cell Group Revival Stories)*, 116.

137 Gwi-Sam Cho, *Young Sanui Guyuk-Yeberul Tonghan Kyohoi-Songzang Yunku (A Study of Church Growth through Young San's Guyuk Worship)*, in *Journal of Young San Theology*, vol. 13, Young San Theological Institute of Hansei University, Gunpo, 2008, 279.

138 Gwi-Sam Cho, *Young Sanui Guyuk-Yeberul Tonghan Kyohoi-Songzang Yunku (A Study of Church Growth through Young San's Guyuk Worship)*, 282.

Hong-Rae Park says that when this movement started many pastors from all over the world came to Korea to learn about it and began to adopt the *Home Cell Group* as an instrument of church structure. And the pastors of the two *Cell churches*, which are internationally known as large churches, came to visit the YFGC before starting their cell ministry.[139] And after the 1990s, this system was rapidly diffused in the Korean church.[140] Because many churches in the world are growing using the Cell group principle, Yong-Gi Cho insists that the secret to growth experienced in Korea is an effective principle that transcends race for all the churches. And he is sure that if other churches use this principle with the Pentecostal movement and the Guyuk system, there is no reason not to grow.[141]

The Cell system began when Yong-Gi Cho was 28 years old. He remembers that his body was broken like an old man caring 2,400 faithful. The physician said that "Pastor, you are suffering from nervous fatigue, and the only advice I can give you is to give up pastoral ministry." For Yong-Gi Cho this was a death sentence for his pastoral work.[142] In this situation the Cell system was started and his church grew so quickly.

---

139 Hong-Rae Park, *Cell Group Cell Kyohoi (Cell Group Cell Church)*, Seoro Sarang, Seoul, 2008, 141-142.
140 Gwi-Sam Cho, *Young Sanui Guyuk-Yeberul Tonghan Kyohoi-Songzang Yunku (A Study of Church Growth through Young San's Guyuk Worship)*, 291.
141 Yong-Gi Cho, *Himang Mokhwe 45 Nyun: Guyuk Sogrup Buheung Iyaki (45 years of Hope Ministries: Cell Group Revival Stories)*, 147.
142 Yong-Gi Cho, *Himang Mokhwe 45 Nyun: Guyuk Sogrup Buheung Iyaki (45 years of Hope Ministries: Cell Group Revival Stories)*, 77-78.

The beginning of Yong-Gi Cho's pastoral ministry and the growth of the church can be summarized as follows. He began the first Worship service on 18 May 1958 with five people. The pulpit was made of an apple box covered with a cloth and the day was Wednesday. The participants were Yong-Gi Cho, evangelist Ja-Sil Choi and her three children.[143] In 1964 there were 2,400 believers,[144] after introducing the Guyuk Yebe, the church grew every day. In 1980 there were 150,000 believers with 10,000 Guyuks; in 2008 there were 750,000 believers with so many Guyuk small groups. This church growth was spread through the establishment of *Church Growth Institute* in 1976, and the seminars and education on the principles of Guyuk Yebe pastoral ministry.[145]

Yong-gi Cho handled the double pastoral ministry of the church, that is, the *temple ministry* and the *house-to-house ministry*.[146] Yoido Full Gospel Church insists that Yong-Gi Cho discovered the original form of the Guyuk system from the Old Testament and New Testament. Namely, Yong-Gi Cho discovered: to take care of the Israelites of Exodus with the Word, established a leader and subdivided the organization; the family-centered small community of

---

[143] Yong-Gi Cho, *Himang Mokhwe 45 Nyun: Guyuk Sogrup Buheung Iyaki (45 years of Hope Ministries: Cell Group Revival Stories)*, 22-23.

[144] Yong-Gi Cho, *Himang Mokhwe 45 Nyun: Guyuk Sogrup Buheung Iyaki (45 years of Hope Ministries: Cell Group Revival Stories)*, 89.

[145] Gwi-Sam Cho, *Young Sanui Guyuk-Yeberul Tonghan Kyohoi-Songzang Yunku (A Study of Church Growth through Young San's Guyuk Worship)*, 282.

[146] Gwi-Sam Cho, *Young Sanui Guyuk-Yeberul Tonghan Kyohoi-Songzang Yunku (A Study of Church Growth through Young San's Guyuk Worship)*, 280.

the early church in Acts. Yong-Gi Cho considered that in the early church there was a *temple ministry*, where the disciples met regularly in a temple; there was also a *house-to-house ministry*, where believers met in a house to break bread and share fellowship. (Acts 2:46-47) He says that this discovery was a groundbreaking opportunity to start the lay ministry, especially the Guyuk system. And also it is unique to use the Guyuk structure of the "network pastoral ministry" way to let the lay people participate in the activity for taking care of the believers. Namely, it is to nurture and train the lay leaders so that these lay leaders can lead the Guyuk. It is said to be a more systematic and effective way to grow the church because it is a broader field ministry, like a net.[147]

Yoido Full Gospel Church had a difficulty at the beginning of the Guyuk system. Because lack of meeting place and the Cell leaders were mostly women; at that time the social status of women was low; lay leaders did not recognize, did not trust the Cell system. But after the problem was solved, the Cell system of YFGC became famous internationally. Yong-Gi Cho called the Cell system "the smallest churches within the largest church."

---

147 International Theological Institute, *Yoido Sunbokumkyohoiui Songnyung Undong Ihe (Understanding the Holy Spirit Movement at Yoido Full Gospel Church)*, Seoul Logos, Seoul, 2001, 58-59; Yong-Gi Cho, *Kyohoi Songzang-ui Bikyul (Church Growth Secrets), Church Growth* vol. 2, Seoul Logos, Seoul, 1985, 14-28.

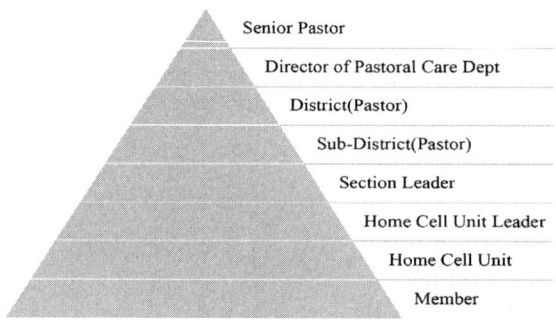

The structure of Guyuk *(Cell Group)*

The Guyuk (Home Cell Unit) is formed like this. Five to seven neighboring families form a Guyuk with its leader and assistant leader, who have a strong spirituality in this group. Five Guyuks form a Section (Jiyuk), 10-15 Sections form a Sub-District (Kyogu), 12-23 Sub-Districts form a District (Dai-Kyogu). Guyuk (Home Cell Unit) leaders and Section leaders are lay people, Sub-District leaders and District leaders are paid pastors. When the Guyuk grows to 10 families, it is divided into two Guyuks of five families each. The assistant leader of the original Guyuk becomes the leader of the new Guyuk. Each Guyuk has one assistant leader. This process repeats itself as the Guyuk grows. The focus of each Guyuk is adjusted according to the need of the Guyuk members. This group includes registered believers and those who will decide to become members of the church. During the Guyuk meeting they pray together for their new member, for the Baptism in the Holy Spirit, for their personal problem and healing.[148]

Guyuk worship uses "Guyuk Yebe Kongkwa (Guyuk Worship Guide)." Yong-Gi Cho defines "Worship is a spiritual sacrifice to God", and explains that "When we worship with God's spirit and truth, God is glorified and gives us blessings." The Guyuk worship lasts one hour, and its order is as follows: praise time, praise God, grace time, thanksgiving, fellowship of believers, closing.

Guyuk worship's order		
Division	Order	Time
Praise time	Hymns	
Praise God	Silence	2 minutes
	The Apostles' Creed	
	Hymns	7 minutes
	Representative prayer	
Grace time	Study the guidebook	30 minutes
	Corporate prayer	5 minutes
Thanksgiving	Offertory	2 minutes
	Offertory prayer	
Fellowship of believers	Title prayer for each other	13 minutes
	Introduce newcomer	
	Hymns	
Closing	Our Father	1 minute
		Total 60 minutes

---

148 Young-Hoon Lee, *The Holy Spirit Movement in Korea*, 106-107.

The "Guyuk Worship Guide (Guyuk Yebe Kongkwa)" has the detailed instructions to let the believers worship well every time: Guyuk worship's order, its successful operation method, how to use this guidebook. Each worship has a theme for worship, and it clearly states the Bible verse related to the theme, the hymn number and the biblical Word to be memorized, the goal of that worship. And there is a summary of the study contents to motivate and to understand better, and then the whole content of the study. The study is concluded with a time of 'Bible study', 'sharing and application.' Yong-Gi Cho suggests that the believers will read together the study contents, Bible study is to find out what they have studied that day. Sharing and application' is to make harmony between faith and action by living what they have learned. And he encourages the believers to recognize, welcome, invite and rely on the Holy Spirit to help and teach them in all this.

How to use the Guyuk Worship Guide
① First, find and read the "Word to read".
② Read together the "Word to memorize" three to five times aloud and memorize it.
③ Have a clear understanding of the goal.
④ Read together the material to be studied.
⑤ The Bible study is to review what you have studied that day.
⑥ "Sharing and applying" is to harmonize faith and action by living what you have studied. A desirable Guyuk Bible study is possible when you share each other and apply what you have learned and

experienced.

⑦ Acknowledge, welcome, invite and rely on the Holy Spirit to help and teach you.[149]

Yong-Gi Cho, says that a church leader is different from a world leader because the church leader has the Holy Spirit as a mentor, emphasizing that a successful leader is one who asks and answers everything to the Holy Spirit. Yong-Gi Cho explains seven attitudes of a pastor to have a successful Guyuk pastoral ministry:

①   Have a vision and assurance for Guyuk pastoral ministry.

②   Supervise thoroughly. The only way to have a successful Guyuk organization in the church is if it is used as an instrument of evangelism. And the pastor should directly supervise Guyuk as a key figure.[150]

③   Start small. Select 12 core lay leaders and train them to be Guyuk leaders. And then let them make their own Guyuk meeting and watch them carefully for 6~8 months. The huge organization also starts small in the beginning.

④   Choose a faithful Guyuk leader. To choose a proper lay leader is the key point of the Guyuk organization. Success or failure depends on them.[151] Therefore, they must learn from the pastor

---

149 Yong-Gi Cho, *Guyuk Yebe Kongkwa 14 (Guyuk Worship Guide)*, Seoul Logos, 2017, 6-8.
150 Yong-Gi Cho, *Himang Mokhwe 45 Nyun: Guyuk Sogrup Buheung Iyaki (45 years of Hope Ministries: Cell Group Revival Stories)*, 153, 176.

who is the leader and receive practical training so that they can communicate well the pastor's teaching to the Guyuk meeting.

⑤ Let them do pastoral ministry for one another. Believers should share their prayer requests with one another, encourage one another, and pray for one another. Because any gathering that is not connected by the circle of love will always have divisions, envy and jealousy will arise, and contradictions will arise that compete with each other rather than build each other up.

⑥ Ask Guyuk to evangelize. Find out non-Christian who can be invited to the Guyuk meeting. Because evangelism is like the veins through which Guyuk can supply true life to the church, and it is a core pastoral ministry of Guyuk.[152]

⑦ Yearn for the anointing of the Holy Spirit and develop commu nion with him. The secret of success is communion with the Holy Spirit. A leader pastor and the leaders of Guyuk, who are the lay leaders must be guided by the Holy Spirit and be filled with the Holy Spirit. And the leaders should have true communion with the Holy Spirit beyond the dimension of being filled and guided.[153]

Gwi-Sam Cho evaluates that Yong-Gi Cho used two kinds of lead-

---

[151] Yong-Gi Cho, *Himang Mokhwe 45 Nyun: Guyuk Sogrup Buheung Iyaki (45 years of Hope Ministries: Cell Group Revival Stories)*, 156.

[152] Yong-Gi Cho, *Himang Mokhwe 45 Nyun: Guyuk Sogrup Buheung Iyaki (45 years of Hope Ministries: Cell Group Revival Stories)*, 158-159.

[153] Yong-Gi Cho, *Himang Mokhwe 45 Nyun: Guyuk Sogrup Buheung Iyaki (45 years of Hope Ministries: Cell Group Revival Stories)*, 162.

ership in the process of church growth by training lay people to be pastoral workers. First, Transformational Leadership. This Leadership means that the leader increases immersion by sharing the vision of future with subordinates and motivating them to achieve the results beyond their original expectation. The other is Servant Leadership, where the leader serves as a servant.[154]

Yong-Gi Cho insists first of all that the requirements for a successful Guyuk are that the senior pastor should have a conviction about the necessity of Guyuk for his church. And he also affirms that many foundation works should be done before the organization is carried out. For example, a pastor, knowing the value of Cell group, told his co-pastor to start the Cell group in his church, but after two years the church stagnated. Yong-Gi Cho points out that the problem of this church came from the lack of active participation of the senior pastor. And he evaluates that the believers considered the Cell group as one of the many different programs of this church, not as the key to revival or a key to evangelism, because the motivation was not well done.

> A pastor of a large church in the USA saw the value of a Cell group (Guyuk) attending the seminar. But instead of directly running the Cell group by studying about the Cell group and trying hard, he gave all the responsibility to his co-pastor. This co-pastor organized everything and the Cell

---

[154] Gwi-Sam Cho, *Young Sanui Guyuk-Yeberul Tonghan Kyohoi-Songzang Yunku (A Study of Church Growth through Young San's Guyuk Worship)*, 295-296.

group was started. But after two years, that church became stagnated. The attendance rate was so terrible, and the believers were not motivated for evangelism. Because the believers considered the Cell group system as one of the many programs of this large church. They did not see the Cell group as a key to revival or a key to evangelism. At all, many other programs were aimed at the goals of the church growth. This pastor did not participate actively. That's why the believers felt that the Cell group couldn't be an important thing.[155]

Yong-Gi Cho clearly states that if the believers are not convinced that their senior pastor supports the formation of Guyuk, one of these three things will happen. Namely, Guyuk will be only for a fellowship meeting, there will be no true spiritual growth, no evangelism; become a formal meeting or fall under the influence of people's personalities; if the leaders of Guyuk do not report regularly to their senior pastor, Guyuk will become a cancerous presence in the community.

> First, the organization will get bogged down and start to stagnate. Guyuks will gather for a fellowship, there will be no true spiritual growth, no evangelism. As a result, there will be high possibility of stopover. Second, the meeting will be formal or Guyuk will fall under the influence of people's personalities. Eventually, Guyuks will become an organ-

---

[155] Yong-Gi Cho, *Himang Mokhwe 45 Nyun: Guyuk Sogrup Buheung Iyaki (45 years of Hope Ministries: Cell Group Revival Stories)*, 154.

ization that is unnecessary, meaningless and only harmful for the church. Third, if Guyuk leaders do not have to report regularly to the senior pastor, the Guyuk organization will become a cancerous presence in the community. ... If I do not give personal attention, the leaders of Guyuk will not be motivated.[156]

Yong-Gi Cho insists that if the implementation of the Guyuk organization fails, it will be because the senior pastor is not directly involved, and the organization without the senior pastor cannot motivate the believers at all. Therefore, Yong-Gi Cho presents seven principles to motivate lay people: recognize them; praise them; love them; pray for the preaching to be anointed; preach the good God and Christ's Atonement; Preach a sermon that fills a need; proclaim faith, hope and love.

① Recognize them
The church can regularly award a certificate to the leaders in various fields, including the leaders of Guyuk. This award shows that they are recognized and thanked. This really encourages them.

② Praise them
The best way to give motivation is to praise them by finding their merit. When we start praising their merits, they feel motivated to correct their shortcomings.

---

156 Yong-Gi Cho, *Himang Mokhwe 45 Nyun: Guyuk Sogrup Buheung Iyaki (45 years of Hope Ministries: Cell Group Revival Stories)*, 155.

③ Love them

Another motivating factor is true love.

④ Pray for the preaching to be anointed

Preaching, church growth and Guyuk revival are connected like a ring. The Pastor's sermon for the week should be the word of God to awaken the believers. But if the pastor's sermon is not anointed by the Holy Spirit, that sermon is just a theory.

⑤ Preach the good God, Atonement of Christ

The important mental attitude of the preacher is to start from the goodness of God. That is the most important theology. The faith and the theology of good God is vitality.

⑥ Preach a sermon that fills a need

If the preach touches their need and presents alternatives, although the church has no air conditioner or heating, they will come and listen. People are not interested in eloquence. They are only interested in their need to be satisfied.

⑦ Proclaim faith, hope and love

The pulpit is there to exalt the faithful and guide them to the path of righteousness. It is not good preaching to condemn the believers and to keep hitting them with moral theology. That is the easiest preaching. Put faith, hope and love into the hearts of the believers and lift them up before God. When a pastor recognizes, cheers up the believers and preaches a sermon anointed by the Holy Spirit, he can motivate them spiritually well.[157]

---

[157] Yong-Gi Cho, *Himang Mokhwe 45 Nyun: Guyuk Sogrup Buheung Iyaki (45 years*

Yong-Gi Cho presents some elements for church growth in the Fourth dimensional faith.

① Prayer

Prayer is truly the most powerful spiritual dynamic for church growth.

② Lay leadership

The pastor's role is to guide and teach the lay leaders and the Guyuk leaders. The church building alone is not the field of pastoral ministry. The church is only the place where the believers gather for worship and education. The real pastoral field is all the places outside the church: the family, the company, the factory, and wherever the feet of the believers arrive.

③ Woman's leadership

The use of women in leadership in the church is actually biblical and God's will. This is because God baptized and used both men and women, and the Holy Spirit broke down the barrier between men and women at Pentecost and gave them the Holy Spirit. Most of the Guyuk leaders of Yoido Full Gospel Church are women, and more than 70% of ministers are women.

④ Discipleship training and church growth

The spiritual faith of the Yong-Gi Cho's Fourth dimension is connected with church growth through the spiritual training of disciples.[158]

---

of Hope Ministries: Cell Group Revival Stories), 177-194.

158 Gwi-Sam Cho, *Young Sanui 4 Chawonui Yungzok-Sekewa Kyohoi Songzang (The Fourth Dimension in Dr. David Yonggi Cho's Ministry and Church Growth)*, in *Journal of Young San Theology*, vol. 12, Young San Theological Institute of Hansei

Through discipleship, Yong-Gi Cho has seen church growth through Guyuk worship. In Jewish society, disciple means those who take lessons to be guided by seniors to follow the traditional piety of rabbis who have religious authority and leadership, to learn the religious commandments and to apply Torah to their real lives.[159]

Gwi-Sam Cho, completing the "Study on Church Growth through Guyuk Worship of Pastor Yong-Gi Cho", concludes that his Guyuk worship has proven to be a precious pastoral work that solves the important problems: fellowship among believers, which is easily overlooked by megachurch, Bible study, evangelism to the neighborhood.[160]

2) The Small Community of the Catholic Archdiocese of Seoul

In order to compare the Guyuk worship of YFGC (Yoido Full Gospel Church) and the Small Community (Sokongdongche Moim) of the Catholic Church in Korea, the reality of the Catholic Archdiocese of Seoul will be presented as both are present in the same city. For a better understanding, before presenting the sit-

---

University, Gunpo, 2008, 109-112.

159 Gwi-Sam Cho, *Young Sanui Guyuk-Yeberul Tonghan Kyohoi Songzang Yunku (A Study of Church Growth through Young San's Guyuk Worship)*, 299.

160 Gwi-Sam Cho, *Young Sanui Guyuk-Yeberul Tonghan Kyohoi Songzang Yunku (A Study of Church Growth through Young San's Guyuk Worship)*, 304.

uation of the Catholic Archdiocese of Seoul, we will look at some general information about the Catholic Church in South Korea.

Most dioceses in South Korea have adopted the Small Community system as one of the new suitable method for the parish pastoral work.[161] Byeong-Soo Ko, a catholic priest, says the two reasons for this choice of Korea. The first is a realistic reason, and the second is the essential reason of the church. The bright side of reality is the increase in the number of newly baptized believers. But its dark shadow is the increase in those who do not attend Sunday Mass. According to him, one reason for this phenomenon is that the church is losing its charm as a church. He says that the charm of the church is to live the life of Jesus, namely the life of sharing and communion. Byeong-Soo Ko thinks that many believers do not attend Sunday Mass for this reason: "The church has become larger with so many believers, so they have rare opportunity to meet with the parish priest and with the other believers. Therefore, little by little, they lose their sense of belonging to the parish, eventually neglect the church losing the charm of faith.

Another reason, according to Byeong-Soo Ko is an essential aspect of the church. He insists that the fundamental reason for activating the Small Community is in line with the vision of the church, which is to build the reign of God. According to him, the reign of

---

[161] Woll-Ki Chung, *HanGuk Chonzukyohoi Sokongdongche Samok Balzonkwazong (The Pastoral Process involved in the Promotion of the Small Community in the Korean Catholic Church)*, Catholic University, M.A. Thesis in Systematic Theology, 2005, 129-141.

God is the reign where God is with us, where there is communion and care for each other, where there is no high and low, jealousy or division. Byeong-Soo Ko says that this is the essence of the church and the vision of the church, insisting that the primitive church is its original form. And he says that the Small Community is a specific plan to realize the vision of the church.[162]

Bishop U-Il Kang (Peter) of Jeju diocese at that time in 2002, affirms that the aim of vivifying the Small Community is to transform the church into a true "community of communion, fellowship, unity and sharing" according to the teaching of the Second Vatican Council. And he insists that this is to change the constitution of the church, furthermore to change the world inside and out, therefore it needs to have a long-term outlook strategy. Changing the constitution of the church, meant by bishop U-Il Kang is to be changed from a passive attitude to an active attitude that builds the church together, to an attitude of seeking God to meet with him, to an attitude of participation in order to satisfy hunger by sharing even small things. And it also means to be an apostle who actually cooperates in the liberation of the world from sin thanks for the help of God.[163]

It is difficult to pinpoint the exact place where the Ecclesial Basic Community first emerged. Joo-Hyun Ro believes, however, that the

---

[162] Byeong-Soo Ko, *Sokongdongche Ihehaki (Understanding Small Community)*, in *Nobundr Handimoyong*, Nohyung, Cheju, 2008, 15.

[163] U-Il KANG, *Kyuk-ryusa (L'Incoraggiamento)*, in Nobundr handimoyong, Nohyung, Cheju, 2008, 3.

most significant region was South America, where groups with the character of Ecclesial Basic Communities began to emerge in the late 1950s or early 1960s - groups in Brazil, Chile, Honduras, Panama and elsewhere - and soon spread throughout the South American continent.[164] It is known that Basic Community began in 1956 in the diocese of Barra do Pirai, in Rio de Janeiro, Brazil.[165] Starting with the Community Evangelization Movement of this diocese, the Basic Education Movement of Natal diocese, and the National Pastoral Programme of Brazil (1965~1970) was carried out, and the Ecclesial Basic Community Movement became official for the first time at a national level. Subsequently, through the Second General Conference of the CELAM (Episcopal Conference of Latin America) in Medellin in 1968, this movement was diffused throughout South America.[166] The bishops gathered in Medellin appreciated the role of the Ecclesial Basic Community, and affirmed that it is the primary cell of the ecclesial structure, the source of the evangelization, and the foundation for the realization and development of humanity.[167]

---

164 Joo-Hyun Ro, *Catholic Kyohoiui 'Sogongdongcheron' Yunku (A Study on 'theory of Small Christian Communities' of Catholic Church)*, Sogang University Master's Thesis Sogang University, Seoul, 2001, 18.

165 Leonardo Boff/Translated by Kwe-Sang Kim, *Seropke Tansenghanun Kyohio (The Church Reborn)*, Joseph, 1987, 15.

166 Joo-Hyun Ro, *Catholic Kyohoiui 'Sogongdongcheron' Yunku (A Study on 'theory of Small Christian Communities' of Catholic Church)*, 19.

167 Secretariado General De CELAM (Consejo Episcopal Latinoamericano), *Medellin Conclusiones*, Translated by Soo-Bok Kim·Yum Sung, Benedict Press, Waekwan, 1989, #10 of Chapter 15; Joo-Hyun Ro, *Catholic Kyohoiui 'Sogongdongcheron' Yunku (A Study on 'theory of Small Christian Communities' of Catholic Church)*, 12.

The bishops in Medellin urged to study more deeply the theological and sociological and historical character of the Ecclesial Basic Community and to exchange and coordinate its various experiences gained in the Ecclesial Basic Community through the Episcopal Conference of Latin America.[168]

The Second Vatican Council (1962~1965) presented the Church as the image of the Mystical Body of Christ, the people of God, and underlined unity and communion. Pope Paul VI, in his Apostolic Exhortation, the *Evangelii Nuntiandi*, said that Ecclesial Basic Communities will be a place of evangelization, for the benefit of the bigger communities, especially the individual Churches. If it meets the following conditions, they will be a hope for the universal Church. Namely, they need to avoid the very real danger of becoming isolated within themselves, remaining firmly attached to the local Church in which they are inserted, and to the universal church, believing themselves to be the only authentic Church of Christ, and condemning the other ecclesial communities; they maintain a sincere communion with the pastors whom the Lord gives to His Church, and with the magisterium which the Spirit of Christ has entrusted to these pastors; they constantly grow in missionary consciousness, fervor, commitment and zeal; they never look on themselves as the sole beneficiaries of sole agents of evangelization, or

---

168 Secretariado General De Celam (Consejo Episcopal Latinoamericano), *Medellin Conclusiones*, Translated by Soo-bok Kim/Yum Sung, Benedict Press, Waekwan, 1989, #10 of Chapter15; Joo-Hyun Ro, *Catholic Kyohoiui 'Sogongdongcheron' Yunku (A Study on 'theory of Small Christian Communities' of Catholic Church)*, 12.

even the only depositaries of the Gospel.[169]

Redemptoris Missio of Pope John Paul II (1990) emphasizes that Ecclesial Basic Communities are a sign of vitality within the Church, an instrument of formation and evangelization, and a solid starting point for a new society based on a "civilization of love." *Ecclesia in Asia* (1999), the Apostolic Exhortation of Pope John Paul II, affirms also that Ecclesial Basic Communities help the faithful to live as believing, praying and loving communities like the early Christians, and are a solid starting point for building a new society to express a civilization of love.[170]

The Korean Catholic Church brought the Small Community programme from the Lumko Institute. The Lumko Institute was established for mission in South Africa. Although Bishop Rosenthal claimed the need to establish a mission institute, the Catholic Biship's Conference of South Africa (CBCSA) did not accept it. So in 1962 he founded the Lumko Missiological Institute in his diocese. The name of the institute comes from the catholic family's name. A man, Lumko, donated his land to Bishop Rosenthal, and then the institute could be founded there, so the name of the institute was called Lumko Institute. In 1972, Lumko Institute became a Pastoral

---

169 Pope Paul VI, *Evangelii Nuntiandi*, #58.
170 Woll-Ki Chung, *HanGuk Chonzukyohoi Sokongdongche Samok Balzonkwazong (The Pastoral Process involved in the Promotion of the Small Community in the Korean Catholic Church)*, 32–33; Pope John Paul II, *Redemptoris Missio: Encyclical on the permanent validity of the Church's missionary mandate* (Dec. 7, 1990), #51; Pope JOHN PAUL II, *Ecclesia in Asia: Apostolic Exhortation* (1999), #25.

Research Institute under the Catholic Bishop's Conference of South Africa. Since 1976, Catholic Bishop's Conference of South Africa (CBCSA) has given priority to the building of the Small Community, understanding the mystery of the Incarnation as the basis of the Small Community. Priest Oswald Hirmer of Lumko Institute developed and diffused the simple way of Bible sharing known as the 'Seven steps.'[171]

Seven steps:
① Invite the Lord
② Read the Bible passage twice
③ Read three times the word or verse that touches each person's heart
④ Listen to the word of God in silence
⑤ Share the word that comes from the heart
⑥ Discuss an activity as a group
⑦ Pray spontaneously together

In 1990, the Fifth Plenary Assembly of FABC (Federation of Asian Bishop's Conferences) in Bandung, Indonesia defined that "A New way of being Church in Asia" is the "Communion of Communities." As one of the concrete way of realizing the "Communion of Communities", the pastoral model and programme of the Small Community of the Lumko Institute of the Republic of South Africa

---

[171] Joo-Hyun Ro, *Catholic Kyohoiui 'Sogongdongcheron' Yunku (A Study on 'theory of Small Christian Communities' of Catholic Church)*, 26-30.

were introduced, and Asian bishops positively evaluated this method.[172] Bishop Peter Kang (U-Il) of the Archdiocese of Seoul, who participated in the Bandung Assembly, sent four people who were priests and nuns to the one-month workshop of the Lumko Institute in Thailand. At the end of 1991, Oswald Hirmer (that time he was a priest), came to Korea and presented Lumko's programme of Small Community to members of the Priest Council in the Archdiocese of Seoul: the majority of the participants expressed a positive reception. Cardinal Stefano Kim (Soo-Whan) was with them from the beginning to the end of the meeting with pleasure. Cardinal Kim proposed to actively study on the introduction of the Lumko's program of Small Community, recognizing that this program is based on the Gospel and it expresses well the spirit of the Second Vatican Council.[173]

The Archdiocese of Seoul reaffirmed that evangelization and the activation of the Small Community, as proclaimed in the 1991 Pastoral Letter is the ultimate and essential goal of the Church; proclaimed 'the Evangelization of the 2000s' as a long-term pastoral plan for the 2000s through the 1992 Pastoral Letter. Through this pastoral letter, the Archdiocese of Seoul announced that it would

---

172 FABC, Fifth Plenary Assembly, *Final Statement: Journeying together toward the Third Millenium* (#8.1.1), July 17~27, 1990; Joo-Hyun Ro, *Catholic Kyohoiui 'Sogongdongcheron' Yunku (A Study on 'theory of Small Christian Communities' of Catholic Church)*, 35-36.

173 Woll-Ki Chung, *HanGuk Chonzukyohoi Sokongdongche Samok Balzonkwazong (The Pastoral Process involved in the Promotion of the Small Community in the Korean Catholic Church)*, 50.

implement its long-term pastoral plan, "Evangelization and Small Communities in the 2000s," in three phases of three years each, from 1992 to 2000.[174] The Bishop of Archdiocese of Seoul, then presented the pastoral goals and tasks for 1992~1994 and the organizational plan for the parish to effectively promote evangelization in the 2000s. He urged the parishes to use these as a basis and to implement them with flexibility and creativity according to the circumstances of each parish.[175]

The long-term effort to Small Community that began in Archdiocese of Seoul in the early 1990s has influenced other dioceses in Korea. The First National Meeting of the Small Community was held in 2001 under the title "The Pastoral Care with the Small Community", which was initiated by the Archdiocese of Seoul and the diocese of Masan with the same spirit, and the several dioceses joined together. It was a good opportunity for frontline priests, parish nuns and lay people to experience the community of the Church.

---

174 Catholic Archdiocese of Seoul, *Seoul Dekyogu Samok Kyoso (Pastoral Letter of Archidiocese of Seoul[1991~1992])*; Dong-Ghun KYUNG, *Kyohoi Zikmuwa Hanguk Chonzukyohoi-ui Zikmu-Ihe (Understanding Church Ministry and the Ministry of the Korean Catholic Church)*, Sogang University, 1998, 53; Woll-Ki Chung, *HanGuk Chonzukyohoi Sokongdongche Samok Balzonkwazong (The Pastoral Process involved in the Promotion of the Small Community in the Korean Catholic Church)*, 51.

175 Catholic Archdiocese of Seoul, *2000 Nyunde Bokumhwa Bondangzozike Kwanhayu ('On the Organisation of Evangelising Parishes in the 2000s)*, Official Documents of the Catholic Archdiocese of Seoul (1992. 4.30), prot No. 92-19; Woll-Ki Chung, *HanGuk Chonzukyohoi Sokongdongche Samok Balzonkwazong (The Pastoral Process involved in the Promotion of the Small Community in the Korean Catholic Church)*, 52.

The purpose of this meeting was to exchange and deepen pastoral experiences in order to promote Small Community in dioceses and parishes. On 23rd November 2001, the Commission for the Evangelization of the CBCK (Catholic Bishop's Conference of Korea), decided to support the exchange activities related to the pastoral care with the Small Community among the dioceses and the international solidarity activities; it established the Sub-Committee for the Small Community under the Commission for the Evangelization. The purpose of the Second National Meeting of Small Communities in 2002 was to provide a forum for the sharing of pastoral experiences, fellowship, and the exchange and deepening of research activities for the vitalization of Small Communities.[176]

The parishes of the Archdiocese of Seoul for a long time had an administrative structure in the name of Ban and Guyuk with their administrative leaders. Since 1992, Ban has been a Small Community with an average of 10~15 families. Guyuk is composed of several Bans.[177] In 1997, during the General Assembly of the priests of the Archdiocese of Seoul, there was a request to evaluate the difference between the experience of Guyuk and Ban meetings before 1991 and the experience of Guyuk and Ban meetings since the beginning

---

176 Woll-Ki Chung, *HanGuk Chonzukyohoi Sokongdongche Samok Balzonkwazong (The Pastoral Process involved in the Promotion of the Small Community in the Korean Catholic Church)*, 6-8.

177 Joo-Hyun Ro, *Catholic Kyohoiui 'Sogongdongcheron' Yunku (A Study on 'theory of Small Christian Communities' of Catholic Church)*, 101.

of the Small Community. In terms of evangelical transformation of the faithful, the priests verified that there was a change in perception of the Bible, a taste for the Gospel and a desire to live a Word-centered life. And in the aspect of lay people's participation in the Church, they verified that in general, the laity can actively participate in the Church's activity, although some faithful are too much involved in the pastoral activity and also the participation of whole parishners is lacking.[178]

Joo-Hyun Ro considers that one of the biggest results of the Seoul Archdiocese's "Evangelization through Small Community" since 1992 is the spread of a proper understanding of the lay ministry and a sense of mission.[179] The school for the Guyuk and Ban leaders to train them as lay leaders was established in 1993. Monthly training sessions for Guyuk and Ban leaders have included lectures on "community building and lay apostolate" as a consistent themes. Through this curriculum, the Guyuk and Ban leaders have been able to recognize the identity of the church as a community, and it is spread a comprehension that Guyuk and Ban is a basic community of the Church, not lower level administrative organization of the

---

[178] Catholic Archdiocese of Seoul, *Discussion Content of the Group Discussions at the 1997 Priestly Assembly (1997 Nyun Sazechonghwe Zobyultoron Naiyong)*, Chonzukyo Seoul Daikyogu Bokumhwa Samuguk (Secretariat for Evangelisation of the Catholic Archdiocese of Seoul), 1997; Joo-Hyun Ro, *Catholic Kyohoiui 'Sogongdongcheron' Yunku (A Study on 'theory of Small Christian Communities' of Catholic Church)*, 97.

[179] Joo-Hyun Ro, *Catholic Kyohoiui 'Sogongdongcheron' Yunku (A Study on 'theory of Small Christian Communities' of Catholic Church)*, 98.

parish.[180]

The Archdiocese of Seoul, while much has come to fruition, in the application of "Evangelization through the Small Community", has been much criticized in the process of establishing and carrying out a pastoral vision. It was also pointed out that there are both limitations and possibilities for the revitalization of Small Communities and the realization of a new ecclesial vision, namely a "community composed of Small Communities."[181] The model and the programme of the Small Community that the Korean Catholic Church tried was criticized because it was not researched and developed by the Korean Church, but the Archdiocese of Seoul imported it directly and used the method of South Africa without the indigenization process.[182]

Joo-Hyun Ro indicates two important factors that made it difficult to activate the Small Community. Firstly, the Archdiocese of Seoul could not lead out the consensus building of the priests and their voluntary participation and cooperation, because the pastoral plan of the diocese was pursued without enough time for an opinion-gathering process of the people and for the consensus building in the Archdiocese of Seoul. Secondly, when the pastoral policy of diocese is carried out at the parish level, the interest and will of

---

180 Joo-Hyun Ro, *Catholic Kyohoiui 'Sogongdongcheron' Yunku (A Study on 'theory of Small Christian Communities' of Catholic Church)*, 100.

181 Joo-Hyun Ro, *Catholic Kyohoiui 'Sogongdongcheron' Yunku (A Study on 'theory of Small Christian Communities' of Catholic Church)*, 103.

182 Joo-Hyun Ro, *Catholic Kyohoiui 'Sogongdongcheron' Yunku (A Study on 'theory of Small Christian Communities' of Catholic Church)*, 108.

the parish priest is the deciding factor. Therefore, the parish priest decides whether or not the parish promotes Small Communities, and the degree of its activation appears in different ways.[183]

The Archdiocese of Seoul asked to respond to the agenda of the group discussion at the General Assembly of the Priests in 1997: Since 1991 the diocese has made an effort to achieve evangelization through the Small Community, what is the reason that only a few parishes had a good result, while the expansion of the base is not yet taking place in the majority of parishes? For this the priests pointed out three aspects. Firstly, when the diocese established the pastoral policy the concrete reality of each parish was not considered. Second, there is lack of consistency in the pastoral direction of each parish according to the transfer of the parish priest.[184] Thirdly, a lack of willingness of the parish priests to follow the pastoral direction of the diocese, because the uniqueness and pastoral individuality of the parish priest himself are well diffused. The priests offered some suggestions to overcome these problems: firstly, have close encounters to build trust between the bishops and the priests; establish a window for mutual exchange and for collecting opinions about the pastoral activity going on in the diocese and in the parish.[185]

---

[183] Joo-Hyun Ro, *Catholic Kyohoiui 'Sogongdongcheron' Yunku (A Study on 'theory of Small Christian Communities' of Catholic Church)*, 105.

[184] The priests of Seoul Archdiocese transfer usually every 5 years, the assistant priests transfer every year or every two years.

[185] Woll-Ki Chung, *HanGuk Chonzukyohoi Sokongdongche Samok Balzonkwazong (The Pastoral Process involved in the Promotion of the Small Community in the Korean*

According to the "Report on Clergy Survey Results" for the Synod of Seoul Archdiocese in 2002, more than 80% of the priests recognized the relationship between the bishops and the priests as an official and formal relationship. And the absolute majority of priests (83.7%) expected the bishop to show respect and consideration for priests in his pastoral ministry. The reasons for priests' criticism, resistance and distrust on the pastoral direction of the diocese with "Evangelization through the Small Community" were no small part came from doubts about the justification or feasibility of the pastoral direction of the diocese, and also from the trial and error of the implementation process. And problems arising from the mistrust of the diocese, the identity of the priest and the pastoral role in the parish were also an important factor. Considering this situation, Wool-Ki Chung, a catholic priest, says that in order to overcome this problem, we need to establish the internal basic order of the church; establish the right relationship between unity and diversity based on the ecclesiology of 'communion.'[186] Especially, he insists on the need to strive to establish the principle of church structure and priests' identity. For this purpose, Wool-Ki Chung suggests that the distance between the bishop and the priests should be reduced by providing the opportunities for a roundtable or a priest's work-

---

Catholic Church), 151.

186 Catholic Archdiocese of Seoul, *Seoul Dekyogu Sinod: Songzikza Desang Solmunzosa Kyulkwabogoso (2002) (Synod of the Archdiocese of Seoul: Report on Clergy Survey Results[2002])*, 8; Woll-Ki Chung, *HanGuk Chonzukyohoi Sokongdongche Samok Balzonkwazong (The Pastoral Process involved in the Promotion of the Small Community in the Korean Catholic Church)*, 152.

shop to share pastoral issues with the bishop. He also suggests that they meet often, using the existing structure, such as the district superintendency system.[187]

Wool-Ki Chung points out that the obstacles in promoting the Small Community: the rejection of the unilateral execution of the bishop and the executioners who help the bishop; the lack of communication between the bishop and the parish priests; the sense of burden that the pastoral ministry of the Small Community gives to the priests. Therefore, Wool-Ki Chung emphasizes these three aspects:

The first is to maintain consistency regardless of the priest's transfer. Therefore, through the ongoing meetings, research, and piloting by parish priests and diocesan pastoral policy promoters, not only the Guyuk, Ban Small Community but also the whole parish pastoral system (Human and material resources, organization and structure) will be arranged in one direction. Secondly, they must study deeply the principle and theories of the Small Community. Therefore, they must strengthen the regular meetings of priests who are carrying forward the Small Community, and must activate the Research Committee of the Small Community under the National Committee of the Small Community's Pastoral Ministry. Thirdly, they need to study the pastoral system that connects the parish, the Small

---

187 Woll-Ki Chung, *HanGuk Chonzukyohoi Sokongdongche Samok Balzonkwazong (The Pastoral Process involved in the Promotion of the Small Community in the Korean Catholic Church)*, 153.

Community and the family, and to deepen the positive value that comes from the meeting between the Church and the world. Wool-Ki Chung suggests that, doing so, they can make the whole church participate in the mission to complete the reign of God, and recover the figure of the Church that bears witness to the figure of God and gives hope to the world.[188] There are some priests who are trying the Small Community meeting in the Archdiocese of Seoul. Here will be presented only on two cases of diocesan priests: Dure community of Father Won Jun and Sarangbang meeting of Father Jae-Ul Lee.

3) The Dure Community of Won Jun

The Catholic Archdiocese of Seoul held a synod with bishop's speech at the beginning of the 2000s. In the early days of the synod, the priests, who showed big interest in the synod, asked for the change and renewal of the organization of the diocese and its operation. They firstly pointed out the various problems of the oversized diocese and the church operation which is unreasonable in adapting to the times. Finally, the Bishop promulgated the Subsequent message of the Synod Bishop, which includes the contents that fully accept the proposals for the church operation. In 2007, Won Jun who was in charge of the Research Institute for

---

188 Woll-Ki Chung, HanGuk Chonzukyohoi Sokongdongche Samok Balzonkwazong (The Pastoral Process involved in the Promotion of the Small Community in the Korean Catholic Church), 165-166.

Integrated Pastoral Ministry of the Archdiocese of Seoul, presented a new form of pastoral structure to realize the outcome of synod. Won Jun says that the main purpose of changing the pastoral structure to administer the diocese and parish, is to realize the ecclesiology of communion, and the pastoral structure is an actual design.[189] He applied a new form, called Dure Community.

Won Jun, a parish priest of the Seoul Archdiocese's Jegi-dong, has been using the 'Dure Community', a pastoral model for a new form of parish structure since April 2009. Dure is a type of traditional agricultural organization. It expresses the unity of a village, which is a small community that gives and receives physical and communal help in farming. A Maul (Village) is made up of several Dures.

This is how Won Jun explains why he founded the Dure Community. According to Won Jun, the Second Vatican Council speaks of the people of God as the institutional Church and the community of communion. In the Korean Catholic Church, the centralized structure of diocese and the parish pastoral council have a subjective role in carrying out the parish ministry. Therefore, Won Jun points out that the participation of lay people is extremely limited, the leaders of Guyuk and Ban are only communicators of the lower transmission structure managed by the Guyuk section of parish pas-

---

[189] Won Jun, *Sinod Jungsine Tarun Kyogu mit Bondangkuzo (Diocesan and Parish Structures in the Spirit of the Synod), in Sinod Silchonul Wihan Hyunankwa Kwaze (Issues and Challenges for Synod Practice)*, Tonghap Samok Yunkuso, Seoul, 2007, 180.

toral council. Won Jun sees that present structure is far from the image of the church as a community of communion that the Second Vatican Council speaks of. That's why he presents this Dure, thinking that the Dure Community is more suitable for the pastoral ministry. Because he believes that the Dure Community forms the participation of God's people, a shared responsibility and a community of communion.[190]

The examples of Dure Community will be from Jegi-dong parish (2008~2013) and Dobongsan parish (2018~2021), where Won Jun served as pastor. The parishes of the Archdiocese of Seoul are usually divided into Guyuk and Ban, according to the district administration. Jegi-dong parish, where Won Jun executed the Dure Community, is also divided into Guyuk and Ban. But Won Jun replaced Guyuk with Dure, emphasizing the mutual cooperation of the Christian community with the aim of evangelization. Dure consists of five or six Bans, each Dure and each Ban has its administrative leader. A Ban is formed with twenty to thirty families, and each Ban has one or two groups of Malssumto, which means "place of the Word." The Malssumto, which has a meeting once a week, is composed of a leader with five to fifteen members. A leader of Ban can be a leader of Massumto, but the leader of Ban can also appoint another person as leader of Malssumto. When the members of Malssumto increase, another Malssumto is born with its spiritual leader.

---

190 Won Jun, *Sinod Jungsine Tarun Kyogu mit Bondangkuzo (Diocesan and Parish Structures in the Spirit of the Synod)*, 212.

In Jegi-dong parish there is also a pastoral council like in other parishes. What is different is that there are nine Dures under the pastoral council. Each Dure has a pastoral council and then the member of the parish pastoral council will be a leader of Dure pastoral council. The Dure pastoral council is a unique form of the Dure Community, this aspect is also different from the other forms of pastoral care attempted in Seoul Korea.[191] The parish priest receives all the information about Dure through the nine Dure leaders. The assistant priest is in charge of the youth, the parish nuns follow the pastoral programs and they are in charge of formation, counselling, visiting the poor and the sick. The leaders are entrusted for two years and participate in diocesan and parish education.[192]

Won Jun sees that the instrument of the community's unity is sharing, service, and communion, saying a new paradigm of the church. In particular, he emphasizes that the role of the leader is to take care of the Word centered church with service and sacrifice. Therefore, he insists that priests, parish nuns and all the parish leaders must look at the life of the parishioners with an attitude of service and sacrifice rather than all eyes in the parish being focused on the parish priest. In particular, he believes that the poor have an important place in pastoral care. Because he sees that if all the leaders in the parish share the pastoral attitude of the parish priest towards the poor, many problems of interrelationships in the parish can be

---

191 Won Jun, *Dure Gyuchik (Dure Rules)*, Jekidong Parish, Seoul, #6, Internet (Sept. 2012), http://jksd.org.

192 Won Jun, *Dure Gyuchik (Dure Rules)*, #9.

avoided and a spontaneous pastoral creativity can arrive.

The members of Dure go through four stages of formation. Using the books and materials produced by the pastoral center of Jegi-dong parish, they participate in the 'post-baptismal re-education' and the 'Bible study.' As a result, the attendance of the Sunday Mass has been increased: for example, in the weekly of Jegi-dong parish of 27, February of 2011, it is written that the 43.42% (1,098) of parishioners (2,529) attended the Sunday Mass, while according to the statistic of Catholic Church in Korea of 2009, the faithful who attended the Sunday Mass were the 25.6%.[193]

Won Jun used the book *Malssum Yuheng (Word Journey)* as the material for the Dure meeting, while running the Dure Community held in Dobongsan Parish of Seoul, in June 2021. Over the past few years, the Gospel sharing materials produced by Won Jun in Jegi-dong parish have been very helpful in activating the Small Community in several parishes. Based on this, a new text, *Malssum Yuheng (Word Journey)* is being published. This book is not studied at a desk, but it is finally written in a new way with revisions and modifications, using it in several parishes, observing the reaction of the faithful in the pastoral field, collecting the opinions of many people: in Jegi-dong parish and Dobongsan parish (Rev. Won Jun); Daebang-dong parish (Rev. Ki-Ju Park), Kwangjang-dong parish (Rev. Wool-ki Chung) and other parishes. This book has contributed to the devel-

---

193 CBCK, *Hanguk Chonzukyohoi Tongke 2009 (Statistics of the Catholic Church in Korea 2009)*, CBCK, Seoul, 2009, 34.

opment of Small Community, which are now bearing fruit in several parishes. Therefore, the text Malssum Yuheng will be introduced in more detail.

Malssum Yuheng (Word Journey)

The outstanding feature of this material is a Jesus-centered way of reading and meditating on the Gospel. Namely, the believers should look at the Bible text to see "with whom Jesus is building a relationship", "what Jesus is saying" and "how Jesus is acting." And the leader will focus on inviting them to meet and love Jesus by constantly asking "who Jesus is in this situation." As a result, many believers testify to a deeper encounter with the Lord and new eyes opened to Bible reading, by Jesus-centered reading and meditating on the Gospel. The experiences of the believers who used the *Malssum Yuheng* for more than a year were very positive:

① "In the past, the Word meditations lacked the unity between the Word and life, but through the *Malssum Yuheng*, there is the joy of living in small actions with different messages depending on the daily situation, expressing 'I love you!', 'I am sorry!'"

② "I experience Jesus coming alive for me in a concrete way, rather than the intellectual emphasis of Bible study or the superficial presentation of Jesus as 'Jesus of mercy' or 'Jesus of goodness.'"

③ "The *Malssum Yuheng* allows the believers, who are mainly listeners, to experience the encounter with Jesus as the protagonist, making the Mass a richer and more heartfelt time of grace leading to a happier life of faith."

④ "On the preacher's side, parishioners also find it easier to communicate with the preacher as they learn more about Jesus."

The characteristic of *Malssum Yuheng* that brings such a good response is to meet the Lord personally in the Word and to realize His wisdom through the Word, rather than to gain intellectual and speculative knowledge. However, if we approach the Gospel from a "self-centered" rather than a "Jesus-centered" perspective, we may fall into the habit of blaming ourselves for being a sinner, self-criticism, or blaming others because we do not live according to the Word of Jesus. As a result, we may live an unhappy religious life, looking at the dark side of ourselves. The Bible is not an ethics textbook. Therefore, the *Malssum Yuheng* leads believers to encounter grace and love, inviting them to the light of the Lord. And it has the characteristic of offering new vitality and joy to the believers, opening new eyes to look at the Gospel focusing on Jesus, not self-centered or ego-centered, and letting the believers deeply meet the Lord of forgiveness, love, healing and consolation in the Word.[194] Here is the way *Malssum Yuheng* is carried out.

① **Opening prayer**: Participants pray to invite the Lord spontaneously.

---

[194] Woll-Ki Chung, Won Jun, *Malssum Yuheng: Marko Bogum (Word Journey: Gospel of Mark)*, Hanguk-Tonghapsamok Center, 2019, 4–5.

— For example: "Lord, please come here and be with us."

② **Reading the Word**: Taking turns, the participants read aloud the whole chapter of the Gospel to be read that day, paragraph by paragraph, or by theme.

— For example: Each person slowly reads aloud a paragraph from the whole chapter 2 of Mark.

③ **Knowing and loving Jesus**: Choose a topic that speaks to your heart or interests you from the whole chapter 2 of Mark. And write down a Bible verse that corresponds to the given question.

— Questions: in your selected topic, "With whom Jesus is meeting? What does he say and do? What happens there?"

(It is necessary to answer Jesus as the Subject always.)

— E.g. Selected topic: "The Disciple and the Sabbath"

ⓐ Jesus is with disciples and Pharisees.

ⓑ Jesus said, "Have you never read what David did." ...

④ **Meditation**: (Stay for a while with a prayerful heart in silence.)

ⓐ In the chosen Word, pause to meditate on what mind Jesus has and who Jesus is (for 3-5minutes).

ⓑ Which sentence is newly realized in the Word?

ⓒ Meditate on where the Lord is inviting me through this Word (for 3-5 minutes).

⑤ **Sharing**: Listen to each other with a prayerful heart, and share the Word invited by the Lord and your personal meditation on it.

ⓐ What is the theme chosen and the Word founded?

ⓑ Jesus' words and actions, and the people and events he encounters.

ⓒ Share what you've been meditating on.

(What kind of heart Jesus had and who he was.)

ⓓ Where does the Lord want me to invite through this Word?

(During sharing, it is necessary to share who Jesus is and to keep Jesus as the Subject always.)

⑥ **Point out the important part**: When a facilitator asks the following question, the faithful find the passage and write it down or underline it. Then one person reads the passage aloud.

ⓐ "What did Jesus say to the paralytic?" (Mk 2: 5v, 11v)

ⓑ How does Jesus answer to this question: "Why does he eat with tax collectors and sinners?" (Mk 2: 17)

⑦ **Word of life**: Choose and write down a "Word of life" that will be deeply remembered in your heart and practiced for one week from among the Words given to you personally by the Lord. Announce to whom you want to transmit this Word.

⑧ **Closing Prayer**: More than two or three people will pray freely, giving thanks for the sharing of the day and asking for the grace they need.

This textbook says that we should choose one Gospel and meditate from the first chapter to the last chapter. It recommends that in a once-weekly meeting we should meditate on a whole chapter of the chosen Gospel. According to their experience, meeting once a month is less fruitful because it breaks the rhythm. If the participants meditate and deepen a favorite subtopic without meditating on the whole chapter, the other parts of the chapter may be neglected. Therefore, in the weekly meeting, a brief knowledge of the Bible and the supplementary part will be offered. For example, give a short explanation of 'synagogue' or 'Galilee' in a common sense line. And the knowledge of the Bible is also complemented by offering the commentary on the small part like what we see in the second chapter of Mark: "The healing of a Paralytic", "The Call of Levi and eating with tax collectors." Four to seven persons are in the meeting for an hour. If there are more, they are divided into two groups so that they have the opportunity to share more deeply.

Malssum Yuheng is to humbly know and learn about the Lord from the Word and to meet Him personally who has come in the Word. Therefore, it is very important to have an attitude of respect and listening to each other. Here are some questions to evaluate once a month to help you mature progress:

① Was there a 'Jesus-centered' sharing rather than a "me-centered" sharing?
② Was there an atmosphere of silence and appropriate time to Meditate well on the Word according to the leading of the Holy Spirit?
③ Did we respect and listen to each other's sharing?
④ Have we been considerate enough to allow all members to participate in sharing?
⑤ Did I try to teach others or speak too much alone?
⑥ Did I tend to interrupt, deny others' words, or contribute to the

discussion?

⑦ Did the sharing turn into a chat or a story that had nothing to do with the Bible?

⑧ Was there a time to share what you wanted to share personally after *Malssum Yuheng*?

4) The Sarangbang Meeting of Jae-Ul Lee

Jae-Ul Lee, Catholic priest of the Archdiocese of Seoul. Since 2006 he has been experimenting in his parish with the *Sarangbang Meeting*, which has the structure of a Small Community. The Archdiocese of Seoul runs the Small Community meeting. Jae-Ul Lee used the diocesan Small Community meeting and the *Sarangbang Meeting* together as the basic structure of the parish. Jae-Ul Lee calls it *Sarangbang* to symbolize a room for conversation with love and the fellowship of Christians. *Sarangbang* is oriented towards a holy, healthy and strong spiritual family. And this is a spiritual family as a community of the Lord that produces the saints who are spiritually healthy. In this family, the members are strengthened, encouraged, and matured through the giving and receiving of recovery, healing, spiritual support, and love.

Jae-Ul Lee had a motivation to start the *Sarangbang Meeting*. He felt a strong thirst for effective evangelization because he was going through pastoral immaturity, limitation, trial and error, while he was constantly trying hard for a better pastoral ministry. During this time, he happened to find a book on Cell church. This book was written by a Korean protestant pastor who had been leading the person-centered Cell church for decades. Jae-Ul Lee confesses that he found the value and vision of a new mission in this book.[195]

Jae-Ul Lee started the *Sarangbang Meeting* with the thought that all classes and generation of modern society and people of many fields must ultimately build a ecclesial community together. Most people today spend more time outside than inside the house, so it is not easy to form only one type of Small Community.[196] Modern people meet differently according to their cultural level, lifestyle, age and generation. This phenomenon can sometimes be seen also in the Small Community meeting of the church: new members find some difficult situation to be with the group together.[197] Jae-Ul Lee sees that the loneliness felt by modern people needs a spiritual community or family, and the *Sarangbang meeting* as ecclesial community can give some help to all the participants. In reality, he experiences that spiritual difficulties or sufferings are healed and recovered in the *Sarangbang meeting*.[198]

Sarangbang has three visions: the personal vision, the Gospel vision, and the mission vision. **The personal vision** reveals the value of each

---

195 Jae-Ul Lee, Sarangbang Sogongdongche (Sarangbang Small Community), Catholicbook, Seoul, 2008, 10-11.
196 Jae-Ul Lee, Sarangbang Kyohoiwa Moimunyung (Sarangbang Church and Running Meetings), Bitkwa Sogum, Seoul, 2009, 29.
197 Jae-Ul Lee, Sarangbang Sogongdongche (Sarangbang Small Community), 7-8.
198 Jae-Ul Lee, Sarangbang Sogongdongche (Sarangbang Small Community), 10.

person and their life through reflection, fellowship, and sharing. In Gospel vision there is Bible reading, reflection, contemplation and dialogue; learning how to listen to the Word and live with each member of the community. In the mission vision, prepare the concrete way of evangelization for community and neighbor, and present three ways (Evangelism plan, Meeting with the evangelism target, Train workers). The Bible is a necessary instrument of salvation for all Christian. Therefore, Word sharing of *Sarangbang* is for the time of Gospel vision. During this time, Bible content and the Bible-centered conversation are essential.[199]

Sarangbang has three core leaders: leader, vice leader and treasurer. When a *Sarangbang* becomes big, it is divided into two *Sarangbangs*. Before a new *Sarangbang* coming out, there must also be three core leaders: reserve leader, reserve vice leader, reserve treasurer. These three persons will lead the new *Sarangbang* group. The existing leader reports to the main leader, who reports to the parish priest about the leader groups and the situation of the *Sarangbang* group. The parish priest interviews the leader groups and provides encouragement and support.[200]

In 2006, Jae-Ul Lee started *Sarangbang* meeting with 12 selected leaders. This meeting forms a *Sarangbang* with their leader and four or five people who have common aspects: age, interest, situation,

---

[199] Jae-Ul Lee, *Sarangbang MalsumNanuki (Sharing of the Word in Sarangbang)*,Catholicbook, Seoul, 2009, 4.

[200] Jae-Ul Lee, *Sarangbang Kyohoiwa Moimunyung (Sarangbang Church and Running Meetings)*, 115.

cultural education benefits. It is a weekly meeting of about 80 minutes. Seven to eight *Sarangbangs* form a Maul, that means village, with a leader. Twice a month there is a training course for the leaders, led by the parish priest and by parish sister. Sometimes the leaders of the Small Community are also the leaders of the *Sarangbang*. But the faithful can choose to belong to either the Small Community or *Sarangbang*. The method and books of the Small Community are different from those of the *Sarangbang* Meeting. The parish priest meets the core leaders every month to form new *Sarangbang* groups and to manage and guide the existing group of leaders. And he makes them know that they are God's workers and encourages them by meeting new leaders of *Sarangbang*.[201]

Jae-Ul Lee sees that although there are 12 parishes are experimenting with the *Sarangbang* method, their growth is very slow. He gives two reasons for this. One is that the parish priest does not consider *Sarangbang* as a fundamental cell of the parish structure, but sees *Sarangbang* together with Small Community as one of the several parish groups. Another is that the parish priest lacks the will to renew his role and function of shepherd by running or participating directly in the basic *Sarangbang* meeting; at the same time, lacks a deep understanding of the actual situation and the ecological environment of other leaders.[202] On the contrary, in the case of Naksongdaedong parish, where Jae-Ul Lee started the *Sarangbang*

---

[201] Jae-Ul Lee, *Sarangbang Sogongdongche (Sarangbang Small Community)*, 190.
[202] Jae-Ul Lee, *Sarangbang Sogongdongche (Sarangbang Small Community)*, 180.

meeting, it can be seen that *Sarangbang* meeting had a great positive impact on the work of the parish: in the weekly of 20 December 2009, 67.4% of the faithful (599 out of 889 parishioners) attended to the Sunday Mass.

Hye-Chong Yun, a Salesian Sister of Don Bosco, has been leading *Sarangbang* meeting of Jae-Ul Lee in different places, not in the parish since 2011. Hye-Chong Yun emphasizes that the Gospel sharing of *Sarangbang* is to speak from heart-to-heart, not to share thoughts. The fruits of the heart-to-heart meeting under the guidance of Hye-Chong Yun can be seen in many places such as the family and the school. In the beginning of the family *Sarangbang* meeting, there were some difficulties due to the habit of not expressing feelings between parents and children, but as time goes by, this aspect has been overcome. Now they are experiencing a very joyful and blessed family church celebrating the holy Sunday. The *Sarangbang* meeting is used in the kindergarten and in the school. Namely, a small faith community has been formed within preschool's mothers and is self-sustaining. On this occasion, the mothers who did not attend Sunday Mass are back in church.

In schools, it became an educational field of empathy and communication, by expanding to "Torae *Sarangbang* (Peer *Sarangbang*)", which consists only of students, and "Parents *Sarangbang*", by registering as an official club meeting. Above all, it has helped students, parents, and teachers to trust each other and build a loving relationship. It is also a good example for frontline education sites that are currently struggling with school violence. Hye-Chong Yun says that by continuing the special class in the school, she has gained confidence that we can lead the students to the light even "outside" of the Church through the *Sarangbang* meeting. And she testifies that the *Sarangbang* meeting can help and satisfy the spiritual thirst of the office workers and the poor youth as a guide to the right faith.

Hye-Chong Yun affirms that what we need to work hard on is first of all to increase the number of Word leaders for the development of the *Sarangbang* meeting. One positive aspect is that the training period for *Sarangbang* leaders is usually shorter than other courses. Hye-Chong Yun sees a need for 'Guides' that meet the needs of different ages, professions, and classis by differentiating training methods and duration. And she expects that the scope and members of *Sarangbang* meeting will be expanded with the '*Sarangbang Meeting Pastoral Team*', which has a systematic organization composed of priests, nuns and lay people together. In particular, '*School Saragbang*' will be spread more in many schools as a tool for prevention education especially for the students who cause problems in school life. Hye-Chong Yun emphasizes the need to revitalize their own meetings by training lay leaders for the *Sarangbang* meeting in the parish and in the family, because it is necessary to overcome the difficulties caused by parish priest turnover.

We will look at the Seven steps of the basic order of the *Saragbang* meeting and its leader.

The Basic Order of the *Sarangbang* meeting[203]		
1. Hymn		Sing lively with a heart of praise and worship.
2. Opening Prayer		Pray that the Lord will guid this meeting from beginning to end, asking for spiritual grace.
3. Fellowship		① Remember the person, the event, the experience in the past, and sometimes have a deep inner reflection. ② After seeing how the Lord has worked in me, in us, in the community, share for 3-5 minutes per person.
4. Prayer of Praise and thanksgiving		Two or three people pray freely with the joy and gratitude of fellowship.
5. Bible Contemplation and Discussion	1) Bible reading	Read 1-2 verses in turn to be enlightened by the light of reason on the meaning of the Word of God.
	2) Peruse the Bible	Concentrate on the biblical Word that gives me inner inspiration under the guidance of the Holy Spirit. (This Word is the Word of the Lord to me, and is the content to be contemplated in the next step)
	3) Dialogue with Jesus (Contemplation)	① Ask a question with the content of the Word to be contemplated, believing in the presence of the Risen Jesus. (Jesus, why are you speaking this Word to me? What and how do you want me to live?) ② Listen to the answer to the question. (The

		answer is the content of the common good in practice: love, justice, conversion, forgiveness, proclamation of the Gospel)
	4) Sharing the Word	Each person shares the answer received from Jesus or the message that touches the heart and will be practiced. (The contents of the sharing is related to my concrete action and event in the church, family, school, office, other community)
	5) Bible Commentary	Explain a selected phrase or passage in relation to the teaching of the church.
	6) Topic Discussion	The leader or guide prepares the topic to be discussed from the biblical message beforehand. (Discuss a topic related to personal or community faith, mission, service, renewal of life)
6. Vision Sharing		Present a vision about believers, non-Christians, those who do not attend Sunday Mass, the spiritually or physically wounded person, formation for leadership group, breeding and doubling of *Sarangbang*, organization operation; and prepare mission plan for the week.
7. Group Prayer		① Write the details of each week's prayer in the personal prayer booklet. ② Pray for each other. ③ Pray for those who are absent from the

	meeting and for those who will come in the future. ④ Experience the Lord's work through prayer.

The *Sarangbang* meeting begins with a heartfelt **Hymn** of praise and worship. The **Opening Prayer** is to ask the Lord to accompany this meeting from beginning to end and to give spiritual grace. In the time of **Fellowship**, each member shares with others the things that have been remembered and organized about all the various works and events of the past week. It is to observe the Lord's help and guidance through the people they meet in these events. Therefore, each member prays for their own partner whom they met and blesses them. In this way, members usually receive the comfort and encouragement of the Lord and spiritual enlightenment. The time of Fellowship is a time to share interest and care for one another.

In the **Bible Contemplation**, each person asks a question to the Risen Lord Jesus and listens to Him inwardly believing that He is present before them. Jae-Ul Lee affirms that in this moment it is necessary to connect the Word with the past events. Pray, "Lord, make me aware of past events, happenings, encounters, and experiences that relate to this Word; help me to remember them" and then listen

---

203 Jae-Ul Lee, *Sarangbang Sogongdongche (Sarangbang Small Community)*, 230-233.

to Him again. After the question and answer, everyone can ask the Lord questions to apply the grace of the experience of the work or event to life: "Lord, when, where, to whom, and in what way should I apply and live out this Word?"

The **Word Sharing** must be a sharing directed to the evangelizing life of the individual and of the community. While the time of fellowship is centered on sharing and thanksgiving, consolation and joy as a time of reflection on life, the Word Sharing during the time of Contemplation is the time for sharing to live the Gospel with the Gospel perspective. Namely, it is a sharing about being a disciple of Jesus Christ and centering my life on the values and actions of the Gospel.[204]

Sarangbang Bible study is not a meeting to study theological theory or knowledge. The leader who leads the Bible study is not a teacher who transmits the knowledge; he is a guide who seeks and searches for truth by meditating and contemplating God's Word together. Therefore, the **Bible Commentary** must make people know and love Jesus more; communicate his saving work in a living way and from the perspective of their faith development, growth, and Gospel practice at the level of the members. The **Topic of Discussion** must be what is presented by the needs of the group members, and it is for the real change and renewal of the community.[205]

The time of **Group Prayer** is the time to experience the love and

---

[204] Jae-Ul Lee, *Sarangbang Sogongdongche (Sarangbang Small Community)*, 204–217.
[205] Jae-Ul Lee, *Sarangbang Sogongdongche (Sarangbang Small Community)*, 218–223.

unity of the community. Take turns praying. When members pray for each other, they receive hope, comfort, courage and strength from the prayers of others. When they pray for the other person with specific intention, they can pray more steadfastly and experience the grace of prayer. Therefore, the leader asks the members to write down each other's prayer intentions by passing around the prayer booklet during the meeting. They are more encouraged from praying for the person next to them than from praying for themselves.

Jae-Ul Lee emphasizes praying in the fullness of the Holy Spirit's guidance and flow, because *Sarangbang* prayer focuses on Gospel practice and discipleship after the meeting. Therefore, after group prayer, there is often a time to listen to the Word of the Lord. Listening to what the Lord is saying to the community is intended to make the meeting spiritual and the Lord's community. This method is: 1) all the members take turns to pray out loud; 2) the leader will invite silence for a while; 3) During the silence, if a man (or a woman) feels the need to share the Word that has touched him, he can proclaim it; 4) the members give thank for the proclaimed Word and end the prayer with Our Father, Hail Mary, Glory Be. Each member prepares a Prayer notebook and writes down every week the content of the prayer and experiences the mercy and love of God who fulfills personal desires. One person writes down all the contents of the meeting in the meeting minutes: names of the participants, the main points of sharing, Gospel theme, mission discussion, decision for the next meeting.²⁰⁶

Jae-Ul Lee underlines the formation of leaders to save the lost souls by considering the leaders of the *Sarangbang* meeting as shepherds. According to Jae-Ul Lee, a leader should be above all a prayerful person who participates in the holy liturgy and sacraments; a pastor who leads the community to communication among the members, and to the relationship of communion and sharing. And a leader prays beforehand for the meeting, visits members before the meeting to encourage them, talks to them and then brings them to the *Sarangbang* meeting.²⁰⁷

The people the leader will encounter are those who are hurting and hurting, those who don't know God or are new to the church, those who are tired of spiritual darkness or are leaving church, and those who are believers. Jae-Ul Lee suggests the following ways and procedures for leaders to meet with them:

① When the person is chosen, firstly begin to pray and dialogue with the Lord, offering this person to the Lord.

② Look at Jesus who is in this person whom a leader will meet, meditate deeply on the Word and have enlightenment on that Word.

③ Ask Jesus, who is present in this person, to make contact with

---

206 Jae-Ul Lee, *Sarangbang Sogongdongche (Sarangbang Small Community)*, 224-226.
207 Jae-Ul Lee, *Sarangbang Sogongdongche (Sarangbang Small Community)*, 79.

the leader himself and then spend time listening to what Jesus wants to say.

④ When the leader meets the person with the appointment, firstly listen to the person. This is to help the person recover from past pain and suffering, fear and conflict.

⑤ Invite the person to the *Sarangbang* meeting. The leader communicates that the *Sarangbang* meeting is no-pressure gathering, but to share feelings of loneliness and solitude, and to energize life through community fellowship.

⑥ Present the method and program of the *Sarangbang* meeting.[208]

4. Conclusion

1) Spirituality of the Fourth dimension

The Fourth dimension theory insisted by Yong-Gi Cho is an essential part of his spirituality, and he presents geometrically that the higher dimension includes and dominates the lower dimension. Yong-Gi Cho sees man as a cubic being, belonging to the Three dimensional world and at the same time to the Fourth dimension; the change of the Fourth dimension necessarily changes also our life, which is in the Three dimension. Yong-Gi Cho affirms that the change of the Fourth dimension depends on how we do the pro-

---

208 Jae-Ul Lee, *Sarangbang Sogongdongche (Sarangbang Small Community)*, 151-155.

gramming of the four elements (thought, faith, dream and word) that compose the Fourth dimension. Yong-Gi Cho understands that there are Fourth dimensional beings: God, man and Satan; man is in the lowest, Satan is in the middle and God is in the highest of the Fourth dimension. Since the Three dimensional world to which we belong, is dominated by Satan, who belongs to the Fourth dimensional world, it is important to win the spiritual war against Satan so that the Three dimensional world will be ruled by the God's sovereignty. Therefore, he emphasizes the discipline of the spirituality of the Fourth dimension, dealing with thought, faith, dream and word. Like this, Yong-Gi Cho explains the existence and activity of Satan with the Fourth dimension theory. But the Catholic Church teaches that Satan or the devil and the other demons are fallen angels who have freely refused to serve God and His plan. Their choice against God is definitive. They try to involve man in their rebellion against God.[209] Therefore, Yong-Gi Cho explains Satan differently, but there is a common aspect to recognize the existence of Satan.

For Yong-Gi Cho, it is very important that God created Adam on God's Sabbath day. Because he sees that Adam was not created to work, but to live for the glory of God, and to rest in God. According to him, God's purpose in creating man is to communicate with man, to make man enjoy the abundant glory of God. And here we see the key words of his pneumatological anthropology: 'dominate', 'rest in God', 'enjoy.' It seems that God and all his creatures exist

---

209 *Catechismus Catholicae Ecclesiale*, #414.

only for man. Therefore, his theology gives the impression of being man-centered, giving less importance to the interrelationship with other creatures.

The catechism of the Catholic Church speaks of the solidarity between the creation of man and all creatures. It teaches that human beings are the culmination of the work of creation, and that the creation story reveals this fact by clearly distinguishing human creation from the creation of other creatures. But it explains that there is a solidarity among all creatures, arising from the fact that all have the same Creator and are all ordered to his glory.[210] And according to this, the 'mastery' over the world that God offered man from the beginning was realized above all in man himself: the mastery of the self. It teaches that the first man was unimpaired and ordered in his whole being because he was free from the triple concupiscence that subjugates him to the pleasures of the senses, covetousness for earthly goods, and self-assertion, contrary to the dictates of reason.[211]

Yong-Gi Cho teaches that the Holy Spirit constantly gives man dreams and visions, which are the language of the Fourth dimension, so that man can creatively dominate the Three dimensional world. He says that man can recover the image of God and rule all things and secure original position of man through the Holy Spirit.

The Catholic Church teaches, in the light of the New Testament

---

[210] *Catechismus Catholicae Ecclesiale,* #343-344.
[211] *Catechismus Catholicae Ecclesiale,* #377.

and Tradition, that Adam and Eve were constituted in an original "state of holiness and justice." This grace of original holiness was "to share in divine life." By the radiance of this grace all dimensions of man's life were confirmed. As long as he remained in the divine intimacy, man would not have to suffer or die. The inner harmony of the human person, the harmony between man and woman, and finally the harmony between the first couple and all creation, comprised the state called "original justice."[212] According to the Catholic Church, Adam and Eve transmitted to their descendants a human nature wounded by their own first sin and hence deprived of original holiness and justice; this deprivation is called "original sin."[213]

The catechism of the Catholic Church says that man is "the only creature on earth that God has willed for himself", and man alone is called to share, by knowledge and love, in God's own life; it was for this end that he was created, and this is the fundamental reason for his dignity. The Catholic Church emphasizes that the human individual possesses the dignity of a person. And man is capable of self-knowledge, of self-possession and of freely giving himself and entering into communion with other persons.[214] Thus we can see that the Catholic Church emphasizes man himself, but also the relationship with other persons and with all creatures.

In his encyclical *Laudato Si'*, Pope Francis explains the word 'dominion' in the book of Genesis as follows. The story of creation

---

212 *Catechismus Catholicae Ecclesiale*, #375-376.
213 *Catechismus Catholicae Ecclesiale*, #417.
214 *Catechismus Catholicae Ecclesiale*, #356-357.

in Genesis suggests that human life is fundamentally based on three intertertwined relationships: with God, with our neighbor, and with the earth. According to the encyclical, these relationships have been disrupted by human beings who see themselves as taking God's place and fail to recognize our limitations as creatures.

> The creation accounts in the Book of Genesis contain, in their own symbolic and narrative language, profound teachings about human existence and its historical reality. They suggest that human life is grounded in three fundamental and closely intertwined relationships: with God, with our neighbor and with the earth itself. According to the Bible, these three vital relationships have been broken, both outwardly and within us. This rupture is sin. The harmony between the Creator, humanity and creation as a whole was disrupted by our presuming to take the place of God and refusing to acknowledge our creaturely limitations.[215]

The Pope's encyclical, *Laudato Si'*, explains that although it is true that we Christians have at times incorrectly interpreted the Scripture, this is how we interpret it today. Namely, what is written in Gen 1, 26v and 28v, that we are created in the image of God and given dominion over the earth, does not justify absolute domination over other creatures. And Gen 2:15 tells us that man is to "till and keep" the garden of the world. 'Tilling' means cultivating, ploughing or

---

[215] Pope Francis, *Laudato Si': Encyclical Letter on Care for Our Common Home* (May 24, 2015), #66.

working, while 'keeping' means caring, protecting, overseeing and preserving. This implies a relationship of mutual responsibility between human beings and nature. Each community can take from the bounty of the earth whatever it needs for subsistence, but it also has the duty to protect the earth and to ensure its fruitfulness for coming generations. *Laudato Si'* emphasizes that the earth with all that is within it (Dt 10:14), belongs to God, and that man is a stranger and sojourner with God (Lev 25:23).

> Judeo-Christian thinking, on the basis of the Genesis account which grants man 'dominion' over the earth (*Gen* 1:28), has encouraged the unbridled exploitation of nature by painting him as domineering and destructive by nature. This is not a correct interpretation of the Bible as understood by the Church. Although it is true that we Christians have at times incorrectly interpreted the Scriptures, nowadays we must forcefully reject the notion that our being created in God's image and given dominion over the earth justifies absolute domination over other creatures. The biblical texts are to be read in their context, with an appropriate hermeneutic, recognizing that they tell us to "till and keep" the garden of the world (*Gen* 2:15). 'Tilling' refers to cultivating, ploughing or working, while 'keeping' means caring, protecting, overseeing and preserving. This implies a relationship of mutual responsibility between human beings and nature. Each community can take from the bounty of the earth whatever it needs for subsistence, but it also has the duty to protect the earth and to ensure its fruitfulness for coming generations. "The earth is the Lord's" (*Ps* 24:1); to him belongs "the earth with all

that is within it" (*Dt* 10:14). Thus, God rejects every claim to absolute ownership: "The land shall not be sold in perpetuity, for the land is mine; for you are strangers and sojourners with me." (*Lev* 25:23)[216]

The *Laudato Si'*, states that the catechism of the Catholic Church clearly and forcefully criticizes a distorted anthropocentrism. And it affirms that an inadequate presentation of Christian anthropology has led to a wrong understanding of the relationship between human beings and the world; human being's dominion over the universe should be more properly understood in the sense of responsible stewardship. And it emphasizes that human being's role is as a cooperator with God in the work of creation, but not to take God's place.

> Where other creatures are concerned, we can speak of the priority of *being* over that of *being useful*. The Catechism clearly and forcefully criticizes a distorted anthropocentrism: "Each creature possesses its own particular goodness and perfection ... Each of the various creatures, willed in its own being, reflects in its own way a ray of God's infinite wisdom and goodness. Man must therefore respect the particular goodness of every creature, to avoid any disordered use of things."[217]
> An inadequate presentation of Christian anthropology gave rise to a wrong understanding of the relationship between human beings and

---

[216] Pope Francis, *Laudato Si'*, #67.
[217] Pope Francis, *Laudato Si'*, #69.

the world. ... Instead, our 'dominion' over the universe should be understood more properly in the sense of responsible stewardship.

Once the human being declares independence from reality and behaves with absolute dominion, the very foundations of our life begin to crumble, for "instead of carrying out his role as a cooperator with God in the work of creation, man sets himself up in place of God and thus ends up provoking a rebellion on the part of nature."[218]

Yong-Gi Cho says that man is created in the image of God, and consists of spirit, soul and body; the spirit is a bowl to welcome God, the soul is a bowl to put oneself, the body is a bowl to put the world. But the catechism of the Catholic Church teaches that the human person, created in the image of God, is a being at once corporeal and spiritual; every spiritual soul does not perish when it separates from the body at death, and it will be reunited with the body at the final Resurrection.[219] Therefore, it is a common aspect that man is created in the image of God; but there is a difference because Yong-Gi Cho sees that man is consisted of spirit, soul and body, while the Catholic Church teaches that man is with soul and body. Yong-Gi Cho affirms that man is created to rest in God and to live for the glory of God; he explains 'dominate' in a human-centered way. The interpretation of Yong-Gi Cho is very different from today's Catholic Church, which explains 'dominate' in terms of solid-

---

218 Pope Francis, *Laudato Si'*, #116-117.
219 *Catechismus Catholicae Ecclesiale*, #362, 366.

arity between creation of man and all creatures. The main cause of environmental destruction comes from the human-centered understanding and development of nature; as a result, the whole world now suffers from Covid 19, weather changes and natural disasters. Therefore, I think that a human-centered understanding of creation is an aspect of Christian theology that is actually lacking in a theology that emphasizes neighborly love.

2) Thought

According to Yong-Gi Cho, thought affects emotion, action, and the body's reaction. Because thought belongs to the Fourth dimension, it can change and lead the Three dimensional world. Therefore, he insists that we need to change our thinking before we change our action, because negative thinking negatively affects all the elements of the Three dimension. But he affirms that unconditional optimism is human thinking and it does not solve all problems. Therefore, Yong-Gi Cho suggests that we should resemble God's thought, and to have a thought that is in God's sovereignty, not our own thought; we will inspect and examine our proper thought, repent and read the Bible regularly, meditate on the Word while having a dialogue with God.

Yong-Gi Cho says that depending on whether we think of a good God or a scary God who scolds and judges, our lives changes very differently. And he suggests to have active thinking with the way of thinking of "can do", together with "thinking bigger and thinking wider." This is because if we think small, we will in reality produce small fruit, and if we think big, we will most likely produce big fruit. He emphasizes that bloody prayer and devotion, research and effort are necessary to make that thought grow in reality.

Therefore, it is important to live a life of sanctification striving to make the thought of Christ one's own thought, living a Bible-centered life and following the sovereignty of a good God. Yong-Gi Cho's view of thought could be helpful in the process of Christification and Sanctification in the spiritual life: "I live, no longer I, but Christ lives in me." (Gal 2:20) Positive thinking can give hope to those who are depressed for many reasons. The more he remains closed and narrow-minded thoughts, the more he is preoccupied with gloomy thoughts, the more he will fall into the pit of depression. But in the moment he realizes that the world he sees now is only very small part of his real world, he can see a small light of hope. Because if he turns the direction towards positive thinking, he can see a big and wide world and can have a positive vision and hope.

3) Faith

Yong-Gi Cho defines faith in different ways. Firstly, he expresses that the true faith is to believe in God who performs a miracle. And he defines that faith as a reality of the heart, invisible to the physical eye, and the ability to make the will and mind of God a reality. He emphasizes that we have to see a reality of what we cannot see, with the eyes of faith, as if it were present, because faith is an absolute condition in the relationship with God, and faith is also the reality of things not seen. He says that when we learn how to live with faith in this way, we can always become a winner of life.

Yong-Gi Cho sees two kinds of faith. One is human belief, which takes place in the Three dimensional world, and the other is God's faith, which comes from the Fourth dimensional world. Cho affirms that when we enter the Fourth dimensional world we can also, like God, call what does not exist as if it were present. But according to him, it is different from self-suggestion because this faith is to accept.

Yong-Gi Cho distinguishes between 'faith in human effort to believe' and 'God's faith' given by the Holy Spirit. God gives God's faith on the seed of faith that we have started. And he suggests waiting for God's time by praying after planting the seed.

Yong-Gi Cho explains that the hatching process of our faith has four basic stages. First, we must be able to visualize a clear object of faith in our mind. This is because faith is the reality of the things we hope for (the obvious things). Secondly, we must have a burning desire. Third, when our burning desire boils, get down on our knees and pray until we have confidence and peace. No matter how long it takes, we must pray until we receive the reality of our faith. Fourth, speak the word of God. Once we are convinced, we must show proof of our faith.

I have a hard time understanding Yong-Gi Cho's teaching where he tells us to pray until we have confidence and peace in the incubation process of faith. How long does it take to have the peace and assurance that comes from God and not self-suggestion? For example, if a Christian cancer patient prayed for a long time to gain such assurance by following the four steps of faith, but ultimately died without spiritual help to organize the end of his life, how would this rule of faith be explained pastorally? Let's look at an example from hospice research.

Since the pastoral care takes into account the integral aspect of human, we will see which part is important for the hospice field. Hae-Sook Lee and Bok-Num Doh had done research on "the spiritual well-being and quality of life of hospice patients and non-hospice patients." They see that the hospice is first of all a loving act to take care of the terminal patient who is near to death and of his family. Therefore, they help the patient to face the last moment of life in peace, maintaining human dignity and a high quality of life, and provide physical, emotional, social and spiritual care.

Another is to provide holistic care to diminish the suffering and sadness of bereaved family. Because the hospice period is the time to say goodbye to each other, to heal divided relationships, to forgive each other, to put neatly released life. Therefore, it could be the most meaningful few months, a few weeks, or the last day of a person's life.[220] The spiritual well-being here means that the inner re-

---

220 Hae-Sook Lee·Bok-Num Doh, *Hospis Huanzawa Bihospis Huanzaui Yungzok Annyungkwa Samuizil Bikyo (Comparison of Spiritual Well-being and Quality of life between Hospice Patients and Nonhospice Patients)*, in Seongin Ganhohakhoizi (Korean Society of Adult Nursing), vol. 15 (#3), Seoul, 2003, 364.

source of the human being is in the holistic healthy situation. Namely, to have a harmonious life in the relationship with the Absolute that transcends time and space, with the highest value, with oneself, with one's neighbor. Quality of life is a subjective sense of well-being experienced by a patient. In other words, it is the patient's self-assessment and satisfaction with his or her current level of functioning, compared with the level of feeling he or she would like to achieve.[221] These two researchers compared spiritual stability, existential well-being, and overall quality of life, mental quality of life between those receiving hospice care and those not receiving hospice care. As a result, the former have a higher level respect to the latter in all aspects.[222] Therefore, it is not easy to affirm that these four basic stages of faith are useful in all cases, as a role of faith, even though Yong-Gi Cho mentioned positive and very successful examples, such as the case of the baby without an ear, which he was able to have.

The Catholic Church teaches that faith is an entirely gift that God makes to man, and a personal adherence of the whole man to God who reveals himself. Namely, she defines that it involves an assent of the intellect and will to the self-revelation that God has made

---

221 Hae-Sook Lee·Bok-Num Doh, *Hospis Hwanzawa Bihospis Hwanzaui Yungzok Annyungkwa Samuizil Bikyo (Comparison of Spiritual Well-being and Quality of life between Hospice Patients and Nonhospice Patients)*, 365.
222 Hae-Sook Lee·Bok-Num Doh, *Hospis Hwanzawa Bihospis Hwanzaui Yungzok Annyungkwa Samuizil Bikyo (Comparison of Spiritual Well-being and Quality of life between Hospice Patients and Nonhospice Patients)*, 371.

through his deeds and Words; faith is a supernatural gift from God. It explains that in order to believe, man needs the interior helps of the Holy Spirit and that faith is a foretaste of the knowledge that will make us blessed in the life to come. But since we can lose this priceless gift, in order to live, grow and persevere in the faith until the end, we must nourish it with the word of God; we must ask the Lord to increase our faith.[223] The Catholic Church emphasizes that the Lord himself affirms that faith is necessary for salvation (Mk 16:16), that we must believe in no one but God: the Father, the Son and the Holy Spirit. And the Church makes it clear that we believe everything "contained in the word of God, written or handed down, and which the Church proposes for belief as divinely revealed."[224]

While Yong-Gi Cho emphasizes faith in a miracle-working God, the Catholic Church emphasizes the sign of Messiah. It seems that the teaching on the faith of the Fourth dimension of Yong-Gi Cho, which emphasizes believing in God who works a miracle, focuses on faith as an instrument to obtain healing and prosperity under the Threefold blessing. But according to the catechism of the Catholic Church, Jesus performed messianic signs by freeing some individuals from the earthly evils of hunger, injustice, illness and death. He did not come to the world to abolish all evils here below. Jesus came to free man from the gravest slavery, sin, which thwarts them in their vocation as God's sons and cauases all forms of human

---

[223] *Catechismus Catholicae Ecclesiale*, #162, 177, 179, 184.
[224] *Catechismus Catholicae Ecclesiale*, #178, 182-183.

bondage.[225]

4) Dream

According to Yong-Gi Cho, dream is a spiritual language of the Holy Spirit, and the Holy Spirit gives dream and fantasy to the believers through the word of God, and guides them to live a creative life. He emphasizes that if the Fourth dimension is not programmed with dream, there is no hope also in the Three dimension. And he explains how dreams and visions can be realized through the four steps. (1) The Holy Spirit continues to speak to us through the word of God, giving us various dreams and visions. (2) If we dream the goal concretely, relying on God, we can hatch our own future. (3) If we keep working towards our goals, we will get good results. (4) Develop dream with the desire to be used preciously by God. Since everything belongs to God's Sovereignty.

Yong-Gi Cho suggests that the goal of the dream, which is the Fourth dimensional element, should be concrete, and suggests fasting prayer to achieve this goal. And he says that it is necessary to go through the tunnel of hardship to make the dream and wishes come true, and he suggests practicing small things first to make the dream come true.

Yong-Gi Cho compares the difference between a right dream and greed. A dream does not need to commit sin, but greed can

---

225 *Catechismus Catholicae Ecclesiale,* #549.

be realized by breaking everything and committing sin. And he considers that no matter how good the dream and idea are, if God is not there, it is just human ambition and greed. I see here some problems. About the word, "greed can be realized by committing sin", firstly Yong-Gi Cho needs to clarify what his definition of sin is. And the judgment that "if God is not together, it is only human ambition and greed", is inappropriate content to apply to all the people who do not believe in God.

Yong-Gi Cho insists that "to look is to possess", gives examples of Abraham and Jacob, and suggests that anyone can look at the wooden Cross stained with blood of Jesus. A question arises. If the two believers of the same church, who live the Fourth dimension spirituality, look at the same thing to possess by trying hard as an object of competition, I wonder how Yong-Gi Cho can explain the winner and the loser of the competition with the Fourth dimension.

Yong-Gi Cho says, "If you dream a concrete goal depending on God, you can hatch your own future, and if you try hard, you can get good result." This word and his theory about dream make us think of God who is always ready to give something to man who asks for it to satisfy his own needs. It needs a spiritual discernment not to remain in the realm of human desire and ambition. This theory of the dream must be deepened with spiritual discernment in order to avoid the temptation: use this method for the satisfaction of individual needs in constant competition, without considering the community level, relationship with others, the social and ecclesial common good, the moral aspect.

5) Word

According to Yong-Gi Cho the word cannot be seen, but it has great creative power to change fate and environment; God created the world with the Word, and we are created in the image of God; what makes us different from other creatures is that we can speak. And he explains that we can receive the word, which has the power to change our life, when the Holy Spirit is with us and when we meditate and pray.

Yong-Gi Cho suggests that we discipline how we speak in daily life. Because the negative word that comes out of a person's mouth programs their Fourth dimension negatively, it can affect their own Fourth dimension. And because the word is the object of God's judgment, it is necessary to proclaim word believing that what we say will come true.

Yong-Gi Cho emphasizes the Fivefold Gospel and the Threefold Blessing with the Pentecostal movement, but he developed his theology in which does not appear much fruit of the Holy Spirit and sanctification (Holiness) that Christians need to live. But the catechism of the Catholic Church emphasizes the fruit of the Holy Spirit, saying that we live by the Holy Spirit; the more we renounce ourselves, the more we "walk by the Holy Spirit." Namely, God's children can bear much fruit by the power of the Holy Spirit: love, joy, peace, patience, kindness, goodness, faithfulness, gentleness, self-control. (Gal 5:22-23)[226]

6) Preaching

Yong-Gi Cho is internationally well known preacher. He uses simple language that touches deeply people's heart and gives hope to the lives of believers. He received the gift of the Word and also prepared the preaching as best as he could with sincere prayer. This aspect is very good example for preachers. Although the catholic theology is very different from the theology of Yong-Gi Cho, there are things to note in the worship of Yoido Full Gospel Church for more effective pastoral ministry. The website of Yoido Full Gospel Church offers all of Yong-Gi Cho's Sunday sermons, both written and recorded video. I think this is a great pastoral sharing because it is always open to all. In particular, their website is available in many languages, including Korean, English, Japanese, Chinese, French, German, Russian and Indonesian. They actively use today's new instrument for Evangelization. In fact, in this aspect they are far ahead than the Catholic Church in Korea.

It could be good to compare the Sunday's preaching of the Catholic Church and the Yoido Full Gospel Church. The Catholic Church uses the same liturgical calendar all over the world. According to this calendar, the same Readings and Gospel are proclaimed in several languages of the faithful. Only the homily connected with the Reading and Gospel of that day is different according to the celebrant of the Mass, and also prayer of the faithful is different.

---

226 *Catechismus Catholicae Ecclesiale*, #736.

On the other hand, each preacher of Yoido Full Gospel Church chooses the theme of the sermon and the Bible text even for the same Sunday's worship.[227] In this aspect, the Catholic Church is very different from YFGC, but also other Protestant Church.

Since the sermon is a center in the worship of Yoido Full Gospel Church, the sermon should be prepared very well. The catholic Mass has the Liturgy of the Word and the Liturgy of the Eucharist, therefore if the homily is sometimes not well-prepared, is not a big problem. In the Catholic Church in Korea there is always homily for the daily Mass. The Sunday service at YFGC lasts about 90 minutes, and they prepare themselves to listen well to the sermon by singing several hymns. After the sermon, there is a time for deepening the sermon and a time for various prayers, healing and offering. Sunday Mass in the Catholic Church lasts about an hour. Although there are some differences like this, Yong-Gi Cho prepares the sermon with a sincere heart, based on the Threefold Blessing and the spirituality of the Fourth dimension. For catholic priests, in reality, their main spirituality does not stand out in homily and life as a priest. Therefore, to have more effective pastoral renewal in the Catholic Church, firstly the priests must try to provide the necessary nutrients for their sheep by deepening the pastoral spirituality of parish priests, and the spiritual life of a good shepherd.

---

227 Yoido Full Gospel Church, *Cho Yong-Gi Moksawa Lee Young-Hoon Moksaui Zuilsolkyo (YungSunday Sermons of Pastor Yong-Gi Cho and Pastor Young-Hoon Lee[Dec. 9, 2012], [Dec. 12, 2012])*, https://davidcho.fgtv.com.

Yong-Gi Cho presents various effective ways to communicate the message of a sermon. Saying that the pastoral ministry of Jesus was a work to solve the problem of life in this world, he insists on having a clear goal of sermon. And he presents the sermon with a counseling form and the message-centered sermon to solve the problem, the sermon that gives dream and hope, and the sermon that has the power to lead people to God by moving their hearts. And mentioning the importance of the content of the sermon and how it should be delivered, he says that the sermon should be prepared and concluded with prayer, and have a creative structure of the sermon together with the eight principles of expression. In particular, Yong-Gi Cho underlines to communicate empirically what the preacher has learned deeply while he preparing the sermon. He emphasizes the importance of responding effectively to the needs of the audience by analyzing the audience before, during and after the sermon. Saying that the preacher must be concerned in all aspects, he explains about preacher's appearance, attitude, body language, voice; he affirms that the prayer after the sermon is a beginning of next sermon.

Pope Francis emphasizes the homily in this way. First, he summarizes that the homily is a touchstone for judging a pastor's ability to approach and communicate with his people; homily is an experience of the Holy Spirit, an encounter with the word of God. Pope Francis in particular emphasizes that the proclamation of the Word in the Eucharistic assembly is a dialogue between God and his people. And he stresses the importance of a brief homily, in which the Lord should be the center of attention rather than the preacher, because the homily is a proclamation within the framework of the Eucharistic celebration. He suggests the preparation of the homily with long time meditation, thorough preparation of the homily, its preparation steps and various methods. Pope says to transmit what the preacher has been touched by the word of God. He emphasizes the importance of discernment along with how to do *Lectio Divina*. Pope suggests the homily that has thoughts, emotions, and image, using the language that people can easily understand, giving hope with a future-oriented and positive language.

Likewise, both the methodological contents of the homily of Pope Francis and the sermon of Yong-Gi Cho could be helpful if we apply them to the real situation. And there are common aspects, such as the importance of preparing the homily with long prayer, in order to transmit to the faithful what the preacher has been touched by.

7) Cell group

The pastoral renewal of the Church requires a paradigm shift in the Church, a shift from the old paradigm to the new. The characteristics of these two paradigms are as follows.

Past paradigm of the Church	New paradigm of the Church
Pyramid shape	Collaborative social form
Western culture-centered	Indigenous culture-centered

Parish-centered organization	Life-centered community
Specific devotion centered	word of God centered (Bible)
Clerical authority system	Shared responsibility
Personal salvation	Community salvation
Triumphal church	Serving church
Church of the clergy	Participating church
*Means of organization's unity: laws and norms * Leader's role: surveillance and control of law and order	*Means of community's unity: sharing, serving, fellowship *Leader's role: service and sacrifice
< Pyramid hierarchy >	< Circular community structure >

Fist, the past paradigm of the Church is with pyramid structure, western culture-centered, parish-centered organization, specific devotion centered. It has characteristic of church with clerical authority system, personal salvation, triumphal church, church of the clergy. Means of organization's unity are laws and norms, leader's role is surveillance and control of law and order with Pyramid hierarchy.

But the new paradigm of the Church has a collaborative social form, indigenous culture-centered, word of God centered with life-centered community. And it is characteristic of the church with the serving and participating church for the salvation of the community and with the system of shared responsibility. Sharing, serving and fellowship are the means of community's unity; the leader has a role of service and sacrifice with circular community structure.[228]

Based on these characteristics, the Cell group could be formed. Up to now, we have seen the three forms of pastoral activity using the Small Community: Guyuk Yebe (Cell group worship), Dure community of Won Jun, *Sarangbang* Meeting of Jae-Ul Lee. David L. Finnell, in his book, "Life in His Body", distinguishes between the traditional church and the Cell church. Finnell insists that the Church that has added the Cell group to the existing traditional program is completely different from the Cell church. Namely, it is not correct to think that the church became a Cell church by adding the Cell group to the various existing programs.[229]

Hong-Rae Park insists that most Korean protestant churches have Guyuk system, therefore we might think that the church is a Cell church, that church is not pure Cell church, but is the church that has only cells. To be a pure Cell church, whole organization of the church must be composed of cells; the Cell leader is in the most important position; the goal and vision of the church is to double the cells. Hong-Rae Park compares these two forms because the Cell church and the church with cells, and traditional church which is program-centered and the Cell church is so different in several aspects.[230]

---

[228] Tonghap Samok Yunkuso, *Samwui-il-che Leadership (Trinity Leadership)*, Tonghap Samok Yunkuso, 2006, 86.

[229] David L. Finnell/Translated by Young-Cheol Park, *Cell Kyohoi Pyungsindo (Life in His Body: A Simple Guide to Active Cell Life)*, NCD, 2009, 15.

[230] Hong-Rae Park, *Cell Group Cell Kyohoi (Cell Group Cell Church)*, 113-114.

Subject	Church with cell	Cell church
Cell group	Programme	Core
Join a Cell group	Optional	Essential
Core leader	Pastoral minister	Cell leader
Leadership	Thematic (e.g. Women's Missionary Society)	Integrative
Who does pastoral care?	Pastoral minister	Cell leader and member
Position of the Cell leader	Periphery of pastoral care	Center of pastoral care
Number of paid staff	Many	Few
Produce lay leaders	Fewer opportunities	Many opportunities
Classdiscrimination	Emphasize discrimination	No distinction between pastoral minister and laity
Discovery of lay leader	Difficult to discover	Easy to discover
Focus on	Nurturing	Preaching the Gospel
Training	Train outside of a Cell group	Train in a Cell group
Cell group's shape	Diversity (Small group)	Similar

The church with cell is programme-centered, and its core leader is pastoral minister. The Cell leader remains on the periphery of pastoral care, it emphasizes class discrimination, and focuses on nurturing. On the other hand, the Cell church is Cell group-centered; its core leader is a Cell leader who is in the center of pastoral work.

And there is no distinction between the pastoral minister and the laity, and focus is on preaching the Gospel.

Programme-centered Traditional church	Cell church
Program-centered: various activities, meetings	Person and relationship-centered, meeting needs
Building-centered: building size limits pastoral work	Community-centered: pastoral work in the family and community
"Come!" structure	"Go!" structure
Church structure based on education: e.g. Bible study	Church structure based on pastoral work: e.g. Spiritual gift
Participation in the activities and programme of the church: Lack of time for evangelism and nurture	Use time for inviting people into cells by relationship evangelism, relationship building, and for caring of non-believers.
Church structure based on western culture: specialist, management, maintain the status quo, bureaucracy	New Testament structure: servering leader, all believers become pastoral workers, extending the reign of God
One-time evangelism, Invitation to Church	Invite people to the cell after relationship evangelism, relationship building.

Programme-centered traditional church has programme-centered various activities and meeting with building-centered and has a "Come!" structure based on education for those who come to the church. And runs the church with maintaining status quo and bureaucracy. The Cell church runs the church with person and relationship-centered, and it approaches to meet the needs of the believers. It gives importance to the community by going out to look for the sheep and with a "Go!" And it has a church structure based on pastoral work with the attitude of serving leader, forming the relationship and trying to work for the expansion of the reign of God. In the Catholic Church of Korea there are many Cell churches are present, but in reality they are with programme-centered pastoral work.

There are some common aspects between Yoido Full Gospel Church and the Catholic Archdiocese of Seoul. YFGC grew so big with the Cell group system. Won Jun and Jae-Ul Lee of the Catholic Church tried hard with pastoral creativity, and as a result, the number of believers attending Sunday Mass also increased. It has been seen that the faithful who belong to these three pastoral styles are constantly growing in fellowship with each other and in the spiritual life. They use their own typical book made for the small group, and use the Bible during the weekly meeting with their leader.

I noticed that the content of their books is so different. In the Protestant Church, even in the same parish, each preacher freely chooses the subject of his sermon and the Bible text. Likewise, the

"Guyuk Yebe Kongkwa (Cell Worship Guide)" of Yong-Gi Cho has a unique framework and a study time at the place of the sermon for their regular worship service. Each Guyuk meeting has a different theme, and examples of themes are as follows:

> "Language life of believers", "Inter-relationship of believers", "Dispute problem among believers", "Life guided by God", "Life attitude", "Martin Luther, reformer", "Reformer Jean Calvin", "Parable of the vineyard", "Parable of the rich young man", "Sermon of Moses", "Sermon of Peter."[231]

On the other hand, as it was seen, the text books of Won Jun and Jae-Ul Lee are for the Bible-centered meeting. Namely, to meditate and share the Sunday's Gospel or the Bible text of the Small Community meeting within basic framework used for each Bible meditation meeting. It is not a study of dealing with general knowledge, but a time to look back on one's life centered on the Word. Each person will have a personal experience of Jesus meditating on the Word of the Lord. This catholic method is very helpful for the re-education of believers after the baptism. I think that the intellectual study of Yong-Gi Cho's way in the "Guyuk Yebe Kongkwa" (Cell Worship Guide) could also be good for the re-education of believers.

Although YFGC and the Catholic Archdiocese of Seoul both conducted the small group meeting, the result was different because

---

231 Yong-Gi Cho, *Guyuk Yebe Kongkwa 14 (Guyuk Worship Guide)*, 4–5.

their history is different. YFGC started the Cell group as a duty of the whole church under the inspiration of Yong-Gi Cho, and the Cell group was strictly managed under his charismatic leadership of the senior pastor. The Small Community of Catholic Archdiocese of Seoul has been influenced by the international catholic movement and follows the teaching of the universal church. Besides the parish priest has the freedom to follow or not to follow in his parish the Small Community system that the diocese is trying. Therefore, the fruit of the Cell group stands out very much in the whole YFGC. On the other hand, in the Catholic Church, the process method and results are very different according to the parish priest's willingness, pastoral interest and creativity. When a catholic priest is transferred to another place, the faithful follow the pastoral direction of a new parish priest. While a new parish priest usually starts his own method from the very beginning, leaving aside the past method of a predecessor, YFGC continues the Cell group without any difficulty when a pastor in charge is transferred to another place. This reality in the Catholic Church is proved by the materials used in the case study of Won Jun and Jae-Ul Lee. In fact, we only had to study the results of the cases implemented in the parish for a limited period of time. But the ways of Bible meditation of Won Jun and Jae-Ul Lee are bearing much fruit and are now spreading positively in several groups and parishes.

I use some aspects of Won Jun, Jae-Ul Lee and also my own method for the catechism class together in the parish to prepare for baptism and confirmation for 90 minutes. I have also a Bible meditation meeting for the leaders during the week. The meeting for the leaders can be used for the ordinary believers outside the catechism class. For example, we have a short life sharing and pray for each other according to Jae-Ul Lee, and Jesus-centered meditation according to the method of Won Jun. The motivation for having this kind of catechism class came from our reality: This is because, while participating in catechetical classes during the preparation for baptism and confirmation, people are able to share in the fellowship of the group and receive support in their faith, but after confirmation, their spiritual walk can be disrupted as they continue on their own.

My method is this. In each catechism class in preparation for baptism, we develop the habit of being close to the Bible by finding a Bible verse. After studying about the Father, the Son and the Holy Spirit, the catechism lasts for 50 minutes, and they learn to meditate on the Bible little by little for 40 minutes, so that when they receive baptism they can meditate on it better. For the confirmation class, the catechism is 45 minutes and the Bible meditation is 45 minutes. I can see that it is a good opportunity to experience Jesus personally, to discover new aspects of Jesus and to feel closer to him through meditation. And it is a time for the community to grow closer spiritually little by little and for inner healing through praying for each other.

The role of the leader is important here. Because new believers do not know how to meditate on the Bible, the leader guides them step by step in the beginning. Later, they can meditate on their own.

Therefore, the training of the leader is necessary and must be continuous. The meditation meeting for leader lasts about 75 minutes. The leader's meditation without the catechism class can give more time for sharing than the catechism class. If necessary, there is also time to deepen basic biblical knowledge. There are many ways of doing a Jesus-centered meditation on the Bible, and I practice the face-to-face and the online way together at the same time:

Hymn Sing it lively, with a heart of praise and worship.
Life sharing
① Remember the person, event, experience in the past and reflect deeply.
② After reflecting on the Lord's work in me, in us and in the community, share. (3-5 minutes per person)
Gospel Reading Read the assigned Sunday Gospel passage aloud, slowly, one at a time, by two people.
Group Sharing After a period of silence, the following steps are taken, one by one, with the leader and shared with the group:
① Where and with whom is Jesus?
② How is Jesus moving?
(Observe the physical movement of Jesus and imagine the heart of Jesus and his facial expression, his posture)
③ What is Jesus saying?
④ What is happening?
⑤ What is the image of Jesus in this Word? (e.g. Healer,

Merciful, Someone I can rely on, always present be side me, Looking with love, Encouraging, etc.)

⑥ In silence, each one reads the given Word again and finds the verses that touch his or her heart personally.

⑦ From the verses that touch the heart, choose one or two key words on a personal level.

⑧ Holy Spirit Song

⑨ Contemplation:

    ⓐ Look at the image of Jesus and key words I have chosen for a whole

    ⓑ Ask and wait what Jesus wants to say through the key words, believing his presence. (e.g. "Jesus, why do you speak this word to me? "How do you want to me to live?")

    ⓒ Share in the group: (1) my selected emage of Jesus (2) my selected key words (3) the response from Jesus to me or the message that touches the heart and invites to live.

(The contents to be shared is related to my concrete action and event in the church, family, school, office, and other community).

⑩ Throughout the week we can often reflect on "Who is Jesus?", "Key words, I", and if possible dialogue with him.

Conclusion

① Pray aloud or in silence, choosing a partner to pray for each other.

② Conclude with the Lord's Prayer.

Guyuk Yebe (Cell group worship) of YFGC uses a Pyramid structure to communicate between the believers and the pastor in charge. Each step of Guyuk Yebe has a distinctive aspect. Namely, there is Bible study, life sharing among members, healing, and it is specifically aimed at the mission of inviting new believers to join the church. The pastor in charge receives all the information about the Cell groups through the Pyramid system. Although the Catholic Archdiocese of Seoul also has a Pyramid structure, it does not work for communication between bishop and priests, faithful and priests. It does very little to invite newcomers or to reach out to resting members. Therefore, it is very necessary to have an active attitude for Mission and Evangelization in the Catholic Church.

Observing the "Guyuk Yebe Kongkwa (Cell Worship Guide)", it is easy to see that its content is more focused on intellectual education, and the believers are able to listen to the sermon passively in the face-to-face worship in the church or in the Guyuk Yebe (Cell group worship). The way of Small Community meeting of the Catholic Church is to face the given word of Bible and to meditate and share it during the Bible meditation time. I think this is very important positive aspect of the Catholic Church.

YFGC emphasizes that the believers will invite newcomers to

the Church by leading the believers through preaching to give hope to the believers who are in many difficulties, and grasping the reality of the believers through Guyuk Yebe together with the visiting pastoral method.

The Catholic Church has Small Community organizations in almost every parish, but it seems to have little interest in what life is really like for the faithful in the sheepfold, waiting for people to come to church on their own. And most priests have an easy pastoral life, centered on the Mass and the sacraments and running organizations. I think this is a big reason why people in Latin America and Africa are moving to Pentecostal churches and other religions, a big dissatisfaction with the way they are being ministered to.

YFGC has Guyuk Yebe (Cell group worship), which focuses on intellectual education. From an objective point of view, it is also possible to live Christian life using the "Guyuk Yebe Kongkwa (Guyuk Worship Guide)" by oneself without participating in the Guyuk Yebe according to individual decision. However, since 2009, the pastors have been the Guyuk Yebe of the believers by posting the weekly sermon video related to "Guyuk Yebe Kongkwa" on the church's website. Furthermore, YFGC is doing its best to make the Guyuk Yebe and fellowship among believers run smoothly through the online video Guyuk Yebe system. In 2022, they use the 1 to 2 (1:2) method for Guyuk Yebe. This is seen as a good breakthrough in a difficult situation to worship together because of Covid-19. Likewise, they are trying hard to activate Guyuk Yebe in various ways to cope with the believers' lifestyle and the environmental change of worship. The unique effort of YFGC to care for the sheep could be evaluated as a good attitude of pastoral ministry. I expect that the Catholic Church will also provide a unique method for pastoral renewal to take care for the sheep and those who are not yet in the sheepfold.

Even though there are many ways to do the Cell system, the positive result of pastoral work depends on the pastoral mind and attitude of pastor. YFGC's management of the Cell system could be a good example for other churches. In reality, there are many participants in the year-round program which is specially prepared for the foreigners. YFGC makes good use of the *Osanri Fast Prayer House*.[232] Because everyone can participate in the programme of this prayer house, pray individually, have an opportunity to heal the 'Han.' Furthermore, the *Osanri Fast Prayer House* provides a good environment for the poor to pray like at home and to regain strength of life through prayer. They are active for in healing using the unique method of Pentecostalism and are getting many positive results. In

---

232 The *Osanri Fast Prayer House* is founded in 1973. In the main church 10,000 persons can participate to the worship, there are 11 other worship rooms. Therefore 20,000 persons can participate to the worship at the same time in the *Osanri Fast Prayer House*. There are 324 very small personal prayer rooms. Many people have experience of speaking in tongues and healing through fasting vigil prayer. Every day there are counsel and the opportunity of healing through prayer, and also YFGC has bus service between Seoul and the *Osanri Fast Prayer House* every day for the convenient of the faithful. Many faithful of other denominations go also there to pray. Namely, Presbiterian (40%), Full Gospel (36%), Methodist, Baptist, Holiness church and other confessions (24%), especially every year more than 10,000 foreigners visit that prayer house. Cfr. YOIDO FULL GOSPEL CHURCH, *Osanri Fast Prayer House*, Internet (April 2020), http://prayer.fgtv.com.

addition, YFGC has several specialized institute composed of many experts and scholars for pastoral study. The Catholic Church has relatively less preparation for the pastoral study institute.

PART IV

Conclusion
-Proposals for the Pastoral Renewal
of the Catholic Church

The motivation for writing this book, as I mentioned in the Introduction, is the problem that many Catholic believers in South America and Africa are turning to Pentecostalism or the other religions. Even in the Catholic Church of Korea, the number of those who do not attend Sunday Mass is constantly increasing. This is not because of the doctrine of the Church, but because of the pastoral method. Therefore, by summarizing the theology and pastoral ministry of Yong-Gi Cho, who was very well known in Korea and also in the international Pentecostal movement, we have seen what aspects moved people's hearts to form the largest congregation in the world. Just as there are differences in theological interpretation among Christian denominations, it is true that Yong-Gi Cho's theology has its own unique characteristics and that his theology also has limitations. However, I believe that we must acknowledge and learn from his tireless pastoral passion for giving hope and courage to the poor he encountered. This is an attitude required of Christian spiritual leaders, especially in a post-religious age, when the gap between rich and poor is widening.

Another difficulty for the Catholic Church is the sharp decline in the number of young people attending church. It is very common for very few young people to attend youth Mass. Some years ago, when I was researching Catholic Mass and Protestant worship, I attended a Sunday service for Protestant youth. This Protestant church was full of young people. At the same time, in the same city (Seoul), the Catholic Church had very few young people, but this

Protestant Church was full of them. There was clearly a spiritual thirst in them. I was very moved to see them listening to the sermon, praising and praying with all their hearts. I think this is the difference in pastoral methods. Just as the paradigms of pastoral methods of traditional churches and Cell churches are different, there is an urgent need to change the paradigm of youth ministry today and in the future.

It is hoped that changes in pastoral practice will act as priming water or catalyst for change in the whole diocese through the synergy of small changes in individual parishes together with the big picture at the diocesan level. No matter how good a diocesan proposal is, if each parish does not recognize its value and put it into practice, it will be little fruit. Therefore, in the hope of change at the diocesan and parish level, I would like to propose contents related to pastoral activities, discernment, the special place of the poor, and the pastoral care of young people in the Age of Scientism.

1. Pastoral activity

In July 2012, the Catholic Archdiocese of Seoul in Korea published the *"Basic Data Collection Survey Report for Revitalizing Parish Pastoral Care <Seoul Dekyogu Bondangsamok Hwalsonghwarul Wihan Kichozaryosuzip Solmunzosa Bogoseo>."* As a result of examining the status of evangelization in the Catholic Archdiocese of Seoul in this data, it can be seen that although the number of new believers is steadily increasing, the number of believers who do not attend Sunday Mass has increased every year. At that time, the percentage of parishioners attending Sunday Mass in the Archdiocese of Seoul was only 27.5%. Therefore, Yong-Suk Oh said, "Jesus went out to find the one lost sheep, but how can the parishes of the Archdiocese of Seoul allow the 'empty sheepfold' to remain as it is, with more than 70 sheep not returned to the fold!"[1] According to the report, the number of faithful who invited newcomers to the church was also very low.[2]

Yong-Suk Oh argues that the urgent task for parishes today is "internal mission" rather than "external mission", that is, "self-evangelization", and that they must show the image of a church that gives hope to the world. If parishes on the frontline of mission focus only on "outward evangelism" without accompanying the qualitative growth of the church, they will end up training "outward believers" like scribes and Pharisees of "superficial outward believers." And if "superficial believers" become the mainstream of the church, Christianity will eventually lose hope. Yong-Suk Oh believes that the rise of atheism and religious indifference in today's world is due to the fact that Christianity, which has dominated world civilization,

---

1 Yong-Suk Oh, 'Seroun Bokeumhwa' Side-ui Songkongzok Bondangsamok Banghyang (Successful Parish Pastoral Direction in the Era of the 'New Evangelisation'), in Seoul Dekyoku Bondangsamok Hwalsonghwarul Wihan Kichozaryosuzip Solmunzosa Bogoso (Gathering Data for Parish Ministry Revitalisation Survey Report), Catholic Archdiocese of Seoul, 2012, 225.

2 Catholic Archdiocese of Seoul, Seoul Dekyogu Bondangsamok Hwalsonghwarul Wihan Kichozaryosuzip Solmunzosa Bogoso (Survey Report on Collecting Basic Data for Revitalising Parish Pastoral Ministry in the Seoul Archdioces), Catholic Archdiocese of Seoul, 2012, 28.

has degenerated into a religion that has lost hope. This is especially convincing to young people, so the Catholic Church must humbly accept this. Hence, according to Yong-Suk Oh, it is a sign of the times and a vocation for the parishes of the Archdiocese of Seoul to create an image of the Church that gives true hope to the world.[3]

Sung-Poong Jo, a catholic priest, makes several suggestions for revitalizing the pastoral ministry. First, specific and practical research on the resting parishioners who do not attend Sunday Mass. Second, specific and practical research on parish priests (Research on priests' leadership, relationships with parishioners, pastoral activities, etc). Third, develop more specific metrics for parish diagnosis. Fourth, research and implementation teams are required to develop and implement various training programs and diagnostic metrics.

We will look at the revitalization of the liturgy, Small Community, spiritual growth, and care of souls in order to achieve qualitative growth in the church, to allow the presence of the Lord to penetrate deeper into the hearts of the believers and to grow in communion with Him.

---

[3] To the question on the number of the 'Missionary Admissions' the 77.4% of faithful answered 'No'. This shows that the mostly faithful of parish in the archdiocese of Seoul do not put into practice the direct mission, namely, 'outer evangelization.' Yong-Suk Oh, *'Sairoun Bokumhwa' Side-ui Songkongzok Bondangsamok Banghyang (Successful Parish Pastoral Direction in the Era of the 'New Evangelisation')*, 226-227.

Revitalization of the Liturgy

In the Catholic Church, there is a very good aspect of receiving the Holy Communion through the liturgy of the Eucharist at every Mass. However, considering the liturgical renewal of the Catholic Church and overcoming the formal and passive aspects of the faithful during the Mass, I would like to suggest the use of various instruments in liturgical music. I also suggest creating an environment in which people can spend their time praying more actively through hymns. Protestant worship focuses on well-prepared sermons and hymns. Some Protestant churches use a variety of musical instruments during worship to create an environment that is conducive to getting closer to God during times of worship. That is, there are organs, piano, drum, orchestras, electronic instruments, etc. Therefore, believers can choose a worship environment according to their preference. On the other hand, the Mass of the Catholic Church includes the Liturgy of the Word and the Liturgy of the Eucharist, and the hymns are accompanied mainly by the organ. In Protestant worship, if a hymn with verses 1 to 4, it is said that believers receive much grace while singing all of them. However, in Catholic Church Mass in Korea, the entrance and concluding hymns are usually sung only to the first or second verse. Therefore, it is necessary to have a prayer time when people sing with all their heart until the fourth verse, like the Protestant praise time. A long time ago, I went to the 11 o'clock Sunday Mass in Croatia. During the Mass the youth choir and all the faithful sang with sincerity, the meaning of each lyric engraved to the accompaniment of various instruments, and it became one in praising the Lord; this remains a truly beautiful and holy memory of mine. Today, for our religious life, it is necessary to reflect more in a creative way and to put it into practice. For example, because of Covid-19, face-to-face worship was limited, and it was difficult to sing hymns to one's heart's content. Even if the congregation could not sing along with the choir, it was actually very helpful to have someone singing into the microphone and leading the congregation in prayer. Therefore, let's look forward to a more gracious time of praise during the Mass.

Small Christian Community

Yong-Gi Cho insists that he was the first in the world to start the Cell system in 1964. But this system began in the Catholic Church of South America in 1956, before Yong-Gi Cho. Many Protestant churches in Korea had Cell systems with different names. Although the Korean Catholic Church mainly uses the names "Small Community" (Sogongdongce) or "Ban Moim", there is no quantitative growth like YFGC. However, there is a change in the perception of the Bible, a taste for the Gospel, and an attempt to live a Word-centered life, and the positive aspect of laypeople actively participating in church activities is noticeable.

Yong-Gi Cho emphasizes that the key to the development of Small Christian Communities depends on the pastoral attitude of the parish priest, and I think this point is not far from truth. And as seen in the case study of the Small Community gatherings of two priests in the Catholic Archdiocese of Seoul, it is confirmed that when

Small Communities are well activated, they are of great help in the spiritual growth of the church community and in increasing attendance at Sunday Mass. The numerical growth of the faithful is important, but it is necessary to focus more on the essential aspect of the church. If too much attention is paid to the number of faithful, there is a danger of focusing only on the size and money of the church and the personal interests of the leader. This is something that is not difficult to find in Korean Protestant churches, especially megachurches.

For the spiritual growth of believers, it is necessary to spread "Jesus-centered Bible meditation" widely so that they can experience Jesus personally in Small Community prayer meetings. In order to achieve this, it will be of practical help for the revival of Small Communities if parish priests participate directly in Small Community meetings and gain field experience. In other words, the parish priest can make specific and wise changes in the way Small Community groups are organized and how they meet to suit local circumstances. Leading believers only with theory without first-hand experience of Small Community may lack a sense of reality.

I would also like to suggest efforts to improve the quality of Bible meditation meetings. It is true that Small Community meetings are difficult these days as we live in a world of multifaceted and constant social change. However, it is possible to share Gospel meditation through face-to-face meetings, online meetings, or both face-to-face and online while adapting to the situation at the time. It is easy to find modern people who are willing to give up their time if they think it will be helpful to them. This is because people will voluntarily attend a Bible meditation meeting if they are determined that it is suitable for their spiritual life and inner muscle training, just as they organize exercise time for their health. When we meet Jesus personally in some way, we will be willing to share the God we have experienced. Based on this, we will be more active in inviting believers who do not attend Sunday Mass and those who want to join the church, and our missionary methods will be creatively researched and put into practice.

Pope Francis speaks of the best incentive for the determination to spread the Gospel. This is to contemplate the Gospel with love, lingering over its pages and reading it with the heart. He says that in this way, its beauty will amaze and constantly excite us, and we will ultimately be able to share the Good News with others.

> The best incentive for sharing the Gospel comes from contemplating it with love, lingering over its pages and reading it with the heart. If we approach it in this way, its beauty will amaze and constantly excite us. But if this is to come about, we need to recover a contemplative spirit which can help us to realize ever anew that we have been entrusted with a treasure which makes us more human and helps us to lead a new life.[4]

---

4 Pope Francis, *Evangelii Gaudium*, #264.

Spiritual Growth

Material abundance cannot satisfy the inner thirst. Rather than simply seeking material satisfaction, the poor seek a deeper experience of God's presence that provides meaning and real hope in life. The Pentecostal movement helps people to experience God personally. This is especially true through speaking in tongues (Glossolalia) and the gifts of the Holy Spirit, which provide emotional and direct experiences. Experiencing God is inevitable for all Christians, but one can live a sanctified life in daily life even without speaking in tongues.

There are different spiritualities in the Christian tradition. However, most ordinary believers are not aware of them. Among them, is the method proposed by Brother Lawrence of the Carmelite Monastery. Brother Lawrence refers to experiencing God through constant communion with Jesus, practicing the presence of God, and sublimating suffering in daily life. He is confident that if he were a preacher or spiritual director, he would advise practicing God's presence more than anything else. According to him, God is much closer than we think and it is not difficult to practice God's presence. This means that we can talk to God with a humble heart and have a conversation with God at any time with a loving heart, rejoicing that the Holy God is with us. He affirms that we must not grow tired of doing little things for the love of God, who does not look at the size of the work but at the love in it.

If I were a preacher, I would not preach anything else than the practice of the presence of God; and if I were a spiritual director, I would advise it to everyone so much do I believe it necessary and yes, even easy.[5] He is closer to us than we think. We do not have to be constantly in church to be with God. We can make our heart a prayer room into which we can retire from time to time to converse with Him gently, humbly, and lovingly.[6]

Practicing the presence of God is the application of our spirit to God; it is the vivid recollection that God is present with us. It can be accomplished either through the imagination or by the understanding.[7] The holiest, most universal and most necessary practice in the spiritual life is the presence of God. To practice the presence of God is to take pleasure in and become accustomed to His Divine company, speaking humbly and conversing lovingly in our hearts with Him at all times and at every moment, especially in times of temptation, pain, spiritual dryness, revulsion to spiritual things, and even unfaithfulness and sin.[8]

Those who consider their sufferings as coming from the hand of God, as effects of His mercy, and as means that He uses for their salvation, commonly enjoy in them such great sweetness and consolations that they can actually feel them.[9] We must not grow weary of doing little things for the love of God, who looks not on the great size of the work,

---

[5] Brother Lawrence, *The Practice of the Presence of God, Paraclete Press*, Massachusetts, 2010, 56.

[6] Brother Lawrence, *The Practice of the Presence of God*, 59.

[7] Brother Lawrence, *The Practice of the Presence of God*, 103.

[8] Brother Lawrence, *The Practice of the Presence of God*, 95.

[9] Brother Lawrence, *The Practice of the Presence of God*, 77.

but on the love in it.[10]

Other monks' story of spiritual growth suggests ways to follow the path of perfection. In other words, many monks worked hard for several years to follow the guidelines given by their spiritual teacher. However, they were unable to reach the level required by their teachers and later confessed that they did not have the strength to endure the daily struggle. The mountain to perfection was too high for them, and there was too much they had to go through to reach the top. In the end, they had no choice but to give up at the first hill, which is a teaching that in order to live as a true Christian, one cannot go far just by training one's will. Believing in the power of the Holy Spirit does not mean not climbing the mountain of perfection. It means taking the second place. In other words, it is a teaching that since God holds us in His arms first and ascends the path of sanctification, we must first be embraced in His arms.[11]

Care of souls

According to Giacomo Morandi caring for the soul is not just caring for a part of a person, but caring for the whole person. Christian growth towards human transformation requires an integrated method. For this reason, he emphasizes that in order to provide pastoral care, the pastor must first take care of himself, especially

---

10 Brother Lawrence, *The Practice of the Presence of God*, 46.
11 Leon-Joseph Suenens, *Lo Spirito Santo nostra speranza: una nuova Pentecoste?*, Edizioni Paoline, Rome, 1975, 88.

his relationship with Christ. As St. Paul said, this is to avoid disqualifying oneself while shouting for others to win. (1Cor 9:27)[12]

St. Bernard talks about the difference between a water pipe and a water basin. The water pipe pours out the water almost at the same time after receiving it, but the water basin waits until the vessel is full and shares the overflow. St. Bernard's advice is to be a spiritually fulfilled basin first, because in the Church of today, there are many water pipes, but very few basins. Because they have to speak before they digest and deepen; they prefer to talk rather than listen; they are ready to teach what they have learned; they lack patience when it comes to guiding others; and above all, they don't know how to handle themselves, he says:

> Likewise, if you are wise, you will show the water basin and not the water pipe. The water pipe receives the water and pours it out almost at the same time, but the water basin waits until the vessel is full and divides the overflow. ... In fact, there are many water pipes and very few water basins in churches today. There are those who wish to pour upon us the fountain of heaven with great love. However, they must speak before digesting and deepening, prefer talking rather than listening, be ready to teach what they have learned, and lack patience when it comes to guiding others. Above all, they don't know how to handle themselves.[13]

---

12 Giacomo Morandi, *Fondamenti Biblici della Cura d'anime*, in *La vita in Cristo Pastora: La cura d'anime minister delle SJBP (Atti del Seminario)*, ed., Sisters of Jesus Good Shepherd (Pastorelle Sisters), Rome, 2010, 43.

2. Discernment

Christianity is a religion of revelation. Revelation means that God reveals religious truths to man that man cannot know for himself. If we want to know for sure who God is and how he loves us, it is only possible if God tells us directly.[14] Therefore, the correct interpretation of revelation is more necessary than anything else, and what all Christians including the Catholic Church must not forget for a true religious life is discernment.

The Pentecostal movement is largely divided into Classical Pentecostalism, Charismatic Movement, and the Third Wave. In this movement, despite the different interpretations of the work of the Holy Spirit and different mystical experiences of denominations or groups, the mystical experience itself occupies an important place. In particular, the New Apostolic Movement (New Apostolic Reformation) of the Third Wave emphasizes direct revelation, prophecy, and the experience of unusual phenomenon. However, the Catholic Church distinguishes between public and private revelation and explains it as follows. First, public revelation has already been completed. In other words, in the past, God spoke to our fathers by the prophets in many and various ways. Then he told everything

---

13 San Bernardo, *Sermoni sul Cantico dei Cantici, XVIII, 3, Opere di st. Bernardo (V/I)* (Milano: Scriptorium Claravallense, Fondazione di Studi Cistercensi, 2006), 237.
14 Catholic Bishop's Conference of Korea, *Catechism of the Catholic Church in Korea*, CBCK, 2015, 21.

through his Son, Jesus Christ. Therefore, according to the Catholic Church, no new public revelation should be expected until Jesus returns. However, even though public revelation is complete, it has not been made completely explicit. Therefore, we must gradually grasp its full significance over the course of the centuries.

> "In many and various ways God spoke of old to our fathers by the prophets, but in these last days he has spoken to us by a Son (Heb 1:1-2). Christ, the Son of God made man, is the Father's one, perfect and unsurpassable Word. In him, he has said everything; there will be no other word than this one.[15]
> No new public revelation is to be expected before the glorious manifestation of our Lord Jesus Christ." Yet even if Revelation is already complete, it has not been made completely explicit; it remains for Christian faith gradually to grasp its full significance over the course of the centuries.[16]

The Catholic Church also explains 'private' revelations. In other words, there have been 'private' revelations in the church, some of which have been recognized by the authority of the church. But this is to help us live more fully according to revelation. These do not belong to the deposit of faith. Therefore, the Catholic Church clearly teaches that private revelations should be discerned and ac-

---

15 *Catechismus Catholicae Ecclesiale*, #65.
16 *Catechismus Catholicae Ecclesiale*, #66.

cepted under the guidance of the magisterium. Also, since Christ is the completion of revelation, the Christian faith cannot accept "revelations" that claim to surpass or correct the Revelation of which Christ is the fulfillment, as is the case in certain non-Christian religions and also in certain recent sects which base themselves on such "revelations."

> Throughout the ages, there have been so-called "private" revelations, some of which have been recognized by the authority of the Church. They do not belong, however, to the deposit of faith. It is not their role to improve or complete Christ's definitive Revelation, but to help live more fully by it in a certain period of history. Guided by the Magisterium of the Church, the sensus fidelium knows how to discern and welcome in these revelations whatever constitutes an authentic call of Christ or his saints to the Church.
> Christian faith cannot accept "revelations" that claim to surpass or correct the Revelation of which Christ is the fulfillment, as is the case in certain non-Christian religions and also in certain recent sects which base themselves on such "revelations."[17]

Let's look at what Pope Francis and St. Ignatius of Loyola, the founder of the Society of Jesus to which he belongs, say about discernment. Pope Francis explains what discernment is in his Apostolic Exhortation, "*Gaudete et Exsultate.*" According to Pope

---

17 *Catechismus Catholicae Ecclesiale*, #67.

Francis, discernment is the only way to know whether something comes from the Holy Spirit or from worldly or demonic spirits. Discernment is also a grace that requires qualities beyond intelligence or common sense and must be requested from the Holy Spirit. The Pope also suggests ways to develop the spiritual gift of discernment through prayer, reflection, reading and good counsel.[18]

According to the Pope's exhortation, discernment is even more important when something new appears, so we must discern whether it is new wine sent by God or an illusion created by the spirit of the world or the spirit of the devil. Sometimes we may face opposition. This is because the power of the devil tempts us to leave things in their original state and to resist change. This blocks the working of the Holy Spirit. Therefore, the Pope says that we are free, with the freedom of Christ, still he asks us to examine what is within us (Our desires, anxieties, fears, questions) and what takes place all around us, namely "the signs of the times", and thus to recognize the paths that lead to complete freedom.

> This is all the more important when some novelty presents itself in our lives. Then we have to decide whether it is new wine brought by God or an illusion created by the spirit of this world or the spirit of the devil. At other times, the opposite can happen, when the forces of evil induce us not to change, to leave things as they are, to opt for a rigid resistance to change. Yet that would be to block the working of the Spirit. We

---

18 Pope Francis, *Gaudete et Exsultate*, #166.

are free, with the freedom of Christ. Still, he asks us to examine what is within us – our desires, anxieties, fears and questions – and what takes place all around us – "the signs of the times" – and thus to recognize the paths that lead to complete freedom. "Test everything; hold fast to what is good." (1 Thess 5:21)[19]

According to Pope Francis, discernment is a means of spiritual combat that helps us follow the Lord more faithfully and is achieved in the seemingly insignificant details. This is because great things are revealed in simple everyday reality. And discernment is a matter of putting all our heart and soul into the small things of the day, without setting limits to the great, the best, and the most beautiful. Therefore, the Pope recommends that all Christians engage in a sincere "examination of conscience" in daily conversation with the Lord.

Discernment is necessary not only at extraordinary times, when we need to resolve grave problems and make crucial decisions. It is a means of spiritual combat for helping us to follow the Lord more faithfully. We need it at all times, to help us recognize God's timetable, lest we fail to heed the promptings of his grace and disregard his invitation to grow. Often discernment is exercised in small and apparently irrelevant things, since greatness of spirit is manifested in simple everyday realities. It involves striving untrammelled for all that is great, better

---

19 Pope Francis, *Gaudete et Exsultate*, #168.

and more beautiful, while at the same time being concerned for the little things, for each day's responsibilities and commitments. For this reason, I ask all Christians not to omit, in dialogue with the Lord, a sincere daily "examination of conscience." Discernment also enables us to recognize the concrete means that the Lord provides in his mysterious and loving plan, to make us move beyond mere good intentions.[20]

The Pope says that spiritual discernment does not exclude existential, psychological, sociological or moral insights drawn from the human sciences, but at the same time it transcends them. Above all, he says that spiritual discernment does not mean only my temporal well-being, my satisfaction at having accomplished something useful, or even my desire for peace of mind. Because it is related to the meaning of my life before God the Father, who knows and loves me, with the real purpose of my life, which nobody knows better than He. And ultimately, discernment leads to the wellspring of eternal life.

Certainly, spiritual discernment does not exclude existential, psychological, sociological or moral insights drawn from the human sciences. At the same time, it transcends them. Nor are the Church's sound norms sufficient. We should always remember that discernment is a grace. Even though it includes reason and prudence, it goes beyond them, for it seeks a glimpse of that unique and mysterious plan that God has for

---

20 Pope Francis, *Gaudete et Exsultate*, #169.

each of us, which takes shape amid so many varied situations and limitations. It involves more than my temporal well-being, my satisfaction at having accomplished something useful, or even my desire for peace of mind. It has to do with the meaning of my life before the Father who knows and loves me, with the real purpose of my life, which nobody knows better than he. Ultimately, discernment leads to the wellspring of undying life: to know the Father, the only true God, and the one whom he has sent, Jesus Christ. (Jn 17:3) It requires no special abilities, nor is it only for the more intelligent or better educated. The Father readily reveals himself to the lowly. (Mt 11:25)[21]

The Pope's exhortation emphasizes the importance of the silence of prolonged prayer for discernment. The Lord speaks to us in various ways and at every moment, and silent prayer enables us better to perceive God's language and see our whole existence afresh in God's light.

The Lord speaks to us in a variety of ways, at work, through others and at every moment. Yet we simply cannot do without the silence of prolonged prayer, which enables us better to perceive God's language, to interpret the real meaning of the inspirations we believe we have received, to calm our anxieties and to see the whole of our existence afresh in his own light. In this way, we allow the birth of a new synthesis that springs from a life inspired by the Spirit.[22]

---

21 Pope Francis, *Gaudete et Exsultate*, #170.

According to the Pope, the starting point for discernment through prayer is an attitude of listening. This is listening to reality itself, which always challenges us. Because as the Pope sees it, only when we are ready to listen that we will have the freedom to break away from our own partial or insufficient ideas, our usual habits and ways of seeing things. And In this way, we become truly open to accepting a call that can lead to a better life.

> Nonetheless, it is possible that, even in prayer itself, we could refuse to let ourselves be confronted by the freedom of the Spirit, who acts as he wills. We must remember that prayerful discernment must be born of a readiness to listen: to the Lord and to others, and to reality itself, which always challenges us in new ways. Only if we are prepared to listen, do we have the freedom to set aside our own partial or insufficient ideas, our usual habits and ways of seeing things. In this way, we become truly open to accepting a call that can shatter our security, but lead us to a better life. It is not enough that everything be calm and peaceful. God may be offering us something more, but in our comfortable inadvertence, we do not recognize it.[23]

Pope Francis mentions obedience to the Gospel as the ultimate standard in his attitude of listening and, unlike Protestantism, emphasizes obedience to the teachings of the Magisterium. The same

---

22 Pope Francis, *Gaudete et Exsultate*, #171.
23 Pope Francis, *Gaudete et Exsultate*, #172.

solution is not valid in all circumstances, and the discernment of spirits liberates us from rigidity, which has no place before the eternal "today" of the risen Lord.

> Naturally, this attitude of listening entails obedience to the Gospel as the ultimate standard, but also to the Magisterium that guards it, as we seek to find in the treasury of the Church whatever is most fruitful for the "today" of salvation. ... the same solutions are not valid in all circumstances. ... The discernment of spirits liberates us from rigidity, which has no place before the perennial "today" of the risen Lord.[24]

According to the Pope's exhortation, an essential condition for progress in discernment is a growing understanding of God's patience and his timetable. And discernment is not about discovering what more we can get out of this life, but about recognizing how we can better accomplish the mission entrusted to us at our baptism.

> An essential condition for progress in discernment is a growing understanding of God's patience and his timetable, which are never our own. ... Discernment is not about discovering what more we can get out of this life, but about recognizing how we can better accomplish the mission entrusted to us at our baptism. This entails a readiness to make sacrifices, even to sacrificing everything. For happiness is a paradox. We experience it most when we accept the mysterious logic that is not

---

24 Pope Francis, *Gaudete et Exsultate*, #173.

of this world.25

The Pope says that discernment is not a form of infantile self-analysis or individualistic self-reflection, but a process of truly breaking away from oneself and moving towards the mystery of God.26

St. Ignatius of Loyola emphasizes that the spirit of evil is "by nature weak and worthless." This is a message of hope to anyone who is worried about falling into temptation. He says that if a believer is not "frightened and discouraged" and "does the exact opposite" to the temptation of an evil spirit, the evil spirit will "lose strength, withdraw from the temptation, and run away." According to St. Ignatius, what we must not forget is that the "most important moment" in the strategy of resisting the temptation of evil spirits is "the moment when this temptation first begins." If one resolutely resists "when temptation begins", the temptation will not be able to increase its power and will no longer be able to increase its power to dominate those who are being tempted. However, it is emphasized that the more a person being tempted reacts indecisively and allows temptations to arise, the more difficult it will be to resist the temptation later.27

---

25 Pope Francis, *Gaudete et Exsultate*, #174.
26 Pope Francis, *Gaudete et Exsultate*, #175.
27 Timothy M. Gallagher/translated by Du-Jin Kim, *The Discernment of Spirits: An Ignatian Guide for Everyday Living (Young-ui Sikbyul: St. Ignatiaga Annaihanun Meilui Sam)*, Ignatian Spirituality Institute, Seoul, 2020, 324-326.

St. Ignatius describes the characteristics of evil spirits as follows: The evil spirit leads people who begin to love and serve God into error, and his first weapon is to place obstacles and impediments in their way. In other words, it tempts us to look at life long-term rather than risk our lives for various reasons.

> The enemy is leading you into error ... but not in any way to make you fall into a sin that would separate you from God our Lord. He tries rather to upset you and to interfere with your service of God and your peace of mind.[28]

> The enemy as a rule follows this course. He places obstacles and impediments in the way of those who love and begin to serve God our Lord, and this is the first weapon he uses in his efforts to wound them. He asks, for instance: "How can you continue a life of such great penance, deprived of all satisfaction from friends, relatives, possessions? How can you lead so lonely a life, with no rest, when you can save your soul in other ways and without such dangers?" He tries to bring us to understand that we must lead a life that is longer than it will actually be, by reason of the trials he places before us and which no one ever underwent.[29]

---

[28] William Young, *Letters of Saint Ignatius of Loyola* (Chicago: Loyola University Press, 1959), 19; Timothy M. Gallagher, *The Discernment of Spirits: An Ignatian Guide for Everyday Living*, 105.

[29] Timothy M. Gallagher/translated by Du-Jin Kim, *The Discernment of Spirits: An Ignatian Guide for Everyday Living*, 107.

Timothy M. Gallagher (OMV) summarizes what St. Ignatius says about discernment of Spirits: the evil spirit weakens the movement toward God; the good spirit strengthens the movement toward God. The inspirations of the good spirit give clarity about how to "go forward in doing good." The good spirit gives such persons a peaceful and strengthening quiet of heart. The action of the good spirit quiets anxieties and instills peace in the Lord. On the other hand, the action of the evil spirit fosters disquiet in the hearts of committed persons, place obstacles through false reasons so that the person may not go forward toward God.[30] Here is an example.

> A dedicated woman has begun to doubt that she will ever grow closer to the Lord in the way she desires. She has tried but finds herself failing again and again in the same habitual ways. Such growth seems impossible. Then one morning the smile of her child reveals afresh to her God's faithful love. She senses now that the obstacles are not insurmountable and that "for God all things are possible" (Matt 19:26). Filled with renewed hope, she will, by God's grace, overcome obstacles and "advance in good works." She embarks on a new journey of spiritual growth. This is what a good spirit does: it "makes all obstacles easier to overcome and removes them.[31]

---

30 Timothy M. Gallagher/translated by Du-Jin Kim, *The Discernment of Spirits: An Ignatian Guide for Everyday Living*, 103-115.

31 Timothy M. Gallagher/translated by Du-Jin Kim, *The Discernment of Spirits: An Ignatian Guide for Everyday Living*, 116.

According to Pope Francis, spiritual discernment does not mean only my present happiness, the self-satisfaction of achieving something useful, or even my desire for peace of mind. Discernment is related to the meaning of my life before God the Father and the true purpose of my life, because it leads me to the source of eternal life. Therefore, as we asked earlier, "What is church growth for?", the question of Church inheritance succession as seen in Korean Protestant megachurches needs to be asked, "What is Church inheritance for?" Also, after reflecting on mystical experience, revelation, and discernment, it is necessary to ask, "For what is mystical experience and prophesy?" "Can we really see the fruit of love and the fruit of the Holy Spirit in the lives of Christians who have had mystical experiences?" One thing that is essential for Christians today, living in the era of the Fourth Industrial Revolution, is a spiritual life that progresses step by step by discerning the flow of good and evil spirits through frequent examination of conscience.

3. A special place for the poor

Pope Francis proposes a Church that is poor and for the poor. According to him, we are called to recognize Christ in the poor and to give voice to their needs. He emphasizes that we are called to be their friend, to listen to them, to understand them and to receive the mysterious wisdom that God wants to share with us through them.[32]

In order to be a poor church, we must first identify areas of poverty. In other words, it is necessary to consider poverty in many aspects, including not only material poverty, but also spiritual poverty, physical poverty, mental poverty, social poverty, and psychological poverty. Although a person may be materially poor, he or she may be mentally or spiritually wealthy, and although he or she may enjoy great material benefits, he or she may experience extreme poverty in other ways. Jesus was with the poor in many ways.

Specific and effective pastoral care practices are needed to ensure the spiritual growth of the church and to give priority to the poor. Therefore, parish priests and parish leaders must look at the reality of not only believers but also local residents, especially the poor, with the compassion of Jesus, the Good Shepherd. This is because it gives Small Community members the opportunity to practice love, discover the poor, especially those in blind spots, and to extend a helping hand to them.

The Catholic Church is very active in social welfare projects for the poor throughout the world through charitable organizations. This is very necessary and has the advantage of reaching directly those who are suffering. While the poor need financial help, sometimes they expect more: to be listened to, comforted, and respected. People who have received help from others or had their heartfelt stories accepted and listened to during difficult times will be better to support others in similar situations.

---

32 Pope Francis, *Evangelii Gaudium*, #198.

In caring for the soul, it is inevitable to accept and embrace a listening attitude that gives encouragement and hope to overcome difficult moments. Therefore, I would like to make some suggestions to create this opportunity. Firstly, it is necessary to provide spiritual directors to accompany parish priests and parish sisters at the diocesan level or beyond the diocese. There should also be training in listening skills for parish priests and parish sisters. In addition, the collaboration of retired priests and nuns who are active in this field provides opportunities to listen to believers and non-believers. Especially for those in mental distress, it would be good to have a garden or farmland for prayer and nature care at the parish level. Such examples are easy to find in the 'Cenacle Community', which was founded in Italy and has now spread to many other countries. Young people who are addicted to alcohol or drugs are healed through contact with nature, prayer and simple physical labor.

Pope Francis emphasizes that there is a special place in God's heart for the poor, to the extent that God himself "became poor" (2 Cor 8:9), and that mercy shown to all is the key to heaven.[33]

> For I was hungry and you gave me food, I was thirsty and you gave me drink, a stranger and you welcomed me, naked and you clothed me, ill and you cared for me, in prison and you visited me. (Mt 25:35-36)

The Pope also recommends paying attention to new forms of

---

33 Pope Francis, *Evangelii Gaudium*, #197.

poverty and vulnerability, because we are called to recognize Christ suffering in them. He thinks of the homeless, addicts, refugees, indigenous people, the elderly who are increasingly isolated and abandoned, and many others.[34]

The Pope also mentions abortion. This is because among the weakest for whom the Church wishes to care with particular love and concern are unborn children, the most defenseless and innocent among us. Asserting that the human person is an end in itself and never a means to solve other problems, he strongly opposes attempts to deny the human dignity of unborn children, such as passing laws that encourage abortion, as a crime against the Creator.[35]

At present, the Catholic Archdiocese of Seoul conducts various sharing movements, suicide prevention, care for the suicide bereaved and various life movements targeting over 50 countries around the world, including Korea, under the *Hanmaum-Hanmom-Undong* (One Mind, One Body Movement). The Society of St. Vincent de Paul, founded in 1962, also have missions within parishes and dioceses as part of social pastoral care by seeking out those in need of sharing and care.

Modern people, who are experiencing poverty and hard times in many ways due to Covid-19, must make efforts to overcome the Lonely Century together. Regarding this, the antidote to a lonely

---

34 Pope Francis, *Evangelii Gaudium*, #210.
35 Pope Francis, *Evangelii Gaudium*, #213.

century, says Noreena Hertz, is for us to be there for each other. Firstly, he recommends a change in mindset. In other words, changing the role from a receiver to a giver and from an indifferent observer to an active participant. For example, it is an attempt to first talk to a neighbor you have never spoken to before, a lost stranger, or someone who seems lonely. It can also include stroking the arm of a sick patient, talking on the phone with a friend who is going through a difficult time, or smiling at a neighbor.[36]

Words of Encouragement Movement

In concluding this book, I would like to suggest that all Christians unite and spread the "Words of Encouragement Movement." This is about putting into practice the love for neighbor that Jesus talked about. It is a word of encouragement to our neighbors, those who are very close to us, and who are in unspeakable pain due to the rapid pace of change in the age of AI and postmodernism.

Yi-Kyung Kim says that the best encouragement is self-encouragement, and explains the similar yet different aspects of compliment and encouragement as follows. In other words, compliment is a kind of reward that recognizes a job well done. Encouragement can be given before doing something or even after failure. Compliments and encouragement are both motivators, and build confidence. However, the foundation of compliment is often com-

---

36 Noreena Hertz/Translated by Jung-In Hong, *The Lonely Century (Koripui Sidai)*, Woongjin Think Big, 2021, 392-394.

paring with others. Encouragement focuses on the process, effort, and change rather than the result, so there is less risk of falling into the trap of comparison. Therefore, not only the main character who is encouraged, but also other people feel encouraged. Compliment is sweet but last short, encouragement is subtle but last long. Encouragement is something small and trivial, and when there is a noticeable positivity, it reads the behavior specifically and immediately. In order to practice the encouragement movement, it would be good to refer to the following examples she gives.

> Compliments and encouragement are similar but different. A compliment is a kind of reward that speaks highly of a job well done. Encouragement can be given not only when results are achieved, but also before doing something or when it has failed. The most important thing for building courage is encouragement.
> Compliments and encouragement are both words that motivate and build confidence. However, compliments are often based on comparison with others. Comparison can give the person being praised a sense of superiority or arrogance as well as self-confidence. When someone else receives a compliment, it creates a level of competition and motivates others to work hard, but there are also cases of feeling jealous or inferior to that friend. Encouragement focuses on the process effort, and change rather than the result, so there is less risk of falling into the trap of comparison. Therefore, it is said that not only the main character who is encouraged, but also others feel encouraged. We may think, "I can do it if I just work hard!"

Compliments are sweet but last short, encouragement is subtle but last long. The more encouragement is given consistently every day, the more powerful it becomes. If there is a noticeable positivity in something small and trivial, encourage it immediately to become habitual. And encouragement is more specific to reading behavior.

"It's getting faster."
"You're working meticulously."
"You have organized all the toys by box. Your organizational skills are improving."
"It's nice to see you playing together."
"It's good to see you working hard."
"I believe you will make it."
"You must be proud of what you have achieved, right?"
Best encouragement = Self-encouragement:
"It is okay. If I try harder, I'll be able to do well!"
Non-verbal encouragement: Pat the person on the back.
Wink and give thumbs up.[37]

---

37 I-Kyung Kim, *Chingchankwa Kyuknyu (Compliments and Encouragement)*, in *Anjou* (July), 2016.

4. Pastoral care for young people in the age of scientific omnipotence

There are many reasons why it is difficult to find young people in religious gatherings today. Do-Hyun Kim, a physicist and Catholic priest, believes that this is because they are influenced by scientific omnipotence. Therefore, in order to have a conversation with young people, it is necessary to look at what scientific omnipotence is and its limitations, as well as the teachings of the Catholic Church and how much the faithful know about it.

Scientism refers to the belief that "Science can explain everything in the world." According to Do-Hyun Kim, young people are strongly influenced by the atheistic and materialistic scientific omnipotence that they have naturally learned in school and society. And the tendency to no longer need a religion of faith is increasing. He says that we need to know as much and as deeply as we need to about science, but we should not indiscriminately embrace the idea of scientific universalism.[38]

Do-Hyun Kim emphasizes that we must recognize that science cannot answer all questions and phenomena in the world. For example, science cannot answer ontological questions such as "Why do I exist in this world?" and "How should I live in the future?" It does not answer semantic or ethical questions such as "How is it right

---

38 Do-Hyun Kim, *Gwahakgwa Sinang Sai (Between Science and Faith)*, Bible and Life, 2022, 165.

to live?"³⁹ He also points out three shortcomings of evolutionary theory. First, 'intermediate fossils', which are accepted as the most important evidence in explaining the process of macroevolution from one species to another, are not as abundant as expected. Second, because there is not yet an integrated theory that authoritatively explains the process of macroevolution, various theories are in disarray. Third, there is a much more serious loophole in macroevolution. This means that we still do not properly understand how the first living organisms (on Earth) emerged, which is the starting point for all evolutionary processes of living organisms.⁴⁰ But he argues that "even in this scientific age, faith is meaningful." This is because faith can provide answers to questions that exist outside the realm of science.⁴¹ They also say that miracles officially confirmed by the Catholic Church for canonization are a sure way of destroying scientific omnipotence. Miracles mean that there are supernatural events outside the realm of science, which means that God really exists.⁴²

The Catholic Church's teaching on the Big Bang and evolution is as follows. Those with scientific omnipotence say, "At some point, 'probably by chance', the universe was created by the Big Bang. After that, as the universe expanded, it went through a process of cosmic evolution in which stars, planets, galaxies etc. were created.

---

39 Do-Hyun Kim, *Gwahakgwa Sinang Sai (Between Science and Faith)*, 159.
40 Do-Hyun Kim, *Gwahakgwa Sinang Sai (Between Science and Faith)*, 129-131.
41 Do-Hyun Kim, *Gwahakgwa Sinang Sai (Between Science and Faith)*, 161.
42 Do-Hyun Kim, *Gwahakgwa Sinang Sai (Between Science and Faith)*, 152-154.

Afterwards, it is argued that 'probably by chance', suitable conditions (Temperature, Pressure, Water and Air, etc) for life to survive were formed on Earth, and life eventually formed and gradually evolved." However, Pope Francis explains, "The Big Bang theory, which is proposed today as the origin of the universe, does not contradict the intervention of God the Creator, but depends on it." And he explains it by changing the part of 'by chance' with 'by the intervention of God the Creator.'[43]

The theory of evolution states that all things are products of evolution. It is said that human beings also evolved and developed from lower animals over a long period of time. The Catholic Church does not exclude theories concerning the evolution and development of man and things since creation, as long as they acknowledge the basic fact that God created man and all things in the universe. However, the church does not accept 'atheistic evolutionism' or 'fundamentalist creationism.' 'Atheistic evolutionism' claims that the human mind also arose spontaneously through the synthesis of matter, and was never created by God. 'Fundamentalist creationism' believes literally the story of the creation of heaven and earth in Genesis chapters 1-3 and claims that the world was created in the order described in the Bible.[44]

On 26 April 1985, an academic conference was held in Rome on "Christian Faith and Theory of Evolution." Here, Pope John Paul

---

43 Do-Hyun Kim, *Gwahakgwa Sinang Sai (Between Science and Faith)*, 140–142.
44 Catholic Bishop's Conference of Korea, *Catechism of the Catholic Church in Korea*, 71.

II states that "Properly understood belief in creation and properly understood theory of evolution do not go their separate ways. Rather, when viewed through the eyes of faith, it becomes clear that God is the Creator of heaven and earth. And when viewed in the light of evolution, creation appears as a 'continuous creation', an event that continues in time."[45]

Cardinal Christoph Schonborn summarizes the four elements of creation theology presented in the Catechism of the Catholic Church as follows, saying that natural science does not hinder faith in creation but rather strengthens faith in the Creator. First, the doctrine of creation maintains that there is an 'absolute beginning.' 'In the beginning God created the heavens and the earth.' (Gen 1:1) This 'absolute beginning' means that God freely and without any influence brought existence out of nothing. Second, the doctrine of creation maintains that there is "distinction" between creatures. (Gen 1:21, 25) Third, God sustains the existence of all that He has created. Theology calls this 'continuous creation.' Fourth, God directs what He has created to a purpose. Therefore, the doctrine of creation also considers the teaching of God's 'providence' as a part of the doctrine of creation.[46]

---

45 Christoph Schonborn/Translated by Hyuk-Tai Kim, *Cardinal Schonborn and Darwin's Delightful Dialogue (Swonborm Chukikyungkwa Dawinui Yukwehan Dehwa)*, Bible and Life, 2017, 44.
46 Christoph Schonborn/Translated by Hyuk-Tai Kim, *Cardinal Schonborn and Darwin's Delightful Dialogue (Swonborm Chukikyungkwa Dawinui Yukwehan Dehwa)*, 54.

It is necessary to evaluate how well these teachings of the Catholic Church have been communicated to young people by asking the following questions. "Have you discussed the relationship between faith and science in adult catechism classes, First communion and Confirmation classes, or youth groups?" "Was the method of discussion scientific and logical?" "What efforts have the church made to lead young people who are influenced by the omnipotence of science, especially the atheistic omnipotence of science, to the light of faith?"

In order to renew the youth ministry, I would like to suggest that the church distribute audio-visual textbooks on creation and evolution that are appropriate for today. If we use them to teach the relationship between science and faith in a more logical way, we will more deeply acknowledge and accept the existence of God the Creator. Furthermore, when the belief in His existence is firm, the teachings and Christian beliefs about the Savior Jesus Christ and the Holy Spirit can take root more naturally and deeply based on this belief.

One of the things that young people nowadays readily approach is a fortune teller. They are so scientifically minded that they believe that science will prove everything, and they don't see the need for religion. So why go to a fortune teller? Is this phenomenon increasing despite our strong belief in the existence of a God Creator? The fact that young people want fortune tellers reminds me that many baptized Catholics in South America are moving to Pentecostal churches because of the Catholic Church's pastoral methods. Why has the church carried out youth ministry up to now and what has it focused on? For young people who have been away from the church for a long time, has the church welcomed them as new workers for existing youth activities rather than responding to their needs? Could it be that the focus has been on events rather than deepening fellowship with Jesus? What specific efforts have been made to investigate and address the reasons why children may have attended church with their parents up to Sunday school, and then drifted away from the church? Did the church listen to their concerns?

There are some things I would like to suggest for better youth ministry. First, create a new paradigm for youth ministry by having a research team study the thoughts and expectations of young people in each parish about the church and their reality. This is to break the pastoral method that has been practiced for a long time as a tradition, and to respond to the reality of those who will lead the church of the future from the big picture. And it is intended to be a concrete pastoral renewal according to the conditions of the parish. Although the truth of Christianity is the same, the method of communicating and applying the truth must be adapted to the needs of the times. Second, the church's priests and nuns need to reflect on their qualities as spiritual directors, asking, "Are we living a life that is a good witness to the Lord in the eyes of young people?" Thirdly, the church needs to make time and space available at parish or diocesan level to simply listen to young people's stories. In St.

Peter's Basilica in Rome we can see that there are permanent confessionals in several languages. However, the proposal here is not for the sacrament of confession, but for the priest or nuns to simply listen to what they want to say. What they need more than a solution is a neighborhood where they know they are never alone and that someone is listening to them. They need a neighbor who understands their hearts and offers words of encouragement, and a neighbor who is an instrument of the Lord to help them regain a sense of purpose and hope in life.

The world needs Christians as true light and true salt. Although the Catholic Church and Protestant Church are the same Christians, it is clear that there are theological differences. However, it is true that in multi-religious era, the phenomenon of De-churchisation phenomenon and the acceleration of scientific omnipotence, to have spiritual renewal, especially pastoral renewal, is necessary not only for the Catholic Church but also for all Christianity.

I hope that the poor churches, Small Community management, personal encounter with the Lord through the Bible, sharing with the poor, spiritual discernment, and the 'Word of Encouragement Movement' that we have looked at so far will be helpful. To this end, I would like to conclude with these things.

Materially poor Church

It requires the church to keep what is necessary to run the church and to share the rest with the poor. Of course, this will not be easy, but the proclamation of the Word of hope by the poor church as a true light has a deeper appeal to the hearts of the world than the materially rich church.

Revitalization of Small Community

In the case of the Catholic Church, the Small Community movement began in South America, and the Korean Catholic Church implemented the African Lumko method. However, it is important to note that Catholic baptized people in South America and Africa are moving to other denominations, and in Korea, the number of believers who do not attend Sunday Mass is increasing. I think it is essential to study the reasons for this increase at the diocesan and parish level. In terms of pastoral methods, there is a particular need to re-examine the methods and content of the work of the Small Community. This is because the larger church has a limited capacity for parish priests, so it is necessary to make use of Small Communities. Is it true that the number of parishioners who leave the church is increasing, even though the parish priest feels deeply about the need for Small Communities and has implemented them? Isn't this the superficial maintenance of a Cell church? Aren't we satisfied and rationalized that pastoral care only takes care of the sheep that come to the sheepfold on their own without much effort? Creative and active pastors are needed, who not only care for the sheep in the sheepfold, but also seek out the sheep like St. Paul.

Personal encounter with the Lord through the Bible

There are times when young people or adults who have been

very active in volunteer work in the church, give up their religious life completely because of the wounds they have received in the church. Of course, there are individual situations and clear reasons, but I wonder if it's the atmosphere of the church that produces activists who are more concerned with events than with spiritual growth? Isn't it basically a lack of personal encounter with the Lord? Could it be that the increase in the number of believers taking a break and moving to other religions is due to a lack of spiritual accompaniment to enable them to experience the Lord with their hearts, to communicate with Him, and to live a life of faith that is close to Him along with the core teachings of the church? Is the environment prepared to welcome those who have been away from the church for a long time and are waiting for their return? Therefore, above all, it is necessary to create a specific environment for a personal encounter with Jesus, I also think that the revision of the catechism is helpful for re-education of the faithful. This is because the catechism learned in children's Sunday school can be deepened in adult catechism classes.

Sharing with the poor

There are many believers who want to provide material help or volunteer work, but cannot because they do not know how. However, in reality, both Protestant and Catholic churches are doing a lot of work to help the less fortunate, both nationally and international levels. In many places, priests and nuns look after the underprivileged and the needy. These include children from broken families, free soup kitchens, shelters for runaway girls, places for young people in difficulties, elderly people living alone, free clinics and hospitals, tiny room villages, the homeless, intercultural children's study rooms, care centers for migrant workers, care centers for single mothers. In addition to this, we are also practicing the role of light and salt in society on a much broader scale. We can also visit these places individually and serve together. Furthermore, as a place to practice Bible meditation in Small Communities, it is necessary to find people in blind spots, among the neighbors, and make efforts to accompany them beyond religion. I think this is a good way to proclaim the Gospel to the world through action. Through the sincerity of our small hearts, they receive the comfort that they are not alone. In addition, by offering a small helping hand, volunteers can experience true inner joy by feeling that Jesus is with them.

Direct sharing with the poor is essential, but the evangelization of the wealthy and social leaders is also important. Rather than simply recognizing them as baptized believers, it is necessary to provide consistent spiritual accompaniment for their evangelization. If they are accompanied, for example, by Small Community gatherings, they can become God's instruments for influencing social change that takes into account the poor and marginalized.

Spiritual discernment

Karl Rahner, a famous German theologian, says that Christianity has not only a history of dogma but also a history of holiness. According to him, many saints have shown the way to live as a true

Christian, and St. Ignatius is one of them. Karl Rahner argues that just as logic became the first discipline of philosophy through Aristotle, the discernment of the spirit became the study of the saints through St. Ignatius.[47]

St. Ignatius emphasizes the distinction between the spirit that brings us closer to God and the spirit that hinders us. All Christians should strive to improve their discernment in prayer, by seeking the grace to discern the great and small temptations in their lives and the word of God that invites them to the path of sanctification.

Word of Encouragement Movement

Problems in relationships are part of the difficulties we exchange in everyday life. Above all, it can be said that it is my relationship with myself, with God, with my neighbors, and with nature. Words of encouragement give life to these relationships. Words of encouragement accompanied by a little interest and love, will change me, change the church, and then change the world. We will build a church community where true children of God are present, living the fruit of the Holy Spirit and the fruit of love.

The Word of Encouragement Movement is a simple movement that I can start practicing now, and at the same time, it will be a movement that lights a small candle that gives hope in a dark world.

---

47 Timothy M. Gallagher, *The Discernment of Spirits: An Ignatian Guide for Everyday Living*, 14.

References

A. Book

Boff, Leonardo/Translated by Kim, Kwe-Sang, *Seropke Tansenghanun Kyohio (The Church Reborn)*, Joseph, 1987.

Brother Lawrence, *The Practice of the Presence of God*, Paraclete Press, Massachusetts, 2010.

Catechismus Catholicae Ecclesiale, CBCK, 2003.

Catholic Archdiocese of Seoul, *Discussion Content of the Group Discussions at the 1997 Priestly Assembly (1997 Nyun Sazechonghwe Zohyultoron Naiyong)*, Chonzukyo Seoul Daikyogu Bokumhwa Samuguk (Secretariat for Evangelisation of the Catholic Archdiocese of Seoul), 1997.

_____, *2000 Nyunde Bokumhwa Bondangzozike Kwanhayu ('On the Organisation of Evangelising Parishes in the 2000s)*, Official Documents of the Catholic Archdiocese of Seoul (1992. 4. 30).

_____, *Seoul Dekyogu Bondangsamok Hwalsonghwarul Wihan Kichozaryosuzip Solmunzosa Bogoso (Survey Report on Collecting Basic Data for Revitalising Parish Pastoral Ministry in the Archdiocese of Seoul)*, Catholic Archdiocese of Seoul, 2012.

_____, *Seoul Dekyogu Samok Kyoso (1991~1992) (Pastoral Letter of Archidiocese of Seoul [1991~1992])*.

_____, *Seoul Dekyogu Sinod: Songzikza Desang Solmunzosa Kyulkwabogoso (2002) (Synod of the Archdiocese of Seoul: Report on Clergy Survey Results[2002])*.

Catholic Bishops' Conference of Korea, *Byungza Songsa Yesik (Rite of the Anointing of the Sick)*, Committee for Liturgy of CBCK, 2018.

_____, *Catechism of the Catholic Church in Korea*, CBCK, 2015.

_____, *Hanguk Chonzukyohoi Tongke 2009 (Statistics of the Catholic Church in Korea 2009)*, CBCK, Seoul, 2009.

Cho, Yong-Gi, *Chiryoui Kang (Healing River)*, complete works of Dickens, vol. 8.

_____, *Geui Narawa Geui Uiga Muosin-ga? (What is his kingdom and what is his righteousness?)* in Sermon Collections, vol. 17.

_____, *Guyuk Yebe Kongkwa 14 (Guyuk Worship Guide 14)*, Seoul Logos, 2017.

_____, *Himang Mokhoi 45 Nyun: Guyuk Sogrup Buheung Iyaki (45 years of Hope Ministries: Cell Group Revival Stories)*, Church Growth Institute, 2006.

_____, *Hwahe (Reconciliation)*, complete works of Dickens, vol. 11.

_____, *Kyohoi Songzang-ui Bikyul (Church Growth Secrets)*, Church Growth vol. 2, Seoul Logos, Seoul, 1985.

_____, *Maum Hanul (Heaven in Heart)*, Kyohoisongzang-yunkuso, Seoul, 2009.

_____, *Nanun Iroke Solkyohanda (I preach like this)*, Seoul Logos, Seoul, 2010.

_____, *Naui Kyohoi Songzang Iyaki (My Church Growth Stories)*, Seoul Logos, Seoul, 2005.

_____, *Nohui-ane Kyesin Christ (Christ present in you)*, complete works of Dickens, vol. 7.

_____, *Ozung Bogumkwa Samzung Chukbok (Fivefold Gospel and Threefold Blessing)*, Seoul Logos, Seoul, 2009.

_____, *Sinyuron (Divine Healing)*, Seoul Logos, Seoul, 2009.

_____, *Sipzaga Wiesobon Yesu (Jesus seen on the Cross)*, complete works of Dickens, vol. 4.

_____, *Solkyonun Naui Inseng (Preaching is my life)*, Seoul Logos, 2009.

_____, *Song-nyung Gang-nimkwa Hananim Nara*, in Sermon Collections, vol. 16.

_____, *Sonkyowa Mokhoi (Mission and Pastoral Ministry)*, vol. 4, 1988.

_____, *Sunbokumui Jinli (Trouth of Full Gospel)*, vol. 2, Seoul Logos, 1979.

_____, *The response of pastor Yong-Gi Cho to the personal letter of Sr. Son. Chung-Myung*, 4 December of 2012.

_____, *Yesunimui Buhwal, Nomuna Kippun Sosik (Resurrection of Jesus, So Good News)*, complete works of Dickens, vol. 19.

_____, *Zu Yesurul Baraboza (Let us look at Lord Jesus)*, complete works of Dickens, vol. 7.

_____, *4 Chawonui Yungsung (4th Dimension of Spirituality)*, Church Growth Institute, 2010.

_____, *4 Chawonui Yungsung – Silchonpyun (4th Dimension of Spirituality-Practice)*, Church Growth Institute, 2010.

_____, *4 Chawonui Yungzokseghe (The Fourth Dimension)*, Seoul Logos, 2010.

Cho, Yong-Gi David, *Salvation, Healing & Prosperity, Creation House*, Westmonte Drive, 1987.

Choi, Ja-Sil, *Nanun Halleluia Azummayutda (I was Halleluia Woman)*, Seoul Logos, Seoul, 2010.

Chung, Woll-Ki, *HanGuk Chonzukyohoi Sokongdongche Samok Balzonkwazong (The Pastoral Process involved in the Promotion of the Small Community in the Korean Catholic Church)*, Catholic University, M.A. Thesis in Systematic Theology, 2005.

_____, Jun Won, *Malssum Yuheng: Marko Bogum (Word Journey: Gospel of Mark)*, Hanguk Tonghap Samok Center, Seoul, 2019.

Chung, Yong-Sub, *Sokbinsolkyo Kwagchansolkyo (Hollow preaching and Full Preaching)*, The Christian Literature Society of Korea, Seoul, 2006.

Cox, Harvey, *Fire from Heaven*, Addison-Wesley Publishing Company, New York, 1995.

_____, *Yungsong, Umak, Yusong (Fire from Heaven)*, translated in Korean by Yu Ji-Hwang, Dong Yeon, Seoul, 1998.

Donald W. Dayton, *Theological Roots of Pentecostalism,* Hendrickson, 1996.

Dr. Paul Cho Yong-Gi, *The Fourth Dimension,* vol. 1, Rhema Publication Ministry, 1979.

FABC, *Fifth Plenary Assembly, Final Statement: Journeying together toward the Third Millenium* (#8.1.1), July 17~27, 1990.

Finnell David L./Translated by Park Young-Cheol, *Cell Kyohoi Pyungsindo (Life in His Body: A Simple Guide to Active Cell Life),* NCD, 2009.

Gallagher, Timothy M./translated by Kim Du-Jin, *The Discernment of Spirits: An Ignatian Guide for Everyday Living (Young-ui Sikbyul: St. Ignatiaga Annaihanun Meilui Sam),* Ignatian Spirituality Institute, Seoul, 2020.

Hertz, Noreena/Translated by Hong Jung-In, *The Lonely Century (Koripui Sidai),* Woongjin Think Big, 2021.

Hong, Yung-Gi, *Cho Yong-Gi Moksaui Yungsongkwa Leadership (Spirituality & Leadership of Rev. Yong-Gi Cho),* Kyohoisongzang-yunkuso, Seou, 2003.

International Theological Institute, *Hananimui Songhoi Kyohoisa (The History of the Assemblies of God),* Seoul Logos, Seoul, 2008.

_____, *Yoido Sunbokumkyohoiui Songnyung Undong Ihe (A Comprehension about the Holy Spirit Movement of the Yoido Full Gospel Church),* Seoul Logos, Seoul, 2001.

_____, *Yoidoui Mokhoiza (The Pastor of Yoido),* Seoul Logos, Seoul, 2010.

Introvigne, Massimo, *Pentecostali,* Elledici, Torino, 2004.

Jun, Won, *Sinod Jungsine Tarun Kyogu mit Bondangkuzo (Diocesan and Parish Structures in the Spirit of the Synod),* in *Sinod Silchonul Wihan Hyunankwa Kwaze (Issues and Challenges for Synod Practice),* Tonghap Samok Yunkuso, Seoul, 2007.

Kim, Do-Hyun, *Gwahakgwa Sinang Sai (Between Science and Faith)*, Bible and Life, 2022.

Kyung, Dong-Hyun, *Kyohoi Zikmuwa Hanguk Chonzukyohoi-ui Zikmu-Ihe (Understanding Church Ministry and the Ministry of the Korean Catholic Church)*, Sogang University, 1998.

Lee, Jae-Ul, *Sarangbang Kyohoiwa Moimunyung (Sarangbang Church and Running Meetings)*, Bitkwa Sogum, Seoul, 2009.

_____, *Sarangbang MalsumNanuki (Sharing of the Word in Sarangbang)*, Catholicbook, Seoul, 2009.

_____, *Sarangbang Sogongdongche (Sarangbang Small Community)*, Catholicbook, Seoul, 2008.

Lee, Young-Hoon, *The Holy Spirit Movement in Korea: Its Historical and Theological Development*, Regnum Books International, Oxford, 2009.

Menzies, William, *Anointed to Serve: The Story of the Assemblies of God* (Springfield, MO: Gospel Publishing House, 1971).

Neuner J., sj – Dupuis J., sj, *La Fede Cristiana nei documenti dottrinali della Chiesa cattolica*, San Paolo, Milano, 2002, 29 (#39.20).

Park, Hong-Rae, *Cell Group Cell Kyohoi (Cell Group Cell Church)*, Seoro Sarang, Seoul, 2008.

Park, Jun-Yang, *Jongmallon-Yungwonhan Sengmyungul Hyanghayo (Eschatology-Towards Eternal Life)*, Bible and Life, 2011, 104-105.

Pope Francis, *Evangelii Gaudium: Apostolic Exhortation to the Bishops, Clergy, Consecrated Persons, and the Lay Faithful on the Proclamation of the Gospel in Today's World* (2015).

_____, *Gaudete et Exsultate: Apostolic Exhortation on the Call to Holiness in Today's World* (March 19, 2018).

_____, *Laudato Si': Encyclical Letter on Care for Our Common Home* (May 24, 2015).

Pope John Paul II, *Ecclesia in Asia: Apostolic Exhortation* (1999).

_____, *Redemptoris Missio: Encyclical on the permanent validity of the Church's missionary mandate* (Dec. 7, 1990), CBCK, 2014.

Pope Paul VI, *Evangelii Nuntiandi: Apostolic Exhortation* (Dec. 8, 1975), CBCK, 2009.

Ro, Joo-Hyun, *Catholic Kyohoiui 'Sogongdongcheron' Yunku (A Study on 'theory of Small Christian Communities' of Catholic Church)*, Sogang University Master's Thesis Sogang University, Seoul, 2001.

San Bernardo, "*Sermoni sul Cantico dei Cantici*," XVIII, 3, *Opere di st. Bernardo (V/I)* (Milano: Scriptorium Claravallense, Fondazione di Studi Cistercensi, 2006).

Schonborn, Christoph/Translated by Hyuk-Tai Kim, *Cardinal Schonborn and Darwin's Delightful Dialogue (Swonborm Chukikyungkwa Dawinui Yukwehan Dehwa)*, Bible and Life, 2017.

Secretariado General De CELAM (Consejo Episcopal Latinoamericano), *Medellin Conclusiones*/Translated by Kim Soo-Bok – Sung Yum, Benedict Press, Waekwan, 1989.

Shim, Sang-Tai, *2000 Nyundeui Hankug Kyohoi (Korean Church in 2000 Year[15])*, FSP, Seoul, 1993, p. 23-26.

Suenens, Leon-Joseph, *Lo Spirito Santo Nostra Speranza: Una Nuova Pentecoste?*, Edizioni Paoline, Rome, 1975.

Sullivan, Francis A., *Carismi e Rinnovamento Carismatico*, Ancora, Milano, 1983.

Tonghap Samok Yunkuso, *Samwui-il-che Leadership (Trinity Leadership)*, Tonghap Samok Yunkuso, Seoul, 2006.

Williams, Cyril G., *Tongues of the Spirit: A Study of Pentecostal Glossolalia and Related Phenomenon*, University of Wales Press, Cardiff, 1981.

Yang, Jae-Cheol, *Hankug Osunzol Kyohoiui Sinangkwa Sinhak (Pentecostal*

Churches in Korea), Hanulmokzang, Seoul, 2005.

Yong-Gi Cho'S Sermon, *"Narai Imhaopsimyo" ("Thy Kingdom Come")*, (1986, 8, 6).

Yong-Gi Cho'S Sermon, *"Narai Imhaopsimyo" ("Thy Kingdom Come")*, (1986, 8, 31).

Young San Yunguwon, *Ozungbokumkwa Samzungkuwonui Chukbok (Fivefold Gospel and the Blessing of Threefold Salvation)*, Seoul Logos, Seoul, 1991.

Young William, *Letters of Saint Ignatius of Loyola*, Loyola University, Chicago, 1959.

B. Magazines

Bae, Dawk-Mahn, *"Ciryo-hasinun Yesunim": Ciryoza Yesu Cristorul Tonghebon Yong Sanui Gidoknon Yunku ("Healing Jesus": A Study on Young San's Christology Focusing on Jesus Christ as a Healer)*, in *Young Sanui Mokhoiwa Sinhak (Ministry & Theology of Young-San)*, vol. 1, ed. Young San Theological Institute, Hansei University Logos, Gunpo 2008.

Catholic Bishops' Conference of Korea, *Chiyu Gidoekwanhan Hunlyung (Instructions on Healing Prayer)*, in *the Teachings of the Catholic Church*, vol. 18, 2001.

Cho, Gwi-Sam, *Young Sanui 4 Chawonui Yungzok-Sekewa Kyohoi Songzang (The Fourth Dimension in Dr. David Yong-Gi Cho's Ministry and Church Growth)*, in *Journal of Young San Theology*, vol. 12, Young San Theological Institute of Hansei University, Gunpo, 2008.

_____, *Young Sanui Guyuk-Yeberul Tonghan Kyohoi-Songzang Yunku (A Study of Church Growth through Young San's Guyuk Worship)*, in *Journal of Young San Theology*, vol. 13, Young San Theological Institute of Hansei University, Gunpo, 2008.

Cho, Young-Mo, *Young San Cho Yong-Gi Moksaui Hananim Nara Ihe (Dr. Yong-Gi Cho's Theology on the Kingdom of God with Reference to the*

NT), in *Ministry & Theology of Young San*, vol. 3, ed. Young San Theological Institute, Hansei University Logos, Gunpo, 2008.

Choi, Mun-Hong, *Young Sanui Kuwon Ihe (Understanding of Young San about Salvation)*, in *Young Sanui Mokhoiwa Sinhak (Ministry & Theology of Young San)*, vol. 1, ed. Young San Theological Institute, Hansei University Logos, Gunpo, 2008.

_____, *Young-san Cho Yong-Gi Moksawa Hananimui Nara (Young-san Rev. Yong-Gi Cho and the Kingdom of God)*, in *Journal of Young San Theology*, Vol. 14, Young San Theological Institute of Hansei University, Gunpo, 2008.

Dayton, Donald W., *The "Good God" and The "Theology of Blessing" in the Thought of David Yong-Gi Cho*, in *Young San International Theological Symposium (2005)*, ed. Young San Theological Institute of Hansei University, Hansei University, Gunpo, 2005.

Hong, Lok-Young, *Young San Cho Yong-Gi Moksaga Mannan Ciyuhasinun Yesu Cristo (Understanding of Young San's Divine Healing)*, in *Young Sanui Mokhoiwa Sinhak (Ministry & Theology of Young San)*, vol.1, ed. Young San Theological Institute, Hansei University Logos, Gunpo, 2008.

Kang, U-Il, *Kyuk-ryusa (L'Incoraggiamento)*, in Nobundr handimoyong, Nohyung, Cheju, 2008.

Kim, Dong-Soo, *Hehanui Sinhakurosoui Young San Sinhak (The Pentecostal Theology as a Theology to make free from Han)*, in *Dr. Yong-Gi Cho's Theology: A Theological Paradigm for the 21st Century*, ed. Full Gospel Theological Institute of Hansei University, Hansei University, Gunpo, 2003.

Kim, Hee-Seong, *Cho Yong-Gi Moksaui Hananimui Nara (Rev. Yong-Gi Cho's Kingdom of God)*, in *16th Young San International Theological*

Symposium, ed. Young San Theological Institute of Hansei University, Hansei University Logos, Gunpo, 2008.

Kim, Hong-Keun, *Young Sankwa Ciyumokhoi (Young San and Divine Healing)*, in *Dr. Yong-Gi Cho's Theology: A theological Paradigm of the 21st Century*, ed. Full Gospel Theological Institute of Hansei University, Hansei University, Gunpo, 2003.

Kim, I-KYung, *Chingchankwa Kyuknyu (Compliments and Encouragement)*, in *Anjou (July)*, 2016.

Kim, Pan-Ho, *Ozungbokumkwa Samzung Chukbok Sasang-e Natanan Hananim Nara (The Kingdom of God Appeared in the Doctrines of Fivefold Gospel and Threefold Blessing)*, in *16th Young San International Theological Symposium*, ed. Young San Theological Institute of Hansei University, Hansei University Logos, Gunpo, 2008.

Ko, Byeong-Soo, *Sokongdongche Ihehaki (Understanding Small Community)*, in Nobundr Handimoyong, Nohyung, Cheju, 2008.

Lee Hae-Sook – Do Bok-Num, *Hospis Hwanzawa Bihospis Hwanzaui Yungzok Annyungkwa Samuizil Bikyo (Comparison of Spiritual Well-being and Quality of life between Hospice Patients and Nonhospice Patients)*, in *Seongin Ganhohakhoizi (Korean Society of Adult Nursing)*, vol. 15 (#3), Seoul, 2003.

Lee, Sang-Bok, *Kungzong Simrihak Kwanzomesobon Osunzol Ciyusinhak: Young San Cho Yong-Gi Moksaui Ciyusinhakul Zungsimuro (Pentecostal Healing Theology from the Positive Psychology Perspective: on the Dr. Yong-Gi Cho's Healing Theology)*, in *Korean Journal of Pentecostal Studies*, vol. 5, ed. Society for Pentecostal Studies in Korea, Hansei University Logos, Gunpo, 2007.

Ma, Won-Suk, *Yong-Gi Cho's Theology of Blessing: New Theological Basis and Directions*, in *Young San International Theological Symposium (2003)*, ed. Full Gospel Theological Institute of Hansei University, Hansei University, Gunpo 2003.

Oh, Yong-Suk, *'Seroun Bokumhwa' Side-ui Songkongzok Bondangsamok Banghyang (Successful Parish Pastoral Direction in the Era of the 'New Evangelisation')*, in *Seoul Dekyoku Bondangsamok Hwalsonghwarul Wihan Kichozaryosuzip Solmunzosa Bogoso (Gathering Data for Parish Ministry Revitalisation Survey Report)*, Catholic Archdiocese of Seoul, 2012.

Park, Won-Kun, *Yebe-esoui Kibok Sinang Muosi Munjeinga? (What's wrong with believing in good luck in worship?)*, in *Hoibo, June* (2011), The Presbyterian Church in the Republic of Korea, Seoul.

Ryoo, Jang-Hyun, *Young Sanui Zongmalone Kwanhan Bipanzok Gochal (A Critical Study of Dr. Yong-Gi Cho's Eschatology)*, in *Journal of Young San Theology*, Vol. 13, Young San Theological Institute of Hansei University, Gunpo, 2008.

Shin, Mun-Chul, *4 Chawonui Yungsong-edehan Sinhkzok Gochal (A Theological Appraisal of the Spirituality of the Fourth Dimension)*, in *Journal of Young San Theology*, vol. 13, Young San Theological Institute of Hansei University, Gunpo, 2008.

_____, *Young Sanui Songnyung-nonzok Ingannon (Pneumatological Anthropology of Young San)*, in Journal of Young San theology, vol.4, Young San Theological Institute of Hansei University, Gunpo, 2007.

Stanley, David, *"S. I. Salvation and Healing," The Way 10* (1970).

Suh, N.D., *Toward a Theology of Han*, in *Minjung Theology: People as the Subjects of History (The Christian Conference of Asia)*, ed. Young-Bok Kim, Singapore, 1981.

Synan, Vinson, *Young San Cho Yong-Gi Moksaui Ciyu Sinhakui Puri (Roots of Yong-Gi Cho's Theology of Healing)*, in *Young San International*

Theological Symposium (2006), ed. Young San Theological Institute of Hansei University, Hansei University, Gunpo, 2006.

Vetrali, Tecle, *Verso Una lettura francescna dell'incontro con il Fratello pentecostale*, in *Studi Ecumenici*, 27, Venezia, 2009.

Yun, Ki-Suk, *Hankug Kyohoiui Kehyuk (1) (The Renewal of Korean Church[1])*, in *Hoibo*, May (2012), the Presbyterian Church in the Republic of Korea, Seoul, 2012.

C. Internet site

Cho, Yong-Gi, *Silpezanun Solgosiopda (Failure has no place to stand[Sept. 11, 2005])*, Sunday Sermon, (Sept. 2012), http://yfgc.fgtv.com.

Jun, Won, *Dure Gyuchik (Dure Rules)*, Jekidong Parish, Seoul, #6, Internet (Sept. 2012), http://jksd.org.

Yoido Full Gospel Church, *Cho Yong-Gi Moksawa Lee Young-Hoon Moksaui Zuilsolkyo (Sunday Sermons of Pastor Yong-Gi Cho and Pastor Young-Hoon Lee[Dec. 9, 2012], [Dec. 12, 2012])*, https://davidcho.fgtv.com.

_____, *Osanri Fast Prayer House*, Internet (April 2020), http://prayer.fgtv.com.

D. Dictionary

Burgess, Stanley M., ed., *Introduction*, in *the New International Dictionary of Pentecostal and Charismatic Movements (Revised and expanded edition)*, Zondervan, Michigan, 2003.

KYDD, R.A.N., *Healing in the Christian Church*, in *The New International Dictionary of Pentecostal and Charismatic Movements (revised and expanded edition)*, ed. Stanley M. Burgess - Eduard M. Van Der Maas, Zondervan, Michigan, 2003.

Lora, Erminio ed., *Enchiridion Vaticanum*, vol. 4, EDB, Bologna, 1978.

_____, *Enchiridion Vaticanum*, vol. 7, EDB, Bologna, 1982.

_____, *Enchiridion Vaticanum*, vol. 19, EDB, Bologna, 2004.

Lovett, L., *Positive Confession Theology*, in *The New International Dictionary of Pentecostal and Charismatic Movements (Revised and expanded edition)*, ed. Stanley M. Burgess - Eduard M. Van Der Maas, Zondervan, Michigan, 2003.

Morandi, Giacomo, *Fondamenti Biblici della Cura d'anime*, in *La vita in Cristo Pastora: La cura d'anime minister delle SJBP (Atti del Seminario)*, ed., Sisters of Jesus Good Shepherd (Pastorelle Sisters), Rome, 2010.

Riss, R.M., *Kenyon, Essek William*, in *The New International Dictionary of Pentecostal and Charismatic Movements (Revised and expanded edition)*, ed. Stanley M. Burgess-Eduard M. Van Der Maas, Zondervan, Michigan, 2003.

The Theology and Pastoral Ministry
of Pastor Yong-Gi Cho:
As Seen by a Catholic Theologian
for the Pastoral Renewal of the Church

First published on Sep. 19, 2025

Author	Chung-Myung Son
Publisher	Young Ho Kim
Published by	Dong Yeon Press
Registration	No. 1-1383 (June 12, 1992)
Address	163-3 World Cup-ro, Mapo-gu, Seoul, South Korea
Phone	+82-2-335-2630
Fax	+82-2-335-2640
Email	yh4321@gmail.com
Instagram	instagram.com/dong-yeon-press

Copyright © Chung-Myung Son, 2025

This book is protected by copyright law,
so unauthorized reproduction and copying are prohibited.

ISBN 978-89-6447-718-2 93230 (pbk.)
ISBN 978-89-6447-719-9 93230 (e-book)